THE
GREAT
POPES
THROUGH
HISTORY

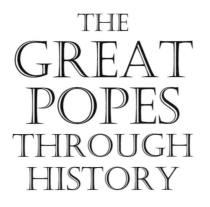

THE
GREAT POPES THROUGH HISTORY

An Encyclopedia
VOLUME II

EDITED BY FRANK J. COPPA

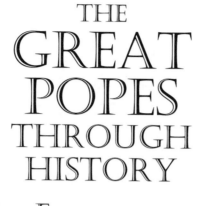

GREENWOOD PRESS
Westport, Connecticut • London

Library of Congress Cataloging-in-Publication Data

The great popes through history : an encyclopedia / edited by Frank J. Coppa.
    p. cm.
    Includes bibliographical references and index.
    ISBN 0–313–29533–6 (set : alk paper)—ISBN 0–313–32417–4 (v. I : alk. paper)—
    ISBN 0–313–32418–2 (v. II : alk. paper)
    1. Popes—Biography—Encyclopedias.   2. Papacy—History—Encyclopedias.
  I. Coppa, Frank J.
  BX955.3.G74   2002
  282'.092'2—dc21   2002023254
  [B]

British Library Cataloguing in Publication Data is available.

Library of Congress Catalog Card Number: 2002023254
ISBN: 0–313–29533–6 (set)
     0–313–32417–4 (vol. I)
     0–313–32418–2 (vol. II)

First published in 2002

Greenwood Press, 88 Post Road West, Westport, CT 06881
An imprint of Greenwood Publishing Group, Inc.
www.greenwood.com

Printed in the United States of America

∞

The paper used in this book complies with the
Permanent Paper Standard issued by the National
Information Standards Organization (Z39.48–1984).

10 9 8 7 6 5 4 3 2 1

CONTENTS

CONTENTS

CONTENTS

CONTENTS

PART IV

THE EARLY MODERN PAPACY

INTRODUCTION

William V. Hudon

The early modern era in the history of the papacy was one marked by dramatic change. The holders of this office inherited a set of policies and practices from their Renaissance predecessors and attempted to remain faithful to both while consolidating the position of the church in early modern society. Their plans for consolidation were only partly implemented, however. Early modern popes failed to implement their plans for consolidation due, among other things, to their personally defining characteristics: their decided inconsistency and shocking contradictions. They failed also due to growing European states that rivaled their authority, and to the jarring cultural realities of a new world. These states and these realities pushed the papacy increasingly into the margins of early modern society. Popes at the end of this era deteriorated into religious and political ineffectiveness, only minimally grasping the necessity of focusing their activity upon pursuit of a more spiritual agenda.

Many early modern popes attempted to maintain the Renaissance traditions of papal artistic support, but others contradicted this trend. One might expect to find such patronage early in the period and disappearing later, but papal interest in this function waxed and waned. It was not uncommon for popes early in the period, like Pius V, to reject the patronage levels attained during the Renaissance out of concern for curial frugality in the post-Reformation world. Even vigorous reformers like Pius V and Sixtus V, however, engaged in the work to a degree. Pius supported poorly endowed monasteries, especially the Dominican house in his hometown. He also made extensive, frescoed additions to the Vatican apartments and assisted in the building of the Jesuit Church of the Gesù. Along the way he supported artists like Giorgio Vasari and Daniele da Volterra. He directed his giving at groups and institutions he considered supportive of his reform agenda. Sixtus V funded extensive projects, but ones that were focused upon urban renewal, while popes like Clement VIII and Innocent XII also engaged in a limited support of the arts. Gregory XIII, Urban VIII, and Benedict XIV were all more lavishly generous patrons, especially Urban VIII. Urban's devotion to the great artist Gian Lorenzo Bernini helped him create some of the most magnificent and commonly identifiable sculpture of the Counter-Reformation. The Renaissance tradition of support for art and artists did not fall into disuse late in this period either, despite the reform ideals of some of these princes of the church. During the administration of Benedict XIV, for example, the Capitoline and Vatican museums were extended, and he even patronized an academy dedicated to the depiction of the naked human form.

While one might argue that the early modern period was a period devoted to ecclesiastical reform, it is important to note that the popes in this age only inconsistently reflected the spiritual renewal and rejection of practices like simony and nepotism that we associate with the Reformation. Some early modern popes, like Pius V and Sixtus V, came from poorer family backgrounds, and this contributed to their frugality and antinepotistic policies. It may also be part of the reason why they autocratically instituted draconian measures upon the Papal States in a largely unsuccessful attempt to squash public vice, in the forms of prostitution and carnival activity. Other holders of the papal office in the early modern period were disciples of the reform ideology of persons like St. Filippo Neri, but advanced in clerical office in a characteristically unreformed fashion, becoming ordained to the priesthood late in life, and sometimes only after appointment to a bishopric. Among these were Clement VIII, Innocent XI, and Benedict XIV. Gregory XIII, for all of his reform credentials and commitment to the implementation of the decrees of the Council of Trent, appointed a bastard son as the governor of Castel Sant'Angelo. Urban VIII applied the same generosity that he showed to artists to his own family, shamelessly promoting their acquisition of stunning wealth. Early modern popes demonstrated inconsistent commitment to the personal reform recommended for prelates by persons on both sides of the contemporary confessional divide.

This was the age of the implementation of the Council of Trent, and while popes were dedicated to this operation, their effectiveness, in the long run, was limited. The prelates at Trent identified the work of the bishops as central to the improvement of the church. Following this lead, many early modern popes claimed Carlo Borromeo, the great reforming bishop of Milan and nephew of Pius IV, as their model. Popes at the end of the period, like Benedict XIV and Clement XIII, extolled the value of

Borromeo's work, just as earlier popes, like Pius V, took up the Milanese example of governance through diocesan visitations in administering Rome itself. Pius's cardinal congregation overseeing bishops promoted visitations throughout the church, while Sixtus V renewed the *ad limina*, or prescribed regular visits to Rome, that brought the prelates to the Eternal City to report on their dioceses. Innocent XI reaffirmed the Tridentine decree on episcopal residence, and Clement XIII likewise reminded bishops of their duties upon his election in 1758. Some of these same popes, and others, reinforced the doctrinal and disciplinary decrees of Trent by promoting the revision of liturgical works used in the rituals of the church and by supervising the publication of new editions of the Scriptures. Here again, however, the results were mixed. Pius presided over the creation of a well-received new general catechism. Sixtus V, on the other hand, ensured his lasting fame—or better, infamy—by commencing work on that well-intentioned but miserably inadequate "Sixtine Vulgate" edition of the Bible. He promoted the work, but in a pushy, unhelpful fashion, requiring scholars to work quickly, incorrectly convinced that he himself could solve any questionable interpretations. Gregory XIV initiated the work to fix the Sixtine mess. Clement VIII deserves great credit for ensuring the reform of the Roman missal and breviary, as does Pius V for his promotion of work on a number of other liturgical texts.

There were elements of inconsistency in the practical implementation of the ideals of Trent, and certain early modern popes reflect this. Perhaps the best example is Benedict XIV. Although he was a bishop who operated closely in line with the Tridentine spirit, and one who wrote a text on the importance of diocesan synods, he never held one of his own, even though it was considered a crucial step in effecting diocesan reform. While the council insisted upon the appointment of duly qualified bishops, Benedict was willing to suspend this, to a degree, by permitting royal nomination and presentation of candidates from Spain. He did so out of diplomatic concerns that connect with longer, wider-ranging negotiation. Negotiation, not dictation, characterized local implementation of the decrees of the Council of Trent from the mid-sixteenth to the mid-eighteenth century. The negotiation operated between bishops and their cathedral chapters, between bishops and monastic institutions, and between bishops and other religious orders. It sometimes even operated between inquisitors and those whose trials were heard.

As the era of "Counter-Reformation," one of the abiding images of the early modern period is that of the battle against heresy. By and large, the popes of this time did indeed conduct a war against heresy, but they did so inconsistently and with varying intensity. In this era Pius V picked up where his mentor, Paul IV, left off. His remodeling of a building to serve as the headquarters of the Roman Holy Office of the Inquisition was the tip of an iceberg. He personally presided over meetings of the body, reopened a case against Pietro Carnesecchi and planned to do the same against Cardinal Giovanni Morone, and literally conducted war with the "infidel" in the form of the Ottoman Turks. Sixtus V was similarly personally invested in the Inquisition and antiheretical operations, as he had been aided in his career by Pius V before he came to the papal throne. Sixtus went so far as to stipulate that papal revenue surpluses could be used only to aid nations threatened by heresy.

After these two, later early modern popes began to illustrate variations in the level of papal determination to fight heterodoxy. Clement VIII and Urban VIII both utilized politics as a vehicle to counteract heresy. Clement worked to try to retain the Catholicism of Henry IV of France and prosecuted Giordano Bruno, who was burned at the stake in 1600. Clement, on the other hand, also sought to mollify the restrictions of the most recent edition of the Index of Prohibited Books. While Urban VIII's positions were ostensibly in support of Catholicism, he moved into an unlikely position of support for France and its ally Sweden. Hence at one point he stood for, not against, a Protestant territory. Urban, then pushed by the Spanish to take an unequivocal stance against heresy, decided—probably in part for this exact reason—to abandon his longtime friend, Galileo Galilei, to the bureaucrats of the Inquisition. Innocent XI and Innocent XII further demonstrated the variations. The former conducted a long and successful war against the Turks and saw both Jansenism and Quietism as threats to the integrity of Catholicism, but he also disapproved of force and persecution to suppress heresy. The latter, as archbishop of Naples, saw firsthand what problems could be caused by local inquisitors. While he did not allow abolition of the office there when a petition to that effect crossed his papal desk, he did insist that heresy trials could be held by the archbishop himself, virtually guaranteeing more lenient treatment. By the turn of the eighteenth century the Inquisition had almost no influence outside of Italy, yet early modern popes clung to its functions. At the end of his reign Benedict XIV, for example, issued one of the more thorough indexes of the period, even though its function had been replaced in some areas by state organs of censorship, as in Spain.

It is against this background of war against heresy that another characteristic of the early modern papacy—its "modernizing" tendencies—is best illustrated. Here too, a general pattern emerges, that of gradual political modernization in the early pontificates, and later of the emergence of spiritualization and moderation of papal policy. Once again, however, this pattern lacks consistency. The first popes of the early modern era demonstrated modernization primarily by mimicking the tendency toward political centralization characteristic of European states more generally. Pius V, Sixtus V, and Gregory XIII presided over the establishment of permanent cardinal commissions, or congregations, charged with overseeing specific functions of the church at large, like missionary activity and the creation of reform legislation. This departmentalization mirrored centralization of administrative functions in the burgeoning monarchies of the early modern world. Sixtus V had the added distinction of directing genuine urban planning and reorganization through the widening of boulevards and the refurbishing of aqueducts and other elements of the Roman infrastructure. Gregory XIII provided real impetus toward inserting the papacy into the developing modern scientific world by expenditures that have led historians to credit him with the founding of the Vatican observatory. Gregory's action in this regard was in line with the direction of Renaissance and Counter-Reformation pontiffs who had earlier encouraged astronomy.

Later popes, like Innocent XII, Benedict XIV, and Clement XIII, moved the image of the papacy closer to that of the modern institution by promoting social service and public assistance operations and by adopting a focus on spiritual concerns. Innocent did so through the expansion of hospices in Rome and through his publicly recognized spiritual devotion. Benedict maintained moderation in both political and theological matters by urging toleration instead of divisive posturing in theological controversies and by supporting scholarship through the Institute of Sciences in Bologna and other academies. He also renewed the condemnations of earlier popes against slavery in colonial territories. Clement worked hard to relieve Roman famine, even at the expense of inflationary economic policies. Still, these popes displayed something less than the "modernism" of later pontiffs. Innocent's social programming in Rome also included enclosure of vagabonds and the establishment of prisons for handling the poor. Benedict relied on a tax system in the Papal States that was widely regarded as inefficient, and for all of his promotion of learning, he considered the developing "Enlightenment" as a serious threat to Christianity. Perhaps the most notorious example of papal action contrary to modernization was taken by Urban VIII in the Galileo affair. Urban's willingness to allow a divided court to have its way with the physicist on the basis of highly irregular evidence created a strain between modern science and religion that persists to this day. This pope who gave extensive audiences to the poor and insisted that the sick be served with viaticum also ran up such debt through his artistic patronage and warfare that by 1640 fully 85 percent of papal income went to servicing that debt. Let the reader decide whether or not this latter fact reflects "modern" fiscal policy.

The early modern papacy stood as well in the midst of an age of evangelization. The popes described in this part went far beyond Protestant initiatives in spreading the Christian faith during this period. Still, some popes were a good deal more active in this operation than others. Those who were not tended to become distracted through what they considered more pressing political matters close to home. Those popes who became leaders in evangelization were Pius V, Sixtus V, Paul V, Innocent XI, Innocent XII, and Benedict XIV. Their activities, too numerous to describe in this introduction, spanned Asia, Africa, and the Americas. Pius could even demonstrate his characteristically hierarchical approach to all things within his missionary policy, by establishing a cardinal commission overseeing these efforts. He did so also by seeking to create an ecclesiastical hierarchy responsible not to religious orders who supplied the majority of missionaries then and now, but to the papacy—that is, to himself—alone. During the administration of Paul V missionaries and the converts they gained suffered under increasing persecution, and Paul considered it his duty to assist their efforts. Dominican universities were established in the Philippines and in Guatemala during the reign of Innocent XI, while his successor Innocent XII permitted probabilist doctrinal positions to promote more frequent reception of the sacraments in missionary lands.

Above all, the age in which these early modern popes found themselves was an era of brewing political upheaval. Papal foreign policies were inconsistent at best and self-contradictory at worst. Early modern popes thus contributed to the rapid decline of the papacy as a player in world affairs. The fundamental contradiction these popes maintained in foreign affairs was to utilize the methods of growing national states while at the same time opposing the interests of these same states. Pius V and Sixtus V began the process of centralizing papal government, creating staff and procedures that resembled governmental centralization elsewhere. Pius used nuncios as emissaries who could accomplish the work of implementing the decrees of Trent by going out from Rome as the center of policy and instruction. Both he and Sixtus established cardinal commissions—Sixtus, in fact, created no fewer than fifteen—that, combined with the work of nuncios and the systematic collection of *relationes* (reports from bishops on diocesan conditions), gathered information used by the pope and curia in decision making. While Sixtus was a more effective revenue raiser and even quasi-mercantilist in seeking Roman agricultural self-sufficiency, he, like Pius, saw his political organization as instrumental, effective in asserting papal authority and in the battle against heresy. These two, plus Clement VIII, were able to retain papal political influence amid the struggles of the world at large, but primarily through determination, and in Clement's case, through a prowess for mediation.

A shift toward papal political weakness began with Paul V and accelerated through the conclusion of the early modern period. Paul relied upon belief in the efficacy of his thunderous condemnations in controversies, first with England over an oath of loyalty required of its subjects, and then with Venice over the Republic's laws violating ecclesiastical rights. In neither case was his belief well founded, and Paul was left, after issuing an interdict against the Republic, in the uncomfortable position of seeking compromise with an excommunicated Venetian Senate that hoped that all

European princes would rally against papal authority. France and Spain came to Paul's assistance in negotiating compromise, but the stage was set for rapid decline in papal political power. The age of effective policy changing through thunderous papal condemnations—if it had ever truly existed—was past.

The religious and political conflicts that mutually affected the papacy and expanding monarchical governments in the seventeenth century and the first half of the eighteenth century exacerbated papal weakness in foreign affairs. While the papacy entered the Thirty Years' War (1618–48) as a relatively influential participant, it exited as a bit player after distracted leadership on the part of Urban VIII defined contradictory alliances. Innocent XI struggled with constant political problems against France, and Innocent XII lacked the political savvy to avoid contributing to the turmoil that led to the War of the Spanish Succession in 1700. What Innocent XII could not do in changing the public perception of the church through cosmetic adjustments, Benedict XIV was able to accomplish through his more spiritualist, moderate positions. Once Benedict had stepped aside, somewhat, from attempts to sway European politics, Clement XIII was unable to reinsert papal considerations when issues such as the expulsion of the Jesuits from Portugal and France had a direct impact upon the church and its personnel. Clement faced the campaign against the Jesuits with the political power only to slow, not to stop it. He died of a stroke in the process, illustrating papal weakness literally. Clement XIV thus caved in on what was virtually inevitable by the time he assumed the papal throne: the dissolution of one of the largest religious orders in the church, one that was, at least symbolically, among the principal buttresses of the papacy.

The contradictions and inconsistencies exhibited by early modern popes were pervasive. Historians seeking an institution that can easily be characterized as a backward opponent of genuine reform, or as a forward-focused contributor to political centralization, or as an anachronistic proponent of authority that no longer existed will be frustrated when they examine these notable popes. The popes of this age faced powerful political, religious, social, and cultural forces in the transition from the Middle Ages to the modern world. Of course, they were not aware of any such transition. Only at the risk of anachronism do we search for signs of "modernity" among them. It is not that such a search for signs of the familiar is wrong in itself, but that our view of contemporary persons and institutions—whether popes and papacy, presidents and presidency, queens and monarchy, or patriarchs and patriarchy—sometimes leads us to identify more than signs of modernity. That view frequently leads us not just to identify "modern" characteristics, but also to identify them as good, as progressive, as "proper" in the context of the past. This form of anachronism leads to the worst kind of history. Study the popes who follow in this part by consideration of what they did and why, not in order to pass judgment upon them as contributors to or obstacles in the way of a modernism to come. It is only in that way that you will understand them.

PIUS V (1566–72)

SERGIO PAGANO, EDITED BY WILLIAM V. HUDON

After the death of Pope Pius IV on 9 September 1565, the three-week conclave to select a successor dissolved several candidacies. One was that of Cardinal Giovanni Morone. He may have been Pius IV's coordinator of the final phase of the Council of Trent, but he was also a victim of the fear and wrath of Paul IV (Gian Pietro Carafa, 1555–59), the pope who imprisoned Morone for suspicion of heresy. Eventually, Michele Ghislieri was elected and chose the name Pius V because he owed his election, in part, to an agreement between Alessandro Farnese and Carlo Borromeo, the nephew of his predecessor. The new pope ironically bore a greater resemblance, both in ideology and in his ecclesiastical policies, to Paul IV. When still a cardinal, the Carafa pope, after all, had nominated Ghislieri to become commissioner-general of the Roman Inquisition in 1551. While pope, Carafa had him elected bishop of Sutri and Nepi (1556) and raised him to the college of cardinals in 1557.

Born in Boscomarengo, near Alessandria, on 17 January 1504, Ghislieri came to the papal throne with a religious mind and mentality that years in the curia, and even life in the shadow of popes, could not change. Historians evaluating the actions he took during his pontificate must acknowledge his upright way of life and determined vision of the faith. Although these characteristics went unnoticed among his more aristocratic colleagues in the college of cardinals who referred to him as "frate scarpone" or "friar Big Boots," denigrating his rustic background, it showed in his every governmental action. Ghislieri developed this outlook and manner of proceeding through long study and life in eight monasteries within the

Lombard province of the Dominican order, including Genoa, where he was ordained a priest in 1528. The Lombard province had committed itself to a reform program since the middle of the fifteenth century. In these houses Ghislieri was novice, priest, professor of theology, and superior. He understood his vocation simply and literally. He dressed himself in the typical Dominican habit, and even when he was called to exercise the power of the "keys of the kingdom," he dressed in pontifical vestments with the same unaffected desire to answer to God rather than to men. Pius V rose above defects like avarice, nepotism, and scant religiosity that many contemporaries criticized in early-sixteenth-century popes from Leo X (1513–21) and Hadrian VI (1522–23) to Clement VII (1523–34) and Paul III (1534–49). Pius V refused to bow to the desire for money, glory, or enrichment of his blood relatives. He made perhaps one concession to the desire to be reputed magnanimous: in ample gifts to the Dominican monastery of Santa Croce e Ognissanti in his native town of Boscomarengo. Pius endowed the Church of Santa Croce, which was attached to the monastery, with precious marble sculptures, reliquaries, and artworks of every kind. He thereby helped that church execute in reality the model for sacred buildings constructed in theory through the decrees of Trent. He also chose it as his burial place.

Ghislieri possessed an inflexible temper that joined virtue with single-minded toughness. He demonstrated mercy while zealously defending Catholic orthodoxy even as a cardinal, and this continued during his papal administration. He showed not only a remarkable affection for poverty and personal humility, but also an energetic determination to secure, if not to expand, papal power and prerogatives. In this latter characteristic he resembled medieval proponents of papal power like Gregory VII (1073–85) and Innocent III (1198–1216). He mixed his interest in theology with an intense desire to restore ecclesiastical discipline and prescribed that desire for those around him. He imposed a more religious way of life on the papal curia that led the great historian of the papacy Ludwig von Pastor to consider him truly unusual. It was rare, according to Pastor, when—as with Pius V—the sovereign was subordinate to the priest.

In a brief overview of the pontificate of Pius V, it would be difficult to overemphasize the importance of his efforts to implement the decrees of the Council of Trent. The organic plan for reformation conceived and promulgated by the council would have been quite useless without an energetic, determined executive committed to the translation of conciliar theory into practice. The good intentions of the Fifth Lateran Council (1512), for example, were wrecked in part because of the disinterest of Pope Leo X. Pius V was convinced of the need for the reforms of Trent. He attended especially to the editing and publishing of key religious texts. In September 1566 the *Catechismo per i parroci* (Parish Catechism) was published. It had been revised and edited by three Dominicans (Egidio Foscarini, Leonardo

De Marini, and Francesco Foreiro) entrusted with that work by the Holy See. Similarly, the *Breviarium Romanum ex decreto sacrosanti Concilii Tridentini restitutum* was published in 1568, followed two years later by the new *Missale Romanum*. The latter, in use until Vatican Council II, was known as the *Messale di Pio V* (Missal of Pius V), recognizing the pope's personal commitment to the revision of such liturgical texts. Pius gave over the work of promoting and diffusing the use of these texts to his apostolic nuncios. He chose them from the administrators closest to him and sent them all over Europe with instructions that explained the use of the texts as part of a broader reform that local bishops were obligated to create. In addition, Pius insisted on the use of these same texts among religious orders that had no liturgical books already formally approved by the Holy See. Pius similarly intended to reform the Latin text of the Holy Scriptures through critical review. He assembled a commission of experts to carry out the work, but the group moved forward very slowly due to the complexity of the project, and it was completed only during the pontificate of Clement VIII (1592–1605), with the so-called Clementine Vulgate edition. Pius paid special attention as well to the reform of regular clergy, insisting on stricter observance of monastic rules where laxity remained a problem after generations of inconsistent reform. He prescribed both solemn profession and attendance at choir, and he reinforced the restriction against regular clergy living outside of cloister.

Pope Pius V. (Courtesy of the Vatican Library)

In his plan for ecclesiastical government Pius saw the application of the disciplinary decrees of the Council of Trent as something that must go hand in hand with defense of Catholic dogma enunciated and confirmed by the council. He therefore maintained a constant, vigilant struggle against heresy and against the infiltration of heterodox theories and practices. He had witnessed the spread of Lutheranism and Calvinism in Catholic countries, including Italy, and the diffusion of evangelism, Waldensianism, Anabaptism, and antitrinitarianism among both elite and lower-class populations. Therefore, he became careful, firm, even suspicious, on the matter of heresy. Pius had previously worked as general commissioner of the inquisitions of Como and Bergamo, places in which heterodox propaganda seemed quite dangerous to him, and had served as the head of the Roman Holy Office as cardinal under Paul IV, who was his model for operation in all matters related to heresy. These experiences simply confirmed the suspicions of Pius and left him convinced that he fully understood not only the defining characteristics of heresy, but also the danger of negotiation, compromise, or conciliation with heretics on matters of Catholic dogma.

With this experience behind him, Pius gave the Holy Office a central position in his administration. An indication of this centrality can be found in his work to restore and remodel a building quite close to St. Peter's Basilica to house the Roman Inquisition. The property was one acquired from Lorenzo Pucci, the cardinal in charge of the Penitentiary. Beyond this physical sign, further evidence can be found in Pius's actions and policies as pope. When any matter of heresy arose, all other considerations, even reasons of state, took a back seat. Neither cardinal nor bishop nor pontifical nuncio could escape his severe censure if, to him, they appeared to support, excuse, or underestimate any heretic. European sovereigns stood in an identical position, as did Italian states, and at times they were forced, as the proud Venetian republic was in 1566, to bow to his will. Pius obliged Venice to turn one Guido Giannetti da Fano over to Roman authorities. A convinced heretic, he had served as secretary to the English ambassador in Rome during the 1530s, and not even the protection of Queen Elizabeth was of the slightest avail.

A similar war of wills developed in numerous other cases during the reign of Pius V. He quarreled with Duke Guglielmo of Mantua in 1568, and earlier with Duke Cosimo I of Florence. The latter battle was over the sad case of Pietro Carnesecchi, perhaps the most famous heretic condemned to death in this period. Pius similarly struggled against both the republic of Genoa and the republic of Lucca over their commercial relations with lands infested with heresy, and against numerous other princes and sovereigns. When Pius V issued an extradition request for a heretic, there may have been opposition, but Pius usually emerged victorious, enjoying an obedience, albeit a grudging one, that his predecessors could not claim. All of these examples are more than just evidence of the zeal of this pope against heresy. They are also part of the reason why dozens of heretics, including the Neapolitan noble Pompeo de Monti (d. 1566), Pietro Carnesecchi (d. 1567), Bartolomeo Bartoccio (d. 1569), and the famous humanist Antonio della Paglia da Veroli (d. 1570) perished under the condemnation of a tribunal personally driven by this inflexible inquisitor.

Pius V extended his absolute approach to the matter of heterodoxy in other celebrated cases as well. He may have been one of the signatories to the absolution Pius IV granted to the Milanese cardinal Giovanni Morone in 1560, but Pius V continued to harbor doubts about him. He considered

Morone too close to the so-called *spirituali* and was apparently preparing to begin a new trial against the cardinal, which he might well have done had his own death not intervened in 1572. Pius also took action in the case of Michael Bajus, a Belgian theologian and professor at Louvain. Bajus, who had been censured by the University of Paris in 1560 for his interpretation of Augustine, had provoked further opposition in the universities of Alcala and Salamanca in 1567 with his ideas about free will, grace, and human nature. When he appealed the charges to the pope, Pius V issued a condemnation of seventy-six theses taken from the theologian's work. Bajus appealed to Cardinal Ludovico Simonetta and even to Pius himself, but finally submitted to the papal censure.

Pius expended great energy toward reform in the curia and in the diocese of Rome. He gradually remodeled the college of cardinals with the appointment of persons favorable to reform. He reformed the Apostolic Penitentiary and restricted its competency to matters of the internal forum. He attempted to eliminate simony in the Datary and other curial offices and formed the Congregation of the Index to monitor printing permissions. Both his creation of the Congregation of the Bishops and the visitation he began of the diocese of Rome in 1566 were designed to promote diocesan reform by direct example. He attempted to do the same by watching over preaching and pastoral work conducted throughout Roman parishes and monasteries.

Pius proceeded with equal energy in consolidating the property, authority, and prerogatives of the Papal States. He considered these compromised, indeed nearly alienated, through privileges conceded by his predecessors to various feudal nobles in central Italy at the expense of the Camera Apostolica. He viewed the loss of ecclesiastical property as among the worst crimes and reinforced his desire to protect the Papal States with a new constitution. Pius issued the document on 29 May 1567 and required that members of the college of cardinals swear to uphold it.

Pius V maintained a foreign policy consistently driven by his intention to implement the decrees of the Council of Trent in all Catholic states. In his actions Pius took inspiration from medieval popes who had stressed a hierocratic image of the papacy, and who had insisted on the absolute autonomy of the church over and against secular authorities, combining religious certainty with the desire for political sovereignty. Both ecclesiastics and lay rulers who had earlier enjoyed special privileges and exemptions from such control, however, had reason to oppose this element of his reform. The former feared that the application of a rigorous canonical discipline would result in the narrowing of religious thought. The latter feared that enhanced ecclesiastical autonomy would diminish their ability to influence church policies and appointments, an ability they had consolidated through direct exemptions as well as through curial practice.

Pius engaged Spain in one of his political struggles. The pope became embroiled in jurisdictional controversies with King Philip II (1527–98) in traditional Spanish territory on the Iberian peninsula and in Spanish holdings in southern Italy. They quarreled over abuses associated with the Spanish Inquisition, which operated autonomously and often in contradiction to the Roman tribunal. They fought also over the dominions of Naples and Sicily, territories that traditionally were considered fiefs of the Holy See, but that, in this period, were under Philip II and the Kingdom of the Two Sicilies. Pius became convinced that resistance to his plan to eliminate Spanish royal influence in ecclesiastical matters was due to adherence to Protestant ideology in places like Spain. For his part, Philip refused to surrender traditional privileges held by the Habsburg crown that had been bequeathed to him by his father Charles V, believing that any concession granted to the Holy See would represent an alienation of royal power. Thus conflicts arose between the two over numerous issues: on when and under what circumstances the royal *placet* (permission for the publication of a papal bull) and the *exequatur* (royal permission for the exercise of a bishop's function) would be issued; on the legitimacy of a royal *recurso de fuerza* (appeal against abuses); and over the exercise of the *monarchia sicula* (the royal control of Sicily).

Once begun, these conflicts survived for a long time, despite exhaustive diplomacy and negotiation. The papal nuncio in Madrid and the orator (or ambassador) of the emperor expended great effort to mend repeated breaks in the relationship between the two powers caused by disagreements between Pius, Philip, and their ministers. This jurisdictional struggle was particularly troublesome in the city of Milan, where senate and archbishop, pope and Habsburg sovereign, waged a war of words. Philip II controlled the city's secular government, against the fierce opposition of its archbishops, throughout this period. These archbishops, in line with their pope, jealously guarded the ancient ecclesiastical autonomy from secular authority that the Council of Trent reasserted in principle and that Pius V was determined to establish in practice.

Relations between France and the Holy See were no less difficult during the reign of Pius V, in part because of his conviction that here, as in Spain, Protestantism subverted the relationship between church and state. At the same time, the queen, Catherine de' Medici (1519–89), struggled to maintain a balance between the Catholic and Huguenot parties for political reasons. Pius would brook no suggestion of any concession to the Calvinist Huguenots, and so he recommended strong measures against them. Catherine employed half-measures instead. The situation was complicated by the generally anti-Spanish attitude of the French Crown and by the French alliance with the Ottoman Turks. The French hoped to counterbalance Spanish hegemony in the Mediterranean through this alliance with the Turks, who threatened both Central Europe and southern Italy.

Pius encountered rough, tension-ridden foreign relations with secular authorities in German-speaking lands as well. The Austrian Habsburg emperor Maximilian II (1564–76) remained far from Pius V on religious questions close to the pope's heart, as he was elusive and inclined to compromise. Pius considered him far too tolerant toward Protestantism, as Maximilian hoped to maintain concessions made in 1555 for adherents to the Augsburg Confession. The two leaders found common ground only in their desire for war against the Turks, but strain developed even in that policy, since Pius linked requirements in imperial religious policy to continued papal war subsidies. Relations were more friendly in one particular German territory, Bavaria, due to its regular procedure in episcopal elections and the benefice assessment that resulted in sizable revenue for Rome.

By the time Pius V reached the papal throne, the split between Anglican and Catholic churches in England was final, and the land remained impervious to his plan to implement the Tridentine decrees. Unlike his predecessor, Pius V had little confidence in the earlier conformity of Queen Elizabeth (1533–1603) to Catholicism during her sister's reign (Mary Tudor, 1516–58) or in the idea that Elizabeth's relative moderation toward Catholics reflected anything more than political expediency. Pius convinced himself that her "moderation" was a tactical illusion, and in February 1570 he began the process of declaring the English sovereign guilty of formal heresy. He received pressure to do so from English Catholics. They desired justification for her overthrow in the form of a papal condemnation. Their wish came true on 25 February 1570 with the publication of the bull *Regnans in excelsis*, which declared her a heretic, usurper of the throne, and fomenter of heresy. Pius excommunicated her and all her followers in this bull. Therein he deprived her of the English crown and absolved her subjects from loyalty. Pius made a serious political mistake in taking this harsh action, the last sentence of deposition pronounced by a pope against a reigning monarch. His bull turned out to be useless, if not completely self-defeating, as the era of papal theocracy had passed. The document served instead as an excuse for the sovereign and her Anglican loyalists to expand anti-Catholic legislation in England.

While his plan in England may have failed, Pius V reached a completely different outcome in operations against the Ottoman Turks. His predecessors had been unsuccessful in such actions due to the rivalry between Spain, France, England, and Germany, but he, on the other hand, succeeded. When the Venetian Marc Antonio Bragadin, the defender of Famagosta, was brutally killed, not to mention flayed, by Turks in 1570, Pius gained an opportunity to press for an alliance of Christian rulers against the Ottoman Empire. Still, it was only after tough negotiations that Pius was able to conceal the opposite interests of Spain and Venice long enough to put together an anti-Turkish league that also included Genoa, the Knights of Malta, and the duke of Savoy. The alliance set off with a fleet of 208 galleys and approximately 25 other vessels under the command of John of Austria. They faced the Turkish fleet near Lepanto, compensated for numerical inferiority with technical superiority, and won a rapid, stunning victory on 7 October 1571. The Battle of Lepanto quickly became a symbol of the triumph of the Cross over the Crescent, and of the papacy over the infidel. Enjoying overwhelming public support, Pius read a religious message into the victory. He dedicated the operation to the Blessed Virgin Mary, establishing a feast day in her honor coinciding with the anniversary of the battle, and thereby also the cult of "Our Lady of Victory."

Pius V actively encouraged missionary activity, especially in the new-world lands of America, Asia, and Africa. In these works he could avoid the institutional struggles he encountered in European affairs, even if religious operations in the Americas had to pass through the so-called Council of the Indies that was controlled by the king of Spain. In mission lands the church lacked the entrenched organizational structure operating in Europe, so Pius worked hard to establish a hierarchy directly subject to the Holy See and outside the control of nonclerics and royal ministers. He established a congregation of cardinals to oversee missionary plans. In 1572 he ordered that two-thirds of the revenue derived from Portuguese tithes be dedicated to the burgeoning missions in Brazil and Japan. He dedicated substantial resources to the Jesuit missions in China as well.

Pius did not possess the reputation for munificence that most of his immediate predecessors enjoyed, and throughout papal Rome he applied the rigid rules concerning patronage inherent in his own personal commitment to poverty and embodied in the decrees of the Council of Trent. After his election Pius refused to fund the traditional opulence and magnificence that often surrounded the papal court. Instead, he preferred to spend large sums in alms to the poor and in contributions to poorly endowed monasteries. Pius was willing, nevertheless, to engage in some expensive building operations. He continued to support the ongoing refurbishing of St. Peter's Basilica and made additions to the Vatican apartments that included three chapels frescoed by such artists as Giorgio Vasari, Jacopo Zucchi, Giulio Mazzoni, and Daniele da Volterra. He completed the construction of Santa Maria dei Angeli and contributed—along with its major patron, Cardinal Alessandro Farnese—to the building of the Church of the Gesù, which became the principal church of the Society of Jesus. During Pius's reign the new convent of SS. Domenico e Sisto al Quirinale was completed. Pius also expended funds for civic improvements, successfully sponsoring the recovery of the water supply known as the Waters of the Virgin that returned to gush from the Trevi Fountain, and restoring walls and fortifications.

Pius V maintained a rigid approach to public morality, which can be likened to his insistence on ecclesiastical discipline. This element of his policy is fairly well known, as he worked to eliminate prostitution in Rome and even to prevent adultery, with the threat of severe punishment. He hoped to eradicate the holding of North African slaves in Christian homes and restricted the licenses of tavern owners in the city of Rome. He loathed the yearly Roman carnival festivities and attempted to curtail them as well. He issued edicts in 1566 against simony, blasphemy, sodomy, and concubinage. For Pius, restrictions placed upon the Jewish population of the city were also part of a coherent moral agenda. In his mind, they were guilty of divination, magic, witchcraft, and usury. In Pius's Rome Jews were forbidden to live together with Christians, to walk about without a distinguishing mark, to purchase real estate, and to employ Christian servants. They were returned to the ghetto designed by Paul IV after the softer treatment they had received under Pius IV. Pius V even restored the walls of the ghetto and obliged Jews to periodically attend religious sermons. Through this latter obligation Pius hoped—as he did in supporting the House of Catechumens—to promote the conversion of Roman Jews to Christianity.

Pius V, whose holiness was celebrated by St. Carlo Borromeo, died in Rome on 1 May 1572. In his will Pius had expressed a desire to be buried in his native land, in the Church of Santa Croce that he had restored, and where he had established a burial vault complete with a funerary inscription he had written himself. Instead, his body was buried first in the Chapel of Sant'Andrea in the Vatican. His remains were moved in 1588 to the Church of Santa Maria Maggiore, where Pope Sixtus V (1585–90) planned a sumptuous monument eventually constructed by the sculptor Domenico Fontana. On the one hundredth anniversary of his death (1 May 1672) Pius was declared blessed by Pope Clement X (1670–76). Clement XI (1700–1721) canonized him on 22 May 1712. The feast of Pius V was originally fixed as 5 May, but now is celebrated on 30 April.

SELECTED BIBLIOGRAPHY

Barzaghi, Cesare. "Schiarimento intorno alla biografia di S. Pio V del P. Giovanni Gabuzio." *Eco dei Barnabiti-studi* 5 (June 1939): 11–24.

Catena, Girolamo. *Vita del gloriosissimo papa Pio Quinto*. Rome: A. Gardano & F. Coattino, 1587.

Chacon, Alfonso. *Vitae et res gestae pontificum romanorum*. Ed. Agostino Oldoini. Rome: Philippi et Antonii de Rubeis, 1677.

Chenna, Giuseppe Antonio. *Del vescovato de' vescovi, e delle chiese della città e diocesi di Alessandria*. Alessandria: Tipografia I. Vimercati, 1786.

Denzler, Georg. "Pius V." *Biographisch-bibliographisches Kirchenlexikon*. Ed. Friedrich W. Bautz. Herzberg: Traugott Bautz, 1994, vol. 6, cols. 665–67.

Duval, André. "Pie V." *Catholicisme hier-aujourd'hui-demain*. Paris: Letouzey & Ané, 1988, vol. 11, cols. 255–58.

Falloux, Alfred-Frédéric-Pierre de. *Histoire de saint Pie V*. Paris: Sagnier & Bray, 1851.

Fuenmayor, Antonio de. *Vida y hechos de Pio quinto pontifice romano*. Madrid: I. Sanchez, 1639.

Gabuzio, Giovanni Antonio. *De vita et-rebus gestis Pii V. Pont. Max. Libri sex*. Rome: Zannetti, 1605.

Ghislieri, P.M. *Elogio istorico di san Pio quinto pontefice massimo*. Assisi: n.p., 1797.

Hernan, E. Garcia. "Pio V y el messianismo profético." *Hispania sacra* 45 (1993): 83–102.

Iacobilli, Lodovico. *Vite del santissimo pontefice Pio V del P. Bonaparte e del P.D. Francesco Ghislieri*. Todi: n.p., 1661.

Kelly, John N.D. *The Oxford Dictionary of Popes*. Oxford: Oxford University Press, 1986.

Labus, Giovanni. *Pio V e suoi tempi*. Ancona: Sartori Cherubini, 1854.

Lemaître, Nicole. "Pie V." *Dictionnaire historique de la Papauté*. Ed. Philippe Levillain. Paris: Fayard, 1994, cols. 1328–30.

———. *Saint Pie V*. Paris: Fayard, 1994.

Maffei, Paolo Alessandro. *Vita di S. Pio Quinto: Sommo Pontefice dell'Ordine Medicatori*. Rome: Francesco Gonzaga, 1712.

Manfredi, Girolamo. *Vita Pii Quinti pontificis maximi*. Cesanae: B. Raverius, 1586.

Mendham, Joseph. *The Life and Pontificate of Saint Pius the Fifth*. London: J. Duncan, 1832.

Mondin, Battista. *Dizionario enciclopedico dei Papi: Storia e insegnamenti*. Rome: Città Nuova, 1995.

Pastor, Ludwig Freiherr von. *The History of the Popes from the Close of the Middle Ages*. Vols. 17 and 18. Trans. Ralph Francis Kerr. St. Louis: Herder, 1951, 1952.

Pierozzi, L. "La vittoria di Lepanto nell'escatologia e nella profezia." *Rinascimento* ser. 2, 34 (1994): 317–63.

Pio V e Santa Croce di Bosco: Aspetti di una committenza papale. Ed. Carlenrica Spantigati and Giulio Ieni. Alessandria: Edizioni dell'Orso, 1985.

Il processo inquisitoriale del cardinale Giovanni Morone. Ed. Massimo Firpo and Dario Marcatto. 6 vols. Rome: Istituto storico italiano per l'età moderna e contemporanea, 1981–95.

San Pio V e la problematica del suo tempo. Ed. Aniceto Fernandez. Alessandria: Cassa di Risparmio di Alessandria, 1972.

Spezi, Pio. *Pio V e i suoi tempi*. Rome: Pustet, 1905.

GREGORY XIII (1572–85): FATHER OF THE NATIONS

Frederick J. McGinness

Ugo Boncompagni (born 1 January 1502; died 10 April 1585; ruled as Pope Gregory XIII, 13 May 1572 to 10 April 1585) was a native of Bologna and the fourth son of the merchant Cristoforo Boncompagni and Angela Marescalchi. He served as pope in the crucial years of the post-Tridentine period, sometimes called the Catholic Reform or Counter-Reformation. A most capable administrator and strategist, Gregory understood and made maximum use of the many strengths of the Roman church to implement the Tridentine reform and, as much as possible, roll back the gains of the Protestants in large parts of Europe. With a profound trust in the transformational value of education, Gregory lavished enormous resources upon scholarship and education to promote Catholicism both at Rome and in the Papal States, and in lands where Protestant sects had gained dominance or were threatening to gain the upper hand. Given to more peaceful than belligerent solutions, he understood the contest with Protestant confessions as being won through solid educational programs and institutions, excellent preaching that boldly proclaimed the truth of the faith, careful strategy, tight ecclesiastical administration, and above all the example of virtuous clergy intent on implementing the decrees of the Tridentine council.

Gregory grew up in Bologna among the prominent members of that society. He took up the study of law at the University of Bologna, where in 1530 he received his doctorate in canon and civil law (*in utroque iure*); he taught law there from 1531 to 1539. Among his more prominent pupils at Bologna were Otto Truchsess, Cristoforo Madruzzo, Reginald Pole,

Francesco Alciati, Alessandro Farnese, and Ippolito Riminaldi. In 1548, long before his ordination to the priesthood, he fathered a natural son, Giacomo, who would later serve his father as papal governor of Castel Sant'Angelo and gonfaloniere of the papal troops. Throughout Gregory's pontificate Giacomo's ambitions for ecclesiastical status often caused problems with which the pontiff dealt firmly to avoid the appearance of favoring his family at the expense of the church. Nonetheless, Giacomo married well, accumulated significant titles, and went on to enrich the Boncompagni family considerably.

Because of a weak voice, Gregory resigned his chair at Bologna and moved to Rome to work for Cardinal Pietro Paolo Parisio. In the early 1540s Boncompagni was appointed by Paul III as a judge in the Capitol, later referendary (*referendarius utriusque segnaturae*), and in 1546 secretary (*abbreviator*) of the Council of Trent (1546). Boncompagni apparently fell from the graces of Julius III (1550–55) and was removed as a *referendarius*; he then withdrew from the curia to resume his studies. However, later in the same pontificate he was appointed by Cardinal Giambattista Cicada as his vice-legate for the Campagna. In 1556 Paul IV availed himself of Boncompagni's legal expertise, appointing him to the Reform Commission; later he served Cardinal Carlo Carafa on papal diplomatic missions to France (1556) and to the court of Philip II at Brussels (1557). In 1558 he was appointed by Paul IV to serve on the Segnatura di Grazia and was made a member of a commission to solve the dispute with Ferdinand I. On 20 July 1558 Boncompagni was made bishop of the southern Italian diocese of Viesti, and toward the end of that year, he was appointed vice-regent to Cardinal Alfonso Carafa, regent of the Camera. Escaping the recriminations against the cardinal nephew after the death of Paul IV in 1559, Boncompagni fell under the influence of the cardinal nephew of Pius IV, Carlo Borromeo, who secured for him an appointment to the Consulta.

In 1561 Boncompagni accompanied the papal legate, Cardinal Ludovico Simonetta, to the last period of the Council of Trent (1561–63), where as papal jurist he helped in the drafting of decrees, among which was that dealing with the obligation of episcopal residence. On 12 March 1565, the feast of Saint Gregory the Great, he was elevated to the purple by Pius IV and made cardinal-presbyter of San Sisto; he was then sent to Spain with Felice Peretti (the future Pope Sixtus V, 1585–90) to review the Inquisition's case against the archbishop of Toledo, Bartolomé Caranza. In 1566 Pius V (1566–72) selected him to preside over the Segnatura of Briefs. Held in almost universal esteem by fellow clergy for his prudence, expertise in canon law, indefatigable labor, organizational skill, and exemplary life, Boncompagni was elected pope on 13 May 1572 on the first ballot. Instrumental in this was the strong approval he enjoyed from the king of Spain, Philip II, who was also not favorable to the man deemed most *papabile*, Alessandro Farnese. Boncompagni's selection of the name

Gregory was in honor of Pope Gregory the Great, on whose feast he had been made cardinal. Influenced profoundly by Carlo Borromeo, Gregory's appointments after his election, such as Tolomeo Galli as secretary of state, and the confirmation of many reformers in their former positions under Pius V made clear his intention to continue the reforms of Trent and the restoration of Catholicism. Though Gregory appointed two of his nephews to the cardinalate, they played very little role in major decisions.

Gregory quickly displayed his skill for organization when he instituted additional special congregations of cardinals to handle the growing complexities of the papal administration. Gregory, in fact, was following the lead of Paul III, who had begun this process with the establishment of the Congregation of the Inquisition (1542), and of other popes as well. Gregory's pontificate included some fifteen congregations to handle diverse questions such as the council, the Index, the Inquisition, the league against the Turks, the reform and publication of a new edition of canon law, and the jubilee year (1575). Many congregations, it seemed, were established to handle questions on an ad hoc basis and submit the matter for the pope's decision. These more efficient organs of administration relieved the excessive burdens that had over the years fallen to the unwieldy papal consistory. To monitor the progress of the Tridentine reform, Gregory augmented the number and importance of nunciatures throughout the Christian world not just for collecting timely information on the political situation in their respective countries, but above all for promoting religious and ecclesiastical disciplinary issues. Gregory created important new nunciatures in strategic areas, such as the one in Lower Germany at Co-

Pope Gregory XIII. (Courtesy of the Vatican Library)

logne (1573), which expanded in 1584 to include Basel, Strassburg, and Flanders, and those at Graz in Styria (1580) and for southern Germany at Salzburg (1573). Gregory also expanded the duties of existing nunciatures, such as that of Lucerne in Switzerland (1579).

With a vision for the restoration of Catholicism throughout Europe, Gregory was well fitted to appreciate the superior resources in the new religious orders such as the Jesuits and the Capuchins for missions to France, Muscovy, England, and the Low Countries, where the example of selfless religious could provide credible examples of virtuous Catholic clergy and so win members of heretical sects, as well as wayward Catholics, back to Rome.

Immediately following his election as pontiff, Gregory turned his attention to the single most important program before him: the implementation of the decrees of the Council of Trent. Foremost among his concerns was the enforcement of the residency requirement for bishops, which Gregory enforced uniformly and with few exceptions. The council had attached the greatest urgency and importance to the necessity of bishops residing permanently in their dioceses and tending to their flocks. One result was to be the departure from Rome of many of the reform's leaders, such as Carlo Borromeo, who returned to Milan as its archbishop, and Giovanni Morone, who took up residence in the diocese of Velletri. But the advantages proved in the end far greater than the loss of administrative expertise at Rome. Gregory insisted that bishops visit the churches and religious institutions of their dioceses once a year and establish seminaries for educating their clergy, and he implemented this in exemplary fashion first by delegating apostolic visitors for the many dioceses within the Papal States, which he then extended to include all of Italy, though at times his program did meet with resistance in some localities, such as Venice. The apostolic visitation looked above all to the religious life of the diocese, but also concerned itself with upholding ecclesiastical liberties, monitoring ecclesiastical discipline, and promoting the authority of the bishop and the standing of his clergy. Gregory also sought to implement the Tridentine directive that bishops conduct annual diocesan and triennial provincial synods, a measure adopted by Carlo Borromeo at Milan that would serve as a model for bishops elsewhere, though in fact few other bishops ever came close to Borromeo's achievement.

At the heart of Gregory's reform initiatives was his attention to the state of religious orders, as well as the advancement of those actively carrying out his reform initiatives. He consolidated the religious houses of the Camaldolese and the Hermits of St. Jerome to accommodate the dramatic decline in membership. To resolve internal disputes within many of the long-established religious orders, he issued ordinances to ensure the free election of superiors and often intervened by appointing his own superiors and forbidding the appeal of members of religious communities to external authorities as a way of circumventing the demands of obedience. He required women's religious orders to enforce the rule of enclosure, as prescribed by Trent, and had reliable visitors inspect Cistercian monasteries of Lombardy and Tuscany to eradicate the impoverishment of these communities because of commendams temporary assignment of revenues of a church or monastery to another cleric or to a layman and irregular monastic elections. Even after Trent, the commendam system often diverted revenues from monastic communities to laymen.

Within Italy Gregory's reforms addressed most major religious orders: the Cassinese Congregation of the Benedictines, Observant Franciscans, Dominicans, and the Knights of Malta, to whom he twice sent nuncios. Gregory's reforms extended beyond Italy to Spain, Portugal, Germany, and France. He also confirmed a number of religious orders such as the Barnabites and the Theatines and brought about some changes in their status and constitutions, such as that of the Ursulines, which he changed from a free association of women dedicated to apostolic work to a canonically approved religious order living under the three vows, and under Carlo Borromeo rather than under a superioress-general, whose office was suppressed. Gregory sought, as well, to eradicate numerous chronic abuses among some religious orders. In some cases, as among Spain's Observant and Alcantarine Franciscans, he intervened directly to settle their disputes. Wherever possible, however, Gregory sought to restore internal discipline by encouraging renewal and by generously fostering clerical education, which he saw as crucial to this end. He warmly supported both old and new religious orders, especially the Capuchins and Jesuits, for their preaching, education, and pastoral ministries; he encouraged the growth and the reorganization of the Basilian order under a single head, as he did for the Servites; and he approved Filippo Neri's Congregation of the Oratory (1575), the new constitution of the Barnabites (1579), and the reforms of Teresa of Avila's Discalced Carmelites (1580).

Gregory's strongest support went to religious who seemed most to be working for the good of the church. In this category, above all, was the Society of Jesus, founded in 1540 by Ignatius Loyola. Gregory's enthusiasm for the work of the Jesuits found its full expression in the confirmation of their order in 1584 and in the restoration of their privileges, which had been diminished by Pius V. These included removing the obligation to recite the divine office in choir, and ordination to the priesthood after the three simple vows. Gregory's generosity to the Jesuits and other religious orders included large subsidies for their numerous colleges in Italy, throughout Europe, and even in newly discovered lands, such as Japan, for the spread of the Catholic faith, especially in those lands of the German empire threatened by Protestants. At Rome he richly endowed special colleges for German students (the Collegium Germanicum [to which was added the Collegium Ungaricum in 1580]), the English (1579), the Greeks (1577), Maronite Christians from Lebanon and Armenia (both in 1577), as well as special colleges for converts from Islam and Judaism (1577), whose direction he entrusted to the Jesuits.

It was, however, his lavish gift of the new Collegio Romano (1584), above all, that signaled Gregory's particular favor to the Jesuits. Remarkable by all educational standards of the time, the new edifice made clear the pope's commitment to the work of education in Catholic reform, and the curriculum of the Collegio Romano (whose successor today is the Gregorian University) would serve as the model of Jesuit education that set a standard for seminaries throughout the world. With papal permission to grant degrees in philosophy and theology, the institution not only educated young Jesuits from throughout the world, but also seminarians from the other colleges of Rome. Gregory also gave generously to the University of Rome (La Sapienza), whose physical fabric he expanded and whose illustrious faculty he richly subsidized. One of the age's most noted humanists and Latinists, Marc Antoine Muret, for example, taught there throughout Gregory's time until his own death in 1585. Muret was known for commanding the highest salary among any of recent memory. Muret, however, was just one of many humanists and scholars whom Gregory warmly accommodated. Though he was a canonist himself, he promoted all branches of learning, both in humanistic and scientific studies, and at the Collegio Romano and the University of Rome. Among the notable scholars flourishing in Gregory's Rome were Uberto Folieta, Paulo Manuzio, Ignazio Danti, Ulisse Aldrovandi, Marc Antoine Muret, Carlo Sigonio, Silvio Antoniano, Guglielmo Sirleto, Fulvio Orsini, Pedro Maldonado, Pedro Chacon, Achille Stazio, Christopher Schlüssel (Clavius), Gerhard Voss, Francisco de Toledo, and Francisco Suarez.

Gregory's enormous success with these educational institutions inspired him in later years to project new educational foundations, which he envisioned as the truest antidote to the spread of heresy and for the propagation of the faith. Gregory's pontificate saw the appearance of new Jesuit colleges throughout Europe in strategically important cities such as Vienna, Graz, Prague, Rheims, and Vilnius. Missionary efforts to India, Japan, China, Brazil, and the Americas were often given hefty papal subsidies for the establishment of new colleges among the promising convert population of these countries.

Gregory valued display and pageantry for proclaiming Catholicism, and the Holy Year of 1575 provided him with a special opportunity to showcase Rome as the universal capital of the Catholic church, where pilgrims could marvel at a reformed, virtuous Rome bristling with holy religious and clergy, lay confraternities, and endless acts of piety. Gregory made elaborate and costly preparations for refurbishing the city's infrastructure and providing for more than 400,000 sojourners. He also monitored every detail for improving the moral appearance of the Romans and for spiritually nourishing pilgrims at Rome. He provided ample occasions for preaching and opportunities for confession and the reception of the Eucharist and made certain that works of charity were much in evidence for everyone's edification. A rich, yet highly tendentious, picture of Rome (as Gregory no doubt wanted it) is that of the English cleric, Gregory Martin, whose *Roma sancta* (1581) piously impresses upon Catholic readers the city's inexhaustible treasure house of graces, the exemplary virtues of her people, and her theological self-understanding as the religious center of the world.

Gregory firmly believed in the special sanctity of Rome and her divine destiny. To this end, he encouraged Carlo Sigonio and Cesare Baronio to prepare ecclesiastical histories to demonstrate the truth of the faith and the church's jurisdictional claims, and he patronized many scholars who published editions of ecclesiastical texts, especially catechisms and the gospel, in numerous languages and types such as Arabic, Armenian, and Slavonic. To this purpose he also set up a printing press at Rome.

Gregory's concern for liturgical practices led to his establishing a reform commission in 1573 for the sacred rites. Among the many changes it wrought were new standard texts for liturgical chant to correspond to the revised liturgical books endorsed by Trent for the reform of the liturgy. The commission also looked into the liturgical practices at the papal court to correct notable abuses, such as the custom of sometimes allowing unsuitable young men to preach before the popes. Gregory also looked into the liturgical practices beyond Rome where other practices prevailed. He confirmed, for example, the ancient and venerable Ambrosian liturgy at use in Milan.

Gregory's interest in scholarship and its value for Catholic reform led to the further enrichment of the Vatican Library when he donated to it his own private library and opened it up to scholars. Montaigne comments on the library's accessibility to anyone who wanted to use it, and he himself speaks with satisfaction of the rich treasures he saw there, such as a "handwritten Virgil" and "handwritten Seneca." Gregory's interest in the early church gave fresh impetus to edit writings of the Fathers, such as John Chrysostom, John Cassian, and St. Ambrose; to gather papal *acta* from Anagni and Avignon; to systematize and reedit fundamental texts for ecclesiastical administration such as the *Decretals* of Gratian, the *Corpus iuris canonici*, the Roman Rituale, the Septuagint, and an early edition of the Roman Martyrology (1584), which would later be revised by Baronio (1586).

On 24 February 1582 Gregory published a reform of the calendar that corrected the Julian calendar's imprecisions and brought the ecclesiastical and civil reckoning of time in line with each other. Though the calendar was accepted first only by Catholic countries, it eventually came to be adopted by all other Christian lands and traditions, with the exception of the Greek Orthodox church.

Gregory's pontificate witnessed the opening of Rome's ancient Christian catacombs, which redirected scholarly attention to early Christian Rome and strengthened the papal argument about the apostolic continuity of early Christian Rome with Gregory's Rome of the sixteenth century. The catacombs brought to one's attention the identity in the use of Christian artistic religious images, the veneration of relics, and other cultic practices, all of which gave credence to the papal claim of an unbroken connection between the church of Peter and the church of Gregorian Rome, or the substantial changelessness of the Roman church.

In his efforts to promote the faith, Gregory closely monitored the condition of religion at Rome, in Italy, and throughout the Catholic world. He maintained the Roman Inquisition to examine the soundness and compatibility of every new theological teaching with the Catholic faith and, whenever necessary, to put on trial authors whose unorthodox doctrines posed a threat to sound doctrine. Gregory personally presided over the last stages of the protracted trial of the archbishop of Toledo, Bartolomé Caranza, and found him free of heretical errors, as he did the chancellor of the University of Louvain, Michael Bajus. Despite such punishments for obvious breaches in social order and ecclesiastical discipline, Gregory in fact decreased the number of trials from those under his predecessor, Pius V. Nonetheless, he zealously continued the institution of the Index of Prohibited Books, but gave the cardinals on its commission wide discretionary powers to deal with each case as they saw fit, whether to demand the complete suppression of the work or merely to excise those passages deemed heretically dangerous or uncertain; the cardinals also kept the Index current. Montaigne on his visit to Rome in 1580 remarked how vigilant, yet well disposed, the master of the sacred palace was toward him, so much so that he allowed this newly made citizen of Rome to cut out what he deemed inappropriate; he was requested, however, to change a reference he made in his *Essays* to "fortune." Nonetheless, he remarked that numerous authors were outlawed and others highly suspect, and city authorities kept close watch at the gates for heretical books coming into the city. Montaigne's impressions of Gregory's Rome, on the whole, were quite positive. Not all infractions, however, were necessarily heretical in abstract theology; many obviously threatened good social order and offended morals. In Gregory's pontificate a number of heretics, magicians, and necromancers found guilty by the tribunal were condemned to the stake, and Montaigne noted in 1581 that nine Portuguese men had been burned a few years before for entering into a homosexual brotherhood and marrying each other at Mass according to the Roman ritual.

Gregory's thirteen-year pontificate experienced little peace among the peoples of Christian Europe. His accession to the chair of Peter came amid some of the most violent sectarian conflicts produced in the Reformation era. Since 1567 Calvinism had made strong headway throughout the Low Countries, where all the provinces showed strong resistance to the oppressive rule of Philip of Spain. The southern Walloon provinces, in addition, found themselves pitted against the Calvinist northern provinces under the leadership of William of Orange (d. 1584). Only with Alessandro Farnese's appointment as leader of the Spanish armies in the Netherlands in 1579 did chances for peace occur in the Treaty of Arras (17 August 1579), as Farnese secured the allegiance of the southern provinces for Spain. Though Gregory sent no money for military support, he made good use of his clergy to collect information and preach in those areas most disturbed by the heretics.

Gregory's concern for the universal church prompted him to send missions to Poland and large parts of Germany, where he opened new nuntiatures, to work for Catholic restoration in Protestant areas and for security in Catholic areas such as Bavaria, the Tyrol, and Salzburg. The nuncios' principal mission was to urge implementation of the decrees of the Council of Trent, which included the establishment of seminaries, the convocation of synods, the eradication of concubinage, the institution of episcopal diocesan visitations, the erection of Catholic schools, and prohibition of heretics within Catholic dioceses. In Bavaria, the Tyrol, Salzburg, the Rhineland, and other lands of Germany, Gregory's strategies paid off. He was also successful in restoring Catholicism to Poland after the coronation in 1576 of Stephen Báthory, who shortly thereafter established nine Jesuit schools and two universities, one in Wilna (Vilnius), Lithuania, and the other in Braunsberg, both within the Kingdom of Poland. Gregory proved less successful with John III of Sweden, who after protracted negotiations about clerical marriage, receiving the Eucharist under both species, and the invocation of the saints sided with the Lutherans and in 1584, after the death of his Catholic spouse, married Gunnila Bielke, a staunch Lutheran. Gregory was equally disappointed in his efforts to win Ivan Vasilievich, "the Terrible," of Muscovy, despite the great skill of his ambassador, the Jesuit Antonio Possevino. Nonetheless, Gregory's efforts paved the way for the eventual reconciliation in 1595 between Rome and the schismatic orthodox Ruthenian church. Gregory's universal vision looked to the very ends of the earth and subsidized the Jesuits and other religious orders in their missionary work in India, China, Japan, the Philippines, and the Americas. His focus also fell on the separated churches within the Ottoman Empire, where he sent Franciscans, Jesuits, and other orders to the many Christian communities from Armenia and Georgia to Egypt and Abyssinia.

In countries closer to home Gregory supported the Catholic Guise faction and Catholic League against the Huguenots during the French Wars of Religion, but had no complicity in Catherine de' Medici's plot to kill Admiral Coligny and his followers on the infamous feast of St. Bartholomew, 24 August 1572. Gregory did, however, laud the event for the good he thought that it would bring the Catholic faith in France, and in gratitude for the Catholic action he had the Te Deum sung in the Basilica of San Marco at Rome and later participated in another solemn thanksgiving celebrated at the Church of San Luigi dei Francesi on 8 September 1572; he later issued a papal bull ordering a general jubilee and ordered a special medal for the occasion. He also commissioned Giorgio Vasari to commemorate the event with a fresco in the Sala Regia. The interminable wars in France, however, brought no positive results for Gregory's papacy, and he could only see the irresolute position of the king and the queen mother, Catherine de' Medici, as the principal reason for the collapse of his principal objective of uniting Christian princes against the Turks. Though he never supported the Guise-led Catholic League with money, Gregory encouraged it strongly in its efforts to rid France of the Huguenots. In the end, all his efforts to bring about a defeat of the Huguenots in France and thwart the accession of the Huguenot Henry of Navarre to the throne of France proved futile.

Gregory was also unsuccessful in regaining the allegiance of England and its monarch Elizabeth I to the church of Rome, despite the full support for the English missionary-priests, many of whom had lived at the venerable English college in Rome and had been trained by the Jesuits. In his support for the captive queen of Scotland, Mary Stuart, and for English Catholics under Elizabeth, Gregory brought pressure on Philip II and the king of France and upon loyal Catholics in England, Scotland, Ireland, and France, as well, to collaborate in ending Elizabeth's rule and heresy and reestablish Catholicism in the British Isles. Gregory hoped that an invasion of England with Spanish and French forces would bring about a general insurrection and replace the queen with Mary Stuart and her son, James VI of Scotland. In the end, all negotiations among interested Catholic parties failed. By 1584 it was obvious to Gregory that he was alone in his resolve to compel England back to the faith.

Gregory's grand hopes for a final victory over the Turks were also doomed to disappointment. Despite the great Christian victory over Ali Pasha at Lepanto in October 1571, the Turks still proved a formidable menace to Western Christendom. Immediately upon his election Gregory appealed again to the king of Spain and to Venice to recommit themselves to a joint enterprise against the Crescent lest the naval advantage be lost. With heady enthusiasm for a decisive confrontation, Gregory used every diplomatic and financial means to forge another holy alliance, only to see it fail because of the mutual jealousies between Spain and Venice. The Holy League lost its chance, and Turkish strength in the Mediterranean grew dominant once again. Any further hopes of countering the Turks were thwarted by Venice's diplomatic and economic arrangements with the Porte in March 1573 and Philip II's armistice with the Turks in 1580, both of which gravely disappointed Gregory and led to a rapid deterioration in relations between Gregory and Philip on ecclesiastical, political, and international issues including Philip's succession to the throne of Portugal (1580), his concession to Philip of ecclesiastical subsidies for the war against the Turks, and matters of ecclesiastical jurisdiction in the *monarchia sicula*, Milan, and elsewhere.

In his administration of the Papal States Gregory had to deal with the endemic problem of banditry, especially in the Campagna and the Romagna, which he never successfully solved, largely because of the support and refuge bandits received from local lords, many of whom were their relatives. Gregory's successor, Sixtus V, is generally credited with ending the problem; in fact, however, banditry would continue to menace travelers and inhabitants for many decades to come.

Gregory's generosity in funding his many diplomatic missions, building projects, and educational and artistic endowments continuously strained papal finances. Noteworthy are his improvements for creating, widening, and straightening Rome's streets for the jubilee year of 1575 and in later years as well, both within the city and in the Papal States. Gregory anticipated the major renovation projects undertaken by his successor, Sixtus V (1585–90). His constitution of 1574 for building in the city made possible major renovations and vast changes that would transform the medieval city into a modern urban setting with its characteristic large palazzi. Gregory undertook the building of the Quirinale Palace, which was to be his summer residence; he rebuilt defenses at Castel Sant'Angelo, repaired bridges (most memorably the Ponte Rotto), and issued numerous decrees for the improvement of civic dwellings and the many churches of Rome, such as San Stefano Rotondo, S. Appolonia, the Pantheon, Santa Maria Maggiore, Santa Maria in Aracoeli, and Santa Sabina. Arguably Gregory's greatest project was the sumptuous Gregorian chapel designed by Giacomo della Porta for St. Peter's Basilica, named in honor of St. Gregory Nazianzen, whose body was translated there with full pomp from the Campo Marzio in 1580, an event celebrated with generous indulgences and an oration delivered by the celebrated Franciscan preacher Francesco Panigarola.

Gregory also had constructed the splendid sacrament altar at St. John Lateran and the imposing Tower of the Winds at the Vatican (later obscured by Sixtus V's renovations for the Vatican Library). Gregory generously funded the new Oratorian Church of S. Maria in Vallicella (Chiesa Nuova di Pozzo Bianco), the Greek College's Church of San Atanasio, and the four fountains of the Piazza Navona, as well as restorations and adornments to many churches and religious sites. Besides lavishing his own resources on major building projects, Gregory encouraged generosity among his cardinals for the building of new churches and the repair of others. During Gregory's pontificate Cardinal Alessandro Farnese, dean of the sacred college, typified this spirit in founding the new Jesuit church, Il Gesù, begun by Giacomo Vignola in 1568 and brought to completion by Giacomo della Porta in 1582. As was papal practice, Gregory continuously encouraged the cardinals of Rome to attend to the fabric of their churches and to give lavishly as need demanded. Gregory's own patronage of artists at Rome resulted in numerous repairs, additions, and frescoes in the Vatican Palace, most notably those of the Sala Regia, the gallery of geographical maps of the Belvedere, and the program in the new papal suite called the Tower of the Winds, all of which proclaimed the constant struggles, yet the ultimate divine triumph of Christianity over the powers of the underworld.

As in many of the paintings and frescoes of Gregory's pontificate, the didactic message was unambiguous: God had created the world and a right order for its running; Gregory saw clearly that it was his purpose as pope to make this clear by restoring to the papacy its divinely bestowed prerogatives throughout the world. His extraordinary energies and projects would prove fundamental for the revival of Catholicism throughout his pontificate and for many to come.

SELECTED BIBLIOGRAPHY *BY WILLIAM V. HUDON*

Baglione, Giovanni. *Le vite de' pittori, scultori, architetti, ed intagliatori; 1572 fino a' tempi di papa Uban. VIII nel 1642.* Naples: n.p., 1733.

Bangert, William V. *A History of the Society of Jesus.* St. Louis: Institute of Jesuit Sources, 1972.

Beltrami, L. *La Roma di Gregorio XIII negli avvisi alla corte Sabauda.* Milan: Allegretti, 1917.

Caraman, Philip. *University of the Nations: The Story of the Gregorian University with Its Associated Institutes, the Biblical and Oriental, 1551–1962.* New York: Paulist Press, 1981.

Caravale, Mario, and Alberto Caracciolo. *Lo stato pontificio da Martino V a Pio LX.* Turin: Unione Tipografico–Editrice Torinese, 1978.

Ciappi, Marco Antonio. *Compendio delle heroiche et gloriose attioni et santa vita di papa Gregorio XIII.* Rome: Stamperia degli Accolti, 1591.

Cochrane, Eric. *Historians and Historiography in the Italian Renaissance.* Chicago: University of Chicago Press, 1981.

Courtright, Nicola. "Gregory XIII's Tower of the Winds in the Vatican." Ph.D. diss., New York University, 1990.

Fernández Collado, Angel. *Gregorio XIII y Felipe II en la nunciatura de Felipe Sega (1577–1581): Aspectos politicos, jurisdiccional, y de reforma.* Toledo: Estudio Teológico de San Ildefonso, Seminario Conciliar, 1991.

Hicks, Leo. "The English College, Rome, and Vocations to the Society of Jesus, March 1579–July 1595." *Archivum historicum Societatis Iesu* 3 (1934): 1–36.

Karttunen, Liisi. *Grégoire XIII comme politicien et souverain.* Helsinki: Suomalaisen Tiedeakatemian Toimituksia, 1911.

Levi della Vida, Giorgio. *Documenti intorno alle relazione delle chiese orientali con la S. Sede durante il pontificato di Gregorio XIII.* Vatican City: Biblioteca Apostolica Vaticana, 1948.

Maffei, Giovanni Pietro. *Degli annali di Gregorio XIII pontefice massimo.* 2 vols. Rome: Girolamo Mainardi, 1742.

Martin, Gregory. *Roma Sancta (1581).* Ed. George B. Parks. Rome: Edizioni di storia e letteratura, 1969.

McGinness, Frederick J. *Right Thinking and Sacred Oratory in Counter-Reformation Rome*. Princeton: Princeton University Press, 1995.

O'Malley, John W. *The First Jesuits*. Cambridge, Mass.: Harvard University Press, 1993.

Pastor, Ludwig Freiherr von. *The History of the Popes from the Close of the Middle Ages*. Vols. 19 and 20. Trans. Ralph Francis Kerr. St. Louis: Herder, 1952.

Prodi, Paolo. *The Papal Prince: One Body and Two Souls: The Papal Monarchy in Early Modern Europe*. New York: Cambridge University Press, 1987.

Ranke, Leopold von. *History of the Popes*. 3 vols. Trans. E. Fowler. New York: Colonial Press, 1901.

SIXTUS V (1585–90): THE PLEBEIAN PAPAL PRINCE

CARLA PENUTI, TRANSLATED BY WILLIAM V. HUDON

Felice Peretti was born on 13 December 1520 (or in 1521, according to some) at Grottamare in the diocese of Fermo. He was the son of Piergentile di Giacomo, called "Peretto," a laboring tenant farmer from Montalto, and a certain Mariana, a native of Frontillo di Pievebovigliana, a little town in the region of Camerino. The family, which moved from Montalto to Grottamare because of warfare, lived in understandable economic hardship. Soon after their return to Montalto, Felice Peretti entered the Franciscan order among the Conventual Friars Minor in the Convent of San Francisco di Montalto, where his uncle, Fra Salvatore, resided. There, after the novitiate period, Peretti made his religious profession, taking the name Fra Felice di Montalto. His education occurred inside the order: in 1538 he was sent to Pesaro to study philosophy, in 1539 to Jesi, and in 1540 to Rocca Contrada. He also studied in Fermo, Ferrara (1540), and Bologna (1543). In the following years he was a second-degree university student at the convent at Rimini (1544) and at Siena (1546), and he was ordained a priest at the latter in 1547. In July 1548 he completed a doctoral degree in theology at Fermo and then began to teach philosophy and theology as a regent in the order's convent school in Siena (1549).

He was highly regarded as a preacher, and his life took a dramatic turn in 1552, when he was called to Rome to serve as a Lenten preacher. There he won the esteem of Cardinal Rodolfo Pio, protector of the Conventuals, by whom he was named a theological advisor some years later. Peretti also gained the attention of the commissioner-general of the Inquisition, Michele Ghislieri, the future Pope Pius VI (1566–72). Within his order he received other appointments: regent at Naples (1553) and in Venice (1556), then later procurator-general (1561) and vicar-general of the Conventual Friars (1566–68). It was thanks to the patronage of Ghislieri, above all, that he gained various important duties within the Inquisition: from 1557 to 1560 he had charge of inquisitors in the Republic of Venice, in 1560 he was named theological consultor of the Holy Office in Rome, and in 1565 he was sent to Spain as a theologian of the Inquisition. In that latter capacity he accompanied the papal legate, Ugo Boncompagni (later Pope Gregory XIII), and the nuncio, Cardinal Giambattista Castegna (later Pope Urban VII) for a trial against Bartolomé Caranza, the archbishop of Toledo. In 1566 Pius V named him bishop of Sant'Agata dei Goti in Benevento, and later he transferred Peretti to the episcopal see of Fermo, which he held from 1571 to 1577. Pius V also made Peretti a cardinal, assigning him the titular church of San Girolamo degli Schiavoni in 1570.

Throughout the years of the pontificate of Gregory XIII (1572–85), with whom he had a misunderstanding at the conclusion of their duties in Spain, Peretti led a secluded life of study, far from the centers of power. During this period of isolation he dedicated himself to work on a new edition of the works of St. Ambrose. In the brief conclave that followed the death of Gregory XIII, the votes of the major factions came to converge around the candidacy of Cardinal Peretti, perhaps with the expectation that he might be a transitional pope. He was elected on 24 April 1585 and assumed the name Sixtus in memory of the preceding Franciscan pope Sixtus IV. He was crowned on 1 May 1585. Both hagiographic works on Sixtus and those of his detractors point to his postelection transformation into a strong, energetic personality.

Once elected, Sixtus clearly manifested the characteristics of a determined centralizer in directing governmental affairs and in designing progressive state consolidation. Beginning with his first governing actions, he showed particular determination to confront problems of public order, especially urban crime and banditry. This banditry was a complex phenomenon and a manifestation of many things: of the reaction to increasing fiscal distress, of the rebelliousness in rural society, and of the tendency of soldiers to disband following the dissolution of mercenary armies. This banditry was above all connected with the destructive attitude of the feudal aristocracy and came up against a repressive politics based on the principle of retributive justice. The measures taken against it aimed to strike at that network of solidarity and connivance that the bandits enjoyed and to isolate them from their protective company. In order to rout the bands from the countryside, they encouraged members to turn one another in with the prospect of a monetary payment or immunity from prosecution. They thus sought to break the contracts of protection the bandits arranged with barons and communities. Pressure placed on the governments of neighboring states in order to obtain their collaboration and the exclusion of outlaws finding refuge by the right of asylum proved decisive. Energetic repressive measures and diplomatic actions put into operation, especially between 1585 and 1587, obtained a temporary decline in the phenomenon of banditry, but not its complete elimination.

Sixtus V carried to completion the reorganization of the central government of the church and the Papal States that his predecessors had begun. With the bull *Postquam verus* (3 December 1586) he restructured the college of cardinals, indicating the requirements for appointment and fixing its number between twenty-four and seventy. The decree included a substantial reduction of the subsidy to the college. With the bull *Immensa aeterni Dei* (22 January 1588) he reorganized the Roman curia into an organizational system of fifteen cardinal congregations that were permanent commissions of cardinals specializing in different areas: six concerned with the government of the Papal States (the congregations of the Consulta, of the Segnatura di grazia, of the Sgravi, of the Strade, ponti, e acque, of the Abbondanza, and of the Armata navale) and nine devoted to ecclesiastical matters (the Congregation of the Inquisition, the commission for the erection of churches, the Congregation of Rites and Ceremonies, the Congregation of the Index, the Congregation for the Council, the commission for the University of Rome, the Congregation of Regular Religious, the Congregation of Bishops, and the commission for the Vatican Press).

Pope Sixtus V. (Courtesy of the Library of Congress)

In the area of political finance Sixtus utilized every possible means to round up revenue. Massive sale of public offices produced a consequent proliferation of venal offices, while expansion of the public debt was accomplished by increasing the number of the state bond funds known as the Monti and their capital base. The overall result was to exacerbate financial burdens. The reinforcement of state finance, although carried out through a well-watered fiscalism and a severe drain on resources, aimed at the accumulation of a reserve fund in Castel Sant'Angelo. At Sixtus's death this enormous treasury in gold and silver amounted to more than six million silver scudi. Fully five million of these were collected under Sixtus. The treasury came to be utilized for extraordinary necessities defined in large part by his successors: to aid Catholic countries in danger of falling into the hands of heretics or infidels, to guard against invasions of the Papal States, to recover territories of the church, to finance crusades, and to cover expenses related to famine or epidemic. Sixtus acted in an attempt to spur the development of agricultural, mercantile, and artisanal work out of the utopian goal to assure a self-sufficient economy in the Papal States, but to no avail. The attempts to drain marshy, malaria-infested land, especially the work to reclaim the Pontine Marshes, recovered territory and increased agricultural production with the aim of resolving food-supply problems in the capital. In the industrial sphere Sixtus sought to facilitate creation of new plants for the wool and silk industries, taking up the same line of action followed by Pius V, but in a fuller and more systematic manner. He granted low-interest loans to foreign contractors and built the necessary infrastructures in Rome, and he supported the cultivation of mulberry groves in state territory.

In foreign policy Sixtus V pursued two principal objectives: combatting the spread of the Reformation and winning a position of independence for papal diplomacy against Spanish power. Sixtus promised his financial support for the disastrous Spanish naval expedition against England, although from the very beginning he focused primarily on the obligations of Spain in the revived war against the Turks. Amid the complex and difficult context of renewed religious civil war in France, he always acted in a prudent and realistic fashion, seeking to restrict the diffusion of Protestant ideas while also avoiding any preponderant influence of Philip II of Spain over France. First, at the urging of Philip II and the Catholic League, he excommunicated the Huguenot Henry of Bourbon, the king of Navarre, as a relapsed heretic. Then he sought to facilitate reconciliation between the league—which was headed by the duke of Guise—and the legitimate sovereign Henry III. The assassination of Henry III and the designation of Henry of Bourbon as his successor (Henry IV) brought about a situation that for the first time favored rapprochement with Spain. Sixtus seized the opportunity and received Catholic supporters of Henry IV. He began such negotiations in the hope of a conversion of Henry to Catholicism, the one secure way to keep France within the family of Catholic powers. Beyond this, Sixtus's nuncios promoted Catholic revival in Central Europe, in Switzerland, and in Germany.

In the religious sphere Sixtus followed the Counter-Reformation directions of his predecessors. In order to establish a firmer contact between pope and bishops, he renewed and regulated the institution of episcopal *ad limina*, or prescribed regular visits to Rome. The regulations required all bishops to come to Rome, with the intervals between visits graduated according to the distance of the diocese from Rome. The new rules prescribed the composition of a set of *relationes*, reports of the bishops on the condition of their dioceses. Sixtus took action to provide a means whereby religious orders and regular congregations could apply the reform decrees of Trent. He approved a new order of regular clerics who ministered to the sick (the Camilliani), the order of the Fogliani (a branch of the Cistercians), and the Caracciolini order of minor clerics regular. He also promoted missionary work in Latin America and in Asia.

Sixtus V had a clear understanding of the role of printing and editing in the work of defending both the church and Catholic orthodoxy. He was preoccupied with the need to move the Vatican Library to a more adequate facility, and he satisfied it through construction of a building at the center of the Belvedere court. He closely linked the 1587 establishment of the Tipografia Vaticana (Vatican Press) to the library, and from the press soon came the first two volumes of Cesane Baronio's *Annales ecclesiastici*. The personal contribution of Sixtus to the revision of the Latin text of the Bible—the Vulgate edition—had an improvident result. In 1586 Sixtus formed a commission assigned to prepare an official text, but showing impatience and dissatisfaction with the proposals it presented, he established the version for publication on his own. This official edition, published in 1590, raised a backlash of criticism, both for the errors it contained and for his arbitrary intervention. The edition was retracted soon after Sixtus's death.

Sixtus only partially completed his urban-reorganization project for Rome, but it proceeded with a speed that impressed his contemporaries. His plan came from a network of religious, political, and socioeconomic motivations tied to the double nature of Rome as the center of Catholicism and as capital of the state. One particular motivation was related to the old devotional practice of visits to the seven cathedral churches, a practice Sixtus intended to revive and enhance with the celebration of solemn pontifical rites in the seven basilicas. He expressed this intention in a bull entitled *Egregia populi Romani* on 13 February 1586. Another objective was to provide a basis for the re-creation of housing in the hilly areas around the city. This plan for urbanization of the less populated areas of Rome was supported by privileges and subsidies granted in the bull *Decet Romanum Pontificem* (13 September 1587) and by provisions for water supply through the Felice aqueduct. New rectilinear roads were opened, public works like the Ospizio (Hospice) of Ponte Sisto were completed, and the new, imposing Lateran Palace and loggia were finished, as were a series of works in St. Peter's, including the cupola and the expansion of Vatican residences. In addition a number of churches and basilicas received restoration. The traces of antiquity took on new importance in this urban context with the reutilization of Egyptian obelisks and classical columns and with the relocation of these to important sites. This desire to redefine classical culture in Christian terms, as an emblematic expression of the victory of faith over paganism, was best represented by the placement of the cross at the tip of these obelisks and by the placement of statues of St. Peter and St. Paul at the capstones of Trajan and Antonine columns.

Sixtus died on 7 August 1590. One year later his remains were placed in the Sistine Chapel of Santa Maria Maggiore, a chapel constructed during his lifetime with a triple function: to serve as a chapel for the Blessed

Sacrament, as a shrine dedicated to the Nativity, and as a papal mausoleum for himself and for his patron, Pope Pius V.

SELECTED BIBLIOGRAPHY

America pontificia primi saeculi evangelizationis, 1493–1592: Documenta pontificia ex registris et minutis praesertim in Archivo Secreto Vaticano existentibus. Ed. Josef Metzler. Vatican City: Libreria Editrice Vaticana, 1991.

La Bibbia "Vulgata" dalle origini ai nostri giorni. Ed. Tarcisio Stramare. Rome: Abbazia San Girolamo; Vatican City: Libreria Vaticana, 1987.

Correspondance du nonce en France, Fabio Mirto Frangipani (1568–1572 et 1586–1587). Ed. A. Lynn Martin. Rome: École française, 1984.

Cugnoni, Giuseppe. "Documenti Chigiani concernenti Felice Peretti, Sisto V, come privato come pontefice." *Archivio della società romana di storia patria* 5 (1882): 1–32, 210–304, 542–89.

Eubel, Konrad, G. van Gulik, and L. Schmitz-Kallenberg. *Hierarchia catholica medii et recentioris aevi.* 3 vols. Regensburg: Libraria Regensbergiana, 1923.

Fosi, I. Polverini. "Justice and Its Image: Political Propaganda and Judicial Reality in the Pontificate of Sixtus V." *Sixteenth Century Journal* 24 (1993): 75–95.

Gamrath, Helge. *Roma Sancta renovata: Studi sull'urbanistica di Roma nella seconda metà del sec. XVI con particolare riferimento al pontificato di Sisto V (1585–1590).* Rome: "L'Erma" di Bretschneider, 1987.

Nuntiatur des Germanico Malaspina und des Giovanni Andrea Caligari, 1582–1587. Ed. J. Rainer. Wien: Verlag der Österreichischen Akademie der Wissenschaften, 1981.

Parisciani, Gustavo. *Sisto V e la sua Montalto.* Padova: EMP, 1986.

Pastor, Ludwig von. *The History of the Popes from the Close of the Middle Ages.* Vol. 21 and 22. Trans. Ralph Francis Kerr. St. Louis: Herder, 1952.

Pistolesi, Francesco. *La prima biografia autentica di Papa Sisto V. scritta dall' Anonimo della Biblioteca Ferraioli di Roma.* Montalto Marche: n.p., 1925.

Prosperi, Adriano. "Sisto V, papa della Controriforma." In *Le diocesi delle Marche in età sistina: Atti del convegno di studi, Ancona Loerto 16–18 ottobre 1986.* Fano: n.p., 1988, 19–35.

Roma di Sisto V. Arti, architettura e città fra Rinascimento e Barocco. Ed. Maria Luisa Madonna and Mario Bevilacqua. Rome: Edizioni de Luca, 1993.

Rosa, Mario. "Sisto V." In *Dictionnaire historique de la papauté.* Ed. Philippe Levillain and Philippe Boutry. Paris: Fayard, 1994, 1593–96.

Sansolini, Cecilia M. *Il pensiero teologico spirituale di Sisto V nei sermoni anteriori al pontificato.* Vatican City: Tipografia Poliglotta Vaticana, 1989.

Sartori, Antonio. *Archivio Sartori: Documenti di storia e arte francescana.* Vol. 1 and 3, pt. 1. Ed. Giovanni M. Luisetto. Padova: Biblioteca Antoniana, 1983, 1988.

Schiffmann, René. *Roma felix: Aspekte der städtebaulichen Gestaltung Roms unter Papst Sixtus V.* Bern: Peter Lang, 1985.

Simoncini, Giorgio. *"Roma restaurata": Rinnovamento urbano al tempo di Sisto V.* Florence: Olschki, 1990.

Sisto V. vol. 1, *Roma e il Lazio*; vol. 2, *Le Marche.* Ed. M. Fagiolo and Maria Luisa Madonna. Rome: Istituto poligrafico e zecca dello stato, 1992.

Spezzaferro, Luigi. "La Roma di Sisto V." In *Storia dell'arte italiana.* XII, 365–405. Torino: Einaudi, 1983.

Stumpo, Enrico. *La gazzetta de l'anno 1588.* Florence: Giunti, 1988.

CLEMENT VIII
(1592–1605)

KATHLEEN M. COMERFORD

Clement VIII (Ippolito Aldobrandini, 1536–1605; reigned 1592–1605) is notable for many reasons, ranging from his reform of the missal and breviary to involvement with religious orders, and from his success in annexing Ferrara to the Papal States to his relationship with Henry IV. A protégé of Pius V (1566–72), who favored the Aldobrandini family, Ippolito began his career with a series of appointments in papal administration, handling difficult international political situations and moving in important circles in Rome. Although he was not always a successful mediator, Aldobrandini's political work provided him with the opportunity to deal with the most pressing political problems of the day. This, along with his continued support from the Roman administration, which continued under Sixtus V (1585–90), allowed Aldobrandini to advance his power in the curia and eventually led to his election as pope. It was his appointment as priest-confessor with the responsibility of hearing the most serious cases under Sixtus that brought him into the inner circle of ecclesiastical power; historians have concluded that Aldobrandini owed his advancement entirely to the favor of the popes, not to any particular achievement.

Aldobrandini studied law at Bologna. He was neither a theologian nor a philosopher and as a result was more at home in politics than in the niceties of doctrine. His political career was rather successful. The high point of Cardinal Aldobrandini's prepapal achievements was his appointment by Sixtus V as *legate a latere* for a specific mission to Poland in 1588. Aldobrandini had earlier held this position for Spain and Portugal, but he proved more successful in the later appointment. In the wake of the succession crisis in Poland following the death of Stephen Báthory in 1586, the mission was a highly important one, and the confidence of Alessandro Farnese, the cardinal-protector of Poland, and Sixtus himself marked a turning point in Aldobrandini's life in the public sphere. His success in convincing Emperor Rudolf II to restore the city of Lubowla/Lublau to the Poles and his work toward the peace treaty of 1589 catapulted him to the most important circles in international ecclesiastical politics. Sixtus wanted to promote him to legate to France after Henry III's assassination, but this was opposed by the Spanish, who preferred a legate with closer ties to Spanish interests.

The opposition of the Spanish to Aldobrandini did not end at this point; in fact, his accession to the papal throne was a source of conflict with the Spaniards, despite the patronage the cardinal had enjoyed from previous popes. After Sixtus V died in 1590, a faction formed for Aldobrandini but was not successful in either of the 1590 elections (Urban VII, Giovanni Battista Castagna, and Gregory XIV, Niccolò Sfondrati) or in the 1591 election (Innocent IX, Giovanni Antonio Facchinetti) due to opposition from the Spanish cardinals, principally Olivares, who advanced his own candidates. Aldobrandini did gain the support of those who believed that the Spaniards were exerting too much influence in the elections, which helped him to win the 1592 election.

Aldobrandini's religious pedigree was no less impressive than his political and administrative background, though not without some blemish. Although Clement VIII's spiritual life has often been emphasized, he did not become a priest until 1581, well into his Roman career. When he did take his vows, it was at an accelerated pace the likes of which the post-Tridentine Catholic church at least formally frowned upon. Over a two-year period (1508–81), at the age of forty-four, Aldobrandini quickly advanced through the seven promotions necessary to become a priest; the council of Trent (Session 23, chapter XI, "The Interstices and Certain Other Regulations to Be Observed in the Reception of Minor Orders") explicitly stated that the final promotions alone (subdeacon, deacon, and priest) must take at least three years. In 1585 he was appointed cardinal by Sixtus V, but was not consecrated bishop until three days after his election as pope. The decision to become a priest at that comparatively late age is widely attributed to the influence of Aldobrandini's spiritual advisor, Filippo Neri. The connection to Neri's Oratorians continued throughout Aldobrandini's life and included the choice of first Giovanni Paolo Bordini and later the annalist Cesare Baronio as his confessors.

Since none of his immediate predecessors held the papal office long enough to have noticeable impact, the very length of Clement VIII's term would afford him notice. However, this pope did more than fill a power vacuum and had a distinguished papal term in his own right, in which he continued to demonstrate his political prowess. He took possession of the

Duchy of Ferrara when the last of the Este dukes died without direct descendants and the only contender, Cesare d'Este of a cadet line, was forced by lack of support to renounce his claims to the duchy. Clement's foreign policy agenda included peripheral involvement with the problems in the Low Countries; advancing the Catholic Reformation in Poland through the work of the Jesuits; and the formation of a league among Catholic European nations (including Poland) to defeat the Turks. He established the congregation that would develop into the Society for the Propagation of the Faith, the purpose of which was evangelization in Latin America (particularly Peru and Chile) and the Far East (particularly the Philippines, China, and Japan). He allowed orders other than the Jesuits, who had enjoyed a monopoly on foreign missions under Gregory XIII, to spread the Catholic faith in the rest of the world. Even more ambitious in political scope, however, were his activities in England and France.

Pope Clement VIII. (Hulton/Archive by Getty Images)

Clement had some involvement with opposition to the English Crown, although the extent is not clear. The pope issued a brief commanding English Catholics to insist on a Catholic monarch, called James I a tyrant by usurpation because of his Presbyterian faith, and authorized his nuncio in France to carry on a secret relationship with the English ambassador to Paris to further the scheme of placing a French Catholic on the English throne. Clement seems not to have been directly involved in planning the Gunpowder Plot of 1605, an attempt to blow up the houses of Parliament. However, his bulls creating the English seminaries at Valladolid (1592) and Seville (1597) and the accompanying attempts to recruit English clergy surely did not endear him to the Protestant majority in England. His connection to political events in France was both more direct and more successful. He has been described as initiating the Catholic Reformation and restoration in France. He not only pursued the adoption there of the canons and decrees of the Council of Trent, but also worked to keep Henry IV "orthodox" and to persuade him to accept the Society of Jesus in France. Henry converted to Catholicism, after a period of equivocation and flirting with Huguenots, in July 1593.

At first Clement VIII refused absolution to the French king and did not accept his conversion as authentic. The conversion was not only religious but also political, and the explosive domestic situation in France (the split among Catholics between supporters of the Holy League, who allied with Spain, and the Loyalists, who supported Henry IV) made the already-delicate international situation of a prominent king changing his religious affiliation all the more tense. The lack of support for Henry IV from Spain's Philip II was no small matter. Clement finally consented in September 1595 to grant absolution to Henry, after a great deal of political intrigue including letters from the king to the pope begging the latter's forgiveness. These letters were annotated and published by Henry duc de Nevers, a Loyalist. The association with Henry IV did not permanently injure the relationship between the pope and Spain, and although there were other difficulties, Clement VIII acted as a mediator between France and Spain on occasion, including the Treaty of Vervins (1598) and the difficulties with Carlo Emanuele I of Savoy that followed.

Some consider the conversion of Henry IV to be the most important event in this pontificate. It was in many ways a defining one due to the fact that it occurred so soon after Clement was elected. However, so many events in Clement's reign were of broad import that choosing a single one is difficult and seems not to be useful; for example, his most recent biographer called him a "tireless mediator" (Boromeo, "Clement VIII," 268). Clement's variety of activities leads one to ask how to characterize the pope. It has been said that the "Tridentine generation" of popes died with Innocent IX (29 October–30 December 1591), begging the question of what is meant by "Tridentine pope" and what "kind" of pope succeeded this group. Surely Clement VIII was also a reformer, and his reforms were clearly compatible with the Council of Trent. For example, Clement made frequent apostolic visitations to the diocese. He was a zealous opponent of heresy and battled it via censorship and the pursuit of particular individuals. He was involved in the activities of several religious orders, including the newer ones, some of which were established under him. In addition, he associated himself with the educational reforms of the Council of Trent; at the time that dioceses began building local seminaries to carry out the decree from Session 23, chapter XVIII, Clement insisted on examining Italian bishops in canon law and theology before confirming them. His connection to the educationally oriented Somaschi Fathers led them to open a school they called the Collegio Clementino in Rome in 1595. He authorized, among others, the organization of the Piarists, the "Workers of the Pious Schools" (Operari delle Scuole Pie), in 1604.

In addition to the connections with the Somaschi and Oratorians, Clement was involved in some other aspects of clerical life, including several regular orders. He found the Society of Jesus very helpful in his international political and religious activities. However, he was not an unwavering supporter of that order. In the controversy over grace between the Dominicans and the Jesuits, Clement first favored the Jesuits but eventually took up the case of the Dominicans. The controversy was not settled at the time of Clement's death. He attempted to improve the episcopate by establishing a congregation to examine candidates for their suitability, thus discouraging the selection by princes of personal favorites. Clement worked as well to revise some of the books used in Catholic worship. In 1592 the Sixtine Vulgate, finished by Clement, was printed in Venice. Clement VIII revived the revision of the translation of the Bible begun by Sixtus V on the advice of Robert Bellarmine, who warned the pope that Sixtus's lack of training had resulted in some serious problems. Nonetheless, the new edition was badly needed, so Clement saw to its completion. Three years later the revised *Pontifical* appeared. The latter produced conflicts over printing privileges between Venice and Rome and a controversy over Venetian changes in the texts. The new *Breviary* appeared in 1602. The literary activity of this pope was not limited to such positive reforms, however, and included a revised Index of Prohibited Books.

Clement's involvement in the prosecution of heresy is well known, and much of that reputation stems from his work on that Index and the case of Giordano Bruno. Repression of Bruno's unorthodox science and questionable writings by others has been termed a part of a papalist counteroffensive around the turn of the sixteenth and seventeenth centuries: a more systematic and intensified campaign against ideological opposition. It was based on a resurgent papacy, increasingly confident in its ability to control heresy in Italy and supported by both the religious orders and the king of France. The opponents to be combatted included scientific as well as philosophical and theological scholars, and the suspicion of heresy was leveled against Giovanni Botero, Antonio Possevino, Pedro da Ribadeneyra, and others. Clement revised the Index of Prohibited Books, a project begun (like the Vulgate) under Sixtus V. Since the 1587-90 version was considered too severe, Clement softened some prohibitions but added more vernacular titles from local indexes. The Clementine Index was promulgated in the spring of 1596, along with an *Instructio* that allowed for individual expurgation according to many strict rules, even allowing readers to correct their own copies; it insisted that printers provide the Holy Office with copies of materials they intended to print; and it required printers and booksellers to swear to the bishop and inquisitor to obey the Index and keep the guild free from heresy. Venetian objections to the Index, the *Instructio*, and the accompanying oath were strong; these led to continued conflicts and eventually escalated into the issue of an interdict against the city under Pope Paul V in 1607.

A final consideration in any pope's notability is in the sphere of cultural patronage. Clement did not equal Sixtus V in this realm because he was not as well educated in art; however, his preparations for the Holy Year

1600 included a foray into more serious art. His most famous favorites were the Alberti brothers, Giovanni and Cherubino, who were known for their perspective drawing. Giovanni was the more able of the two and predeceased his patron. Cherubino enjoyed continued support from the pope, but when Clement died, the artist's career perished along with him. In addition, Clement employed Cristofano Roncalli and il Cavaliere d'Arpino. Of note are the Sala concistoriale and Sala Clementina of the Vatican Palace; the outside of the cupola of St. Peter's Basilica; and the Capella Clementina in the same basilica. In literature Clement VIII admired (and protected) Torquato Tasso and Cesare Baronio; he also enlarged both the manuscript and book collections of the Biblioteca Vaticana.

His personal attributes are more difficult to understand than his public activities and seem at times to be contradictory. He was a spendthrift who was very generous to his family. He had condemned nepotism while he was a cardinal, and he paid close attention while he was pope to the reformation of the clergy; however, he patronized his cardinal nephews Pietro and Cinzio. Clement increased the size of the college of cardinals, but at the same time turned it into a weaker body. He was widely reputed to be indecisive, but he insisted on involvement in decision making rather than delegating that responsibility. He has been described as imperialistic. However, above all, Clement's personal reputation rests on a widespread acknowledgment of deep and sincere piety. In addition to his devotion to Filippo Neri and the Oratorians, Clement was known to attend Mass daily, pray and meditate frequently in his chapel, and confess nightly; he also dined on only bread and water each Friday and made frequent pilgrimages to churches and performed public acts of devotion including walking barefoot in processions.

Clement VIII remains, after close investigation, a difficult person to characterize. More a political leader in spirit than a religious one, he nonetheless was deeply and personally involved in specific religious reforms. Though he was very young while the Council of Trent was in session, he was clearly involved in its implementation and provides further cause to argue that the Catholic Reformation both began and ended later than historians have traditionally argued. Nonetheless, he was guilty of practices condemned by that council that he worked to implement. It would be foolish, however, not to recognize that some of Clement's successes and power can be attributed to his longevity. He remained in office for thirteen years, longer than any other pope since Gregory XIII (1572–85), and certainly longer than his three immediate predecessors (Urban VII, Gregory XIV, and Innocent IX) and his immediate successor (Leo XI), none of whom held office for a full year. He thus had the ability to construct a set of alliances and to follow through his own policies. Without support from Henry IV and the religious orders, which he gained over a period of time of negotiations and cooperation, Clement would have found it difficult to reorganize the Roman curia and revitalize the work of the Catholic Reform—the more militant kind, to be sure—both in Italy and abroad.

SELECTED BIOGRAPHIES

Abromson, Morton Colp. *Painting in Rome during the Papacy of Clement VIII (1592–1605): A Documented Study*. New York: Garland Publishing, 1981.

Andreescu, Stefan. "La Pologne, la Moldavie, et la 'Sainte Ligue' en 1595: Une nouvelle source." *Revue roumaine d'histoire* 22 (1983): 239–55.

Andretta, Stefano and Georg Lutz. *Das Papsttum, die Christenheit, und die Staaten Europas, 1592–1605: Forschungen zu den Hauptinstruktionem Clemens VIII*. Tübingen: Niemeyer, 1994.

Aquilecchia, Giovanni. *Schede Bruniane (1950–1991)*. Rome: Vecchiarelli Editore, 1993.

Baldini, A. Enzo. *Puntigli spagnoleschi e intrighi politici nella Roma di Clemente VIII: Girolamo Frachetta e la sua relazione del 1603 sui cardinali*. Milan: Franco Angeli, 1981.

Barbiche, Bernard, and Segolene de Dainville-Barbiche. "Un Évêque italien de la reforme catholique legat en France sous Henri IV: Le cardinal de Florence (1596–1598)." *Revue d'histoire del l'Église de France* 75 (1989): 45–59.

Baumgartner, Frederick. "Catholic Opposition to the Edict of Nantes, 1598–99." *Bibliothèque d'humanisme et Renaissance* 40 (1978): 525–36.

Benedik, Metod. "Instrukcija Papeza Klemena VIII za obnovo Katoliske Vere na Stajerskem, Koroskem in Kranjskem z dne. 13 Aprila 1592." *Acta ecclesiastica Sloveniae* 1 (1979): 16–41.

Borromeo, Agostino. "Clemente VIII." *Dizionario Biografico degli Italiani* 26 (1982): 259–83.

Bouwsma, William J. *Venice and the Defense of Republican Liberty: Renaissance Values in the Age of the Counter Reformation*. Berkeley: University of California Press, 1968.

Carrafiello, Michael L. "Robert Parsons' Climate of Resistance and the Gunpowder Plot." *Seventeenth Century* 3 (1988): 115–34.

Feigenbaum, Gail. "Clement VIII, the Lateran, and Christian Concord." In *IL 60: Essays Honoring Irving Lavin on His Sixtieth Birthday*, ed. Marilyn Aronberg Lavin. New York: Italica Press, 1990, 167–190.

Fernández, Miguel Aviles. "La censura inquisitorial de 'Los seis libros de la Republica' de Jean Bodin." *Hispania sacra* 37 (1985): 655–92.

Firpo, Luigi. "The Flowering and Withering of Speculative Philosophy: Italian Philosophy and the Counter Reformation: The Condemnation of Francesco Patrizi." In *The Late Italian Renaissance, 1525–1630*. Ed. Eric Cochrane. London: Macmillan, 1970, 266–84.

Fonti per la storia artistica romana al tempo di Clemente VIII. Ed. Anna Maria Corbo. Rome: Archivio di Stato di Roma, 1975.

Frazee, Charles A. *Catholics and Sultans: The Church and the Ottoman Empire, 1453–1923*. London and New York: Cambridge University Press, 1983.

Freiberg, Jack. *The Lateran in 1600: Christian Concord in Counter-Reformation Rome*. Cambridge and New York: Cambridge University Press, 1995.

Grendler, Paul F. *The Roman Inquisition and the Venetian Press, 1540–1605.* Princeton: Princeton University Press, 1977.

Die Hauptinstruktionen Clemens VIII für die Nuntien und Legaten an den Europäischen Fürstenhöfen, 1592–1605. 2 vols. Ed. Klaus Jaitner. Tübingen: Max Niemeyer, 1984.

Jaitner, Klaus. "Memoriale del Cardinale Cinzio Aldobrandini per Clemente VIII." *Archivio storico italiano* 146 (1988): 79–93.

Jaitner, Klaus, and Dagmar Penna-Miesel. "Il nepotismo di Papa Clemente VIII (1592–1605): Il dramma del Cardinale Cinzio Aldobrandini." *Archivio storico italiano* 146 (1988): 57–78.

Lefévre, Renato. "Su un'ambasciata Persiana a Roma." *Studi romani* 35 (1987): 359–73.

Loades, David. "Relations between the Anglican and Roman Catholic Churches in the 16th and 17th Centuries." In *Rome and the Anglicans: Historical and Doctrinal Aspects of Anglican–Roman Catholic Relations.* Ed. Wolfgang Haase. Berlin and New York: Walter de Gruyter, 1982, 1–53.

Macioce, Stefania. *Undique splendente: Aspetti della pittura sacra nella Roma di Clemente VIII Aldobrandini (1592–1605).* Rome: De Luca Edizioni d'Arte, 1990.

Martin, J. "Clément VIII et Jacques Stuart." *Revue d'histoire diplomatique* 25 (1911): 279–307, 359–78.

McCormick, Richard A. "Two Letters and an Inference." *America* 171 (1994): 15–18.

Meyer, Arnold Oskar. *Clemens VIII und Jakob I von England.* Rome: Loescher, 1904.

Nicholls, Mark. *Investigating the Gunpowder Plot.* Manchester: Manchester University Press, 1991.

Paolucci, Riccardo. "La Venuta di Papa Clemente VIII a Fano." *Studia picena* 3 (1927): 9–55.

Pastor, Ludwig Freiherr von. *The History of the Popes from the Close of the Middle Ages.* Vols. 23 and 24. Trans. Ralph Francis Kerr. St. Louis: Herder, 1952.

Sighinolfi, Lino. "Il posesso di cento e della Pieve e la legazione di Cesare Cremonino a Clemente VIII in Ferrara." *Rivista deputazione di storia patria. Atti e memorie per la provincie di Romagna* 25 (1907): 423–467.

Springer, Elisabeth. "Kaiser Rudolf II, Papst Clemens VIII, und die Bosnischen Christen: Taten und untaten des cavaliere Francesco Antonio Bertucci in kaiserlichen Diensten in den Jahren 1594 bis 1602." *Mitteilungen des österreichischen Staatsarchivs* 33 (1980): 77–105.

Witcombe, Christopher. "Some Letters and Some Prints Dedicated to the Medici by Cherubino Alberti." *Sixteenth Century Journal* 22 (1991): 641–60.

Wolfe, Michael. *The Conversion of Henri IV: Politics, Power, and Religious Belief in Early Modern France.* Cambridge, Mass.: Harvard University Press, 1993.

PAUL V (1605–21)

WILLIAM V. HUDON

Camillo Borghese, whose election as successor to Pope Leo XI, who was pope for less than a month in April 1605, came as a surprise. Borghese was born in Rome on 17 September 1552. He was relatively young (fifty-two years old) and not well known outside the curia. Although his family was resident in Rome, it traced its lineage to the town of Siena and—albeit in a distant relationship—to the famous St. Catherine of the same town. They were, as their very name implies, a bourgeois family. Camillo studied law and apparently acquired a love for controversy at universities in Padua and Perugia before beginning a curial career as assistant to his father, Marcantonio. The elder Borghese, who had earlier represented Cardinal Giovanni Morone in his inquisitorial trial, was then a consistorial advocate under Pope Sixtus V (1585–90). Camillo gained prominence through his work for Clement VIII (1592–1605), who appointed him extraordinary envoy to Philip II of Spain in 1593 and then cardinal in 1596. He served as vicar of Rome beginning in 1603. In the second conclave of 1605 he emerged as a compromise candidate after attempts to elect Robert Bellarmine and to convince Cesare Baronio to consider election had failed. While Borghese was considered a scholar and an impartial, nonpartisan prelate, perhaps his principal asset in the conclave was the fact that he had no virulent enemies. After being chosen as pope during the evening of 21 May 1605, Borghese adopted the name of Paul V, apparently out of gratitude for the patronage given to his father by Paul III (1534–49) some sixty years before.

Some might consider Paul V the quintessential "Counter-Reformation" pope because of his love for the law, his propensity for adopting unilateral positions, and his heavy-handed efforts to force religio-political change in Germany, England, and the Republic of Venice. But Paul, like many other popes in the early modern era, was a man of many and deep contradictions. The content of these contradictions defies those who would apply stereotypes like "counter-reformer" or "Renaissance pope" to his character and actions. If the defining characteristic of "early modern" popes, however, was their inconsistency, then perhaps Paul V was the quintessential exemplar after all. He was both humanist and legalist, inquisitor and priest, bombastic rhetorician and diplomat, art patron and parsimonious ascetic, reformer and nepotist.

Paul V is probably best remembered as a player in the religio-political conflicts of the time, although his success was decidedly limited. It is important to remember at the outset that he was an attorney, and one who apparently admired the legalist popes of the Middle Ages. It was he, after all, who oversaw the canonization of his predecessor and role model, Gregory VII (1073–85). Paul maintained policies toward various contemporary states and kingdoms, moreover, that suggest that he was enamored of the bombastic, overwrought claims of papal power that Gregory, not to mention popes like Innocent III (1198–1216), dictated. During Paul's reign religious hostilities in Germany flared into the 1618 beginning of the Thirty Years' War. After initial reluctance to become involved, Paul poured huge subsidies into the Catholic League. He was thus instrumental in obtaining the first substantial league victory—against King Frederick V of Bohemia—just before his death. While Paul professed neutrality in the rivalry between France and Spain, the French could not have seen him operating in such a fashion. He vigorously condemned Gallicanism in the context of French suspicion that Roman clerics would support application of Juan de Mariana's ideas about deposition of kings and tyrannicide to France. Roman reticence in condemning Mariana was tantamount, for the French, to proof that Paul's papacy was a threat to their monarchy. When the French countered Paul's condemnation of Gallicanism with the claim that their king held the crown from God alone, only painstaking diplomacy by Paul's nuncios, not his bombastic rhetoric, could secure removal of the French claim.

Still more famous, and further illustrative of Paul's desire to effect political change, were his actions in the context of the so-called Gunpowder Plot in England, shortly after his election. Paul apparently did not support the use of violence against King James I, even though he did hope to secure the status of Catholics within the Protestant nation. But neither did Paul define what he considered to be proper and improper opposition to the attacks and confiscation of property that English Catholics endured early in James's reign. The Jesuit provincial superior in England, Henry Garnet, had urged such definition, but his recommendations were not considered convincing in Rome. When the plot of eight noblemen to detonate a bomb in the House of Parliament on 5 November 1605 was revealed, it was too late for Paul to act. He wrote to James I expressing hope that Catholics would not suffer as a result of this plan to foment a general uprising against the king, but political partisans in England, of both parliamentary and royal persuasion, quickly defined the plot as a popish conspiracy. The priests who had learned of it in the confessional (the Jesuits Oswald Greenway and John Gerard) fled. Anti-Catholic legislation, not to mention the public execution of Garnet, followed.

That legislation included the famous oath denouncing the papal power to depose kings and to absolve subjects of their loyalty. When Paul did finally act, issuing a condemnation of the oath and forbidding Catholics from swearing it, he divided, rather than unified, the faithful in England.

Seventeenth-century painting of Pope Paul V. (The Art Archive/Museo Storico Aloisiano Castiglione delle Stiviere/ Dagli Orti)

At about the same time that Garnet's fate was being sealed in England (the spring of 1606), Paul worked more quickly in an attempt to have his way in another political context, the Republic of Venice. The Venetian Senate had passed laws that rolled back previously established ecclesiastical rights. Among the laws was one requiring that church construction take place only with the consent of the Senate; another restricted gifts to ecclesiastical persons and institutions. In addition, when Venetian authorities took secular legal action against a canon and an abbot, Paul made an effort to stop it. While clerical immunity in theory went back to privileges granted during the early history of Christianity in the Roman Empire, Venetian authorities commonly prosecuted clerics anyway. Paul excommunicated the Venetian Signoria and laid the entire territory under interdict, forbidding administration of the sacraments. The members of a few religious orders, like the Theatines, the Capuchins, and the Jesuits, supported Paul and were expelled from Venice for their trouble. Venetian bishops and the rest of the clergy, on the contrary, rejected the excommunication and interdict. A tremendous volume of controversial literature was produced on both sides, and while the interdict actually lasted about ten months (17 June 1606–21 April

1607), it was positively ineffective. In most portions of the Venetian territory, sacramental services went on without interruption.

Although Paul ultimately won back the accused clerics captured by Venice, he did not win repeal of Venetian laws claiming secular jurisdiction over the church and its clerics. His position was viewed as an extremist reaction, especially in light of his almost unprecedented action in attempting to stop trial of ecclesiastics in Venetian secular courts. It was only the combined political pressure of France and Spain, not Paul's thundering religious interdict, that brought an end to the controversy. But the compromise under which the interdict was lifted was written in such a way as to suggest that it had never really been imposed. Paul's action in this matter was significant in that he attempted to have his way but really did not, but also because of what he failed to accomplish outright. It appeared that he had lifted the interdict without attaining much that he desired. He did not, moreover, address the underlying issue, the relationship between spiritual and temporal powers. The relationship had long been contested, and that remained the case. The failure of Paul and of his successors to steer a path through which they might exercise spiritual authority without claiming political sovereignty as well contributed to the institutional weakening of the papacy in the early modern period.

Paul V was not notable simply for his continued application of an outmoded papal political agenda, but also for his positive contributions to ecclesiastical reform. He was apparently motivated in this work by sincere piety, as he was known to have confessed his sins and to have said Mass daily. Like many Tridentine reformers, he was committed to the revival of real adherence to the obligation of residence implied in all benefices with the "care of souls" attached, but even in 1605 he illustrated the grave difficulty in bringing about that adherence by demonstrating inconsistency of his own. The long-established requirement had been subverted by exemptions and dispensations for hundreds of years. Reformers who contributed to the Tridentine recovery of the ideal had inveighed against these dispensations even before the challenge of Luther had been issued. Still, when Paul came to power, he felt compelled to reiterate that no exemptions should be granted in the consistory over and against that fundamental pastoral obligation. He himself, however, showed clearly how a rule so frequently invoked could still remain unimplemented. He made his nephew Scipione cardinal at the age of twenty-seven and bestowed upon him—without insisting on residence—benefices sufficient to enable the young man to purchase a vast amount of prime real estate in Latium and to become one of the most popular artistic patrons in Rome. With the income he also built the spectacular Villa Borghese, now a popular Roman art museum, the Galleria Borghese.

Paul showed more consistency in other reform initiatives. He indefatigably promoted the cult of the saints. He indicated his commitment to the canonization of Francesca di Roma from the moment of his election. He raised her to sainthood, along with Carlo Borromeo, in 1610. Paul also beatified a number of the great exemplars of Counter-Reformation spirituality, including Ignatius of Loyola, Teresa of Avila, Francis Xavier, and Filippo Neri. Paul approved new religious organizations as part of his commitment to reform, notably Neri's oratory and the French oratory founded by Pierre de Berulle. Paul exhibited consistent concern over the establishment of ritual and doctrinal uniformity. Thus he chose not only to publish the revised Roman Ritual (the standards for administration of the sacraments), but also to shut down the Thomist-Molinist controversy in 1607. He forbade any further wrangling between the two groups on questions related to the doctrine of grace, such as whether or not it was fundamentally incompatible with human free will.

Paul made substantial contributions to the arts and education, both inside of Rome and beyond. He made large gifts to the Vatican Library, including manuscripts from Bobbio. He purchased the entire library of Cardinal Serafino Olivier, then transferred the collection to the Vatican. These donations were crowned, especially for historians of the papacy, with his establishment of the Vatican Archives in space adjacent to the library itself. Paul had a background as a serious scholar, and apparently this led him to support the teaching of languages (Greek, Latin, Hebrew, and Arabic) by the members of religious orders in the universities of early modern Europe. As a patron of the arts, Paul made contributions that were both financially and artistically significant. While he may have been frugal in his personal and household expenditures, he was a lavish patron. He paid for construction of a chapel in the elegant Basilica of Santa Maria Maggiore. There, in 1613, he presided over the translation of an icon of the Virgin to the chapel he built, in a remarkable event in the history of Tridentine art patronage and Counter-Reformation spirituality. He made additions to the Vatican Palace and built fountains at Ponte Sisto, at Castel Sant' Angelo, and in St. Peter's Square. Paul considered it his principal responsibility as a patron of art to support the completion of St. Peter's Basilica. He entrusted this work primarily to Carlo Maderno, who extended the nave far beyond the original vision of Bramante and Michelangelo, to make the building form a Latin cross. When the facade was completed, Paul underlined the personal responsibility he felt—and took— for the project by having his own name carved in huge characters right over the front door. Modesty was apparently not one of Paul's defining characteristics.

Paul's personal benevolence and charitable aid touched many. He set up a storehouse of grain for the poor in 1607 and later, in 1611, established a credit agency for the farmers of Latium. He worked assiduously on the water-related problems that had long plagued the Papal States. He sponsored the draining of marshes as well as more efficient regulation of river flows, especially in Ferrara and the Romagna. He employed both lay and clerical experts on these matters, including three cardinals. He restored two aqueducts, among them the aqueduct of Trajan, which he renamed the Acqua Paola. These helped to supply the new fountains he built. Such actions, plus the Roman street improvements he made throughout his pontificate, establish him, like Sixtus V before him and Urban VIII (1623–44) after, as one of numerous popes in the early modern era who expended great time and resources enhancing the quality of life in the city.

Paul provided consistent support for missionary activities throughout the world. He sponsored preaching in Japan, China, the Congo, Ethiopia, and the Middle East. He was especially dedicated to Jesuit mission activities and to missions in all areas where persecution was prevalent. The large-scale conversions in Japan—approximately 15,000 between 1606 and 1607, gained primarily by the Jesuits—were reinforced by Paul's acceptance of envoys from Japan in Rome between October 1615 and January 1616. All this work was of little avail in the long run, as persecutions of Christian converts and missionaries by the Tokugawa rulers of Japan began in 1614 and intensified during Paul's reign. During Paul's pontificate Matteo Ricci and his fellow Jesuit missionaries continued making inroads through the mission to China, and the pope took part in these operations also. Paul assisted by, among other things, presiding over approval of the use of the Chinese language in Catholic liturgical services there. Requests like this might have been dismissed out of hand, but Paul did not do so, and when Cardinal Inquisitor Robert Bellarmine spoke up in support of the request, Paul gave the permission. A short-lived persecution of European missionaries began there in 1617, but Jesuit missionaries continued to work in China, with papal support, throughout Paul's reign.

Paul, like the majority of his fellow popes in the early modern period, promoted moderate operation of the Holy Office of the Inquisition. He clearly did not consider such an approach to be incompatible with vigorous pursuit of implementation of the Tridentine synthesis on doctrine and reform. There were few executions for heresy during his pontificate, and the vast majority of cases heard by the tribunal were apparently related to morality, not heterodoxy. There was, moreover, not a single case of prosecution for witchcraft. Paul personally instructed the inquisitors of Italy to operate with justice and understanding. In this matter he provided leadership by example, notably in regard to the most celebrated case of his age, that of Galileo and Copernicanism. During Paul's reign Galileo began his public relations campaign on behalf of the model of the universe espoused by Nicholas Copernicus, as the work of the early-sixteenth-century Polish priest and mathematician was being examined by the Inquisition. When Galileo came to Rome in 1616 and made his case in person, the Florentine physicist was granted multiple audiences with Paul V, who comforted him on the occasion of the tribunal's judgment. He reminded

Galileo that inquisitorial insistence that the Copernican theory could not be taught as truth was not an order to cease the search for proof of the theory. There can be little doubt, however, that the limited prohibition of Copernicus's book *De revolutionibus* and the general prohibition of all books previously written in support of the theory, both of which were published under Paul's watch, had a dampening affect upon European interest in the study of astronomy.

Hence in virtually every major area of his operations as pope, Paul exhibited intentions, attitudes, and commitments that preclude characterization of him and of his administration in any simple manner. His personal piety and status as a vigorous reformer are important characteristics. Paul did not hesitate, however, to promote a young nephew to cardinal or to bestow upon him vast riches in perfectly unreformed fashion. He exhibited the intransigence many persons associate with Counter-Reformation prelates and contemporary ecclesiastical institutions, especially in his jurisprudence and in his defense of papal jurisdictional prerogatives. He was, moreover, a warrior against Protestantism, vigorously subsidizing Catholic forces in the Thirty Years' War. His death in 1621 was the result of strokes suffered during and after the celebration of the defeat of the Calvinist king of Bohemia, Frederick V. There was nothing intransigent, however, about Paul's ability to see beyond simple, lockstep devotional regularity to grasp the value of liturgy in the vernacular, albeit only for the Chinese. It is safe to say, on the other hand, that he generally exhibited precious little political finesse. When his behavior suggested that he might be moving toward more sympathetic relations with another state, he could quickly reverse course. He did just that in his relations with England. Having learned through the interdict crisis with Venice the danger of unilateral positions, he initially expressed his hope to James I that the Gunpowder Plot would not result in backlash against English Catholics, but when the oath was demanded, Paul turned quickly to a policy of simple condemnation. He was a scholar and unquestionably a patron of education. Still, Paul apparently felt no great discomfort in attempting to shut down philosophical inquiry on one of the most nettlesome problems of all: how to account for the operation of grace while retaining the notion of human free will. Paul V was a fascinating, complicated character, a most notable pope, one who richly deserves further study.

SELECTED BIBLIOGRAPHY

Alden, Dauril. *The Making of an Enterprise: The Society of Jesus in Portugal, It's Empire, and Beyond, 1540–1750.* Stanford: Stanford University Press, 1996.

Caravale, Mario, and Alberto Caracciolo. *Lo stato pontificio da Martino V a Pio IX.* Turin: Unione Tipografico–Editrice Torinese, 1978.

Cochrane, Eric. *Italy, 1530–1630.* Ed. Julius Kirshner. New York: Longman, 1988.

Connet, Enrico. *Paolo V. e la repubblica Veneta: Giornale dal 22 Ottobre 1605–9, Giugno 1607.* Vienna: Tendler & Co., 1859.

Corbo, Anna Maria, and Massimo Pomponi, eds. *Fonti per la storia artistica Romana al tempo di Paolo V.* Rome: Ministero per i beni culturali e ambientali, 1995.

Dunne, George H. *Generation of Giants: The Story of the Jesuits in China in the Last Decades of the Ming Dynasty.* Notre Dame, Ind.: University of Notre Dame Press, 1962.

Grendler, Paul F. *The Roman Inquisition and the Venetian Press, 1540–1605.* Princeton: Princeton University Press, 1977.

Hsia, R. Po-chia. *The World of Catholic Renewal, 1540–1770.* New York: Cambridge University Press, 1998.

Iserloh, Erwin, Josef Glazik, Hubert Jedin. *History of the Church.* Vol. 5, *Reformation and Counter Reformation.* New York: Seabury, 1980.

Magistris, Carlo Pio de. *Per la storia del componimento della contesa tra la Repubblica Veneta e Paolo V. 1605–1607.* Torino: Tipografia G. Anfossi, 1941.

Mercati, Giovanni. *Per la storia della Biblioteca Apostolica: Bibliotecario Cesare Baronio.* Perugia: V. Bartelli & Co., 1910.

Moroni, Gaetano. *Dizionario di erudizione storico-ecclesiastica da S. Pietto Siho ai nostri giorni.* 109 vols. Venice: Tipografia Emiliana, 1840–79.

Oakley, Francis. "Complexities of Context: Gerson, Bellarmine, Sarpi, Richer, and the Venetian Interdict of 1606–1607." *Catholic Historical Review* 82 (1996): 369–96.

Ostrow, Steven F. *Art and Spirituality in Counter-Reformation Rome: The Sistine and Pauline Chapels in S. Maria Maggiore.* New York: Cambridge University Press, 1996.

Paschini, Pio, and Vincenzo Monachino, eds. *I papi nella storia.* 2 vols. Rome: Coletti, 1961.

Pastor, Ludwig Freiherr von. *The History of the Popes from the Close of the Middle Ages.* Vols. 25 and 26. Trans. Dom Ernest Graf. St. Louis: Herder, 1952.

Pirri, Pietro. *L'interdetto di Venezia del 1606 e i Gesuiti.* Rome: Institutum Historicum Societatis Iesu, 1959.

Prodi, Paolo. *The Papal Prince: One Body and Two Souls: The Papal Monarchy in Early Modern Europe.* Trans. Susan Haskins. New York: Cambridge University Press, 1987.

Reinhard, Wolfgang. *Papstfinanz und Nepotismus unter Paul V (1605–1621).* Stuttgart: A. Hiersemann, 1974.

Reinhardt, Nicole. *Macht und Ohnmacht der Verflechtung: Rom und Bologna unter Paul V.* Tübingen: Bibliotheca Academica Verlag, 2000.

Stumpo, Enrico. *Il capitale finanziario a Roma fra cinque e seicento: Contributo alla storia della fiscalità pontificia in età moderna, 1570–1660.* Milan: A. Giuffrè, 1985.

Wright, A.D. *The Counter-Reformation: Catholic Europe and the Non-Christian World.* New York: St. Martin's Press, 1982.

URBAN VIII (1623–44): THE BARBERINI ERA

Richard J. Blackwell

In the ebb and flow of human history the rate of change is rather uneven. Occasionally the unfolding of events that are occurring at several different levels comes together in a way that constitutes both a culmination of long-term earlier developments and the initiation of quite new future directions. Such a major turning point characterizes the papacy of Urban VIII (1623–44). During this period the seemingly interminable religious wars in Europe, which were rooted in the Protestant Reformation and the Catholic Counter-Reformation, finally came to an end through the sheer exhaustion of the warring factions. This in turn created the opportunity for the subsequent emergence of the modern national state. At this same time baroque art and architecture had reached their fullest expression, especially in Italy, where much of today's visible face of the cities, particularly Rome, was being produced. At the intellectual level the older medieval cultural paradigm, which was heavily based on a synthesis of Aristotelian philosophy and the Christian religious tradition, was rapidly breaking down to make room for the then only partially understood edifice of what we now call modern science.

It was a time of immense change, of painful abandonment of cherished older world views, of tremendous artistic achievements, of violent warfare, of blatant abuses of power, and of great opportunities lost by the Catholic church. Afterwards the church was destined to play a much less influential role in world affairs for many generations. The man who was elected to the papacy in this critical period was Maffeo Barberini. He was born in Florence in April 1568, the fifth son of a prominent, but not aristocratic, family that had made its money in the wool trade. His father, Antonio, died when he was three years old. His mother, Camilla Barbadori, arranged for him to be educated by the Jesuits, first in Florence and then at the Collegio Romano. Later, in 1589, he was awarded a doctor of laws degree from the University of Pisa.

He entered the service of the church in Rome, where his performance in various appointments led to his consecration as a bishop in 1604 and his designation as a cardinal by Pope Paul V in 1606. In these same years he made several official visits to Paris, including the role of serving as the papal nuncio, and as a result he became well acquainted with Henry IV and the French court, a fact that played an important role later, during the Thirty Years' War. His long and warm friendship with Galileo, a fellow Tuscan, began in about 1611. Many years later (in 1630) he is reported to have said that had it been up to him, the church's decree of 5 March 1616, which condemned Copernicanism as "false and completely contrary to the Sacred Scriptures," would not have been published.

After the death of Pope Gregory XV in July 1623, the cardinal-electors entered into a complex and politically divided conclave (19 July–6 August) that, after a difficult series of votes, finally chose Maffeo Barberini with near unanimity to be the next pope, under the name of Urban VIII. Thus began the longest papacy of the seventeenth century (one week short of twenty-one years), and one of the longer papal tenures in the history of the church. It ended with Urban VIII's death in Rome on 29 July 1644. Urban VIII's election as pope was received with great warmth and enthusiasm on all sides in Rome, but especially among the artists, the literati, and the intellectuals of the day, who correctly anticipated both his encouragement and his financial support of their work. In contrast to the previous two popes, Urban VIII was a man of considerable interest in all matters of high culture, which included his own significant personal accomplishments as a poet. His reign enjoyed a most auspicious beginning.

But the seeds of the abuse of power were sown at the same time. Three days after his coronation Urban VIII made his twenty-five-year-old nephew Francesco Barberini a cardinal. Four years later he made another nephew, the then-twenty-year-old Antonio Barberini, a cardinal. As the years passed, these two cardinal nephews played increasingly major roles in Urban VIII's governance of the church and the Papal States, with Francesco assuming the position of the pope's major advisor and in effect his executive assistant on virtually all matters before the papacy. In 1624 Urban VIII had also conferred the cardinalate on his brother Antonio (the elder), who as a Capuchin monk was less inclined than the two nephews to deal with worldly matters. Another of his brothers, Carlo (the father of the two cardinal nephews), was given the offices of general of the papal armies and governor of the Borgo. Carlo's third son, Taddeo, who was married by the pope to Anna of the powerful and highly aristocratic Co-lonna family, was appointed to various government offices in Rome and in the Papal States and in 1630 succeeded to his father's offices. These various family appointments were made, of course, with the object in mind of solidifying the pope's control of the powers of his office and of establishing his family's status.

All of these people, as well as still other members of the Barberini family, were assigned lucrative benefices and pensions. As a result, the Barberini family acquired a truly immense wealth during Urban VIII's papacy. The abuse of power due to this nepotism was so severe that near the end of his life Urban VIII began to have qualms of conscience over whether his nephews had legal rights to their wealth. After Urban VIII's death the two cardinal nephews took refuge briefly under the protection of Cardinal Mazarin in Paris to avoid any confrontation in Rome over their possessions, but that never developed, and they returned to Rome.

Urban VIII's nepotism was clearly his greatest fault during his years as pope. On the other hand, the vast sums of money so acquired also led to some significant positive results. Although much of the Barberini wealth was used for military campaigns and fortifications, such a great deal also went to the support of art and architecture that the face of Rome was significantly changed during these years. Numerous churches, roads, piazzas, and fountains were built or restored all over Rome. A tell-tale sign of the Barberini influence is the family's ubiquitous symbol consisting of three bees, which were carved or painted

Painting of Pope Urban VIII by Gian Lorenzo Bernini. (The Art Archive/Palazzo Barberini Rome/Dagli Orti)

into many of these artistic works, and which are still visible today. Rome's port city of Civitavecchia was rebuilt, fortifications were added to Castel Sant'Angelo, and the pope's favorite retreat at Castel Gandolfo was reconstructed to take advantage of its spectacular view far down to the waters of Lake Albano below.

Very considerable sums of money from the Barberini fortune were also used to set up and maintain an immense patronage system to support the arts and the literary life of the time. Urban VIII was very fortunate to have a large number of highly talented artists and architects at his disposal to carry out so many of these projects with such great artistic results. Primary among them was Gian Lorenzo Bernini, the leading architect and sculptor of the day, who executed a large number of these commissions. The most famous among them are the Palazzo Barberini on the north slope of the Quirinale and the bronze *baldacchino* constructed over the main altar in the Basilica of St. Peter. Much of the bronze needed for this latter project was taken from the ancient Pantheon in central Rome. This supposedly occasioned the aphorism "Quod non fecerunt barbari, fecerunt Barberini" (What the barbarians did not do, the Barberini have).

While all this was happening in Rome, Urban VIII's reign as pope was constantly in the shadow of the Thirty Years' War (1618–48), his entire papacy falling within these years. This war, which involved most of the major nations of Europe, was actually a series of different military confrontations between various combatants in a wide variety of places in Central Europe. The key question was whether Lutheranism or Catholicism would be the established religion in these areas, although as the years passed, that initial religious issue gradually gave way to the geographical, nationalistic, and dynastic rivalries of the nations involved. By the time the war ended with the Peace of Westphalia, Central Europe was massively decimated and the era of religious wars had finally come to a close.

Urban VIII, of course, would have been most directly concerned for the restoration of Catholicism, which was represented in the war by the two branches of the Habsburg family, in Spain and in Austria. But he was strongly criticized for giving inadequate support to the Catholic side. Part of the reason for this was his long-standing attachment to France, which, under the leadership of Cardinal Richelieu, had become allied in 1631 with King Gustavus Adolphus of Sweden on the other side of the conflict. During the next year Urban VIII had to deal with his most serious internal political crisis over this matter. This culminated in a confrontation on 8 March 1632 in a consistory in which Cardinal Gaspare Borgia, who was also the Spanish ambassador to Rome, openly denounced the pope for protecting heresy, and thus for disloyalty to the church, because of his sympathies with the French and their Swedish allies. This dispute was not resolved until May, when Urban VIII broke off his liaison with the French. This episode, as well as many other events of the war itself, are classic examples of the problems caused by the entanglement of the church with the state.

In the next year Urban VIII was faced with another major crisis that was to have much more lasting and detrimental effects on the Catholic church, namely, the Galileo trial. Urban VIII had long been a personal friend and admirer of Galileo and his work. Shortly after his election Galileo was welcomed to several personal visits with the new pope to discuss, among other things, the status of his work in astronomy. Unfortunately, we have no records of what was specifically said at these meetings, but it is safe to say that they must have included Urban VIII's often-stated conviction about the new debates in astronomy, namely, that neither the Ptolemaic nor the Copernican theory could ever be strictly proven (since God could have created the world in innumerably different ways), and so as a result one should discuss these theories only at a hypothetical, and not at a realistic, level.

Galileo must have felt comfortable enough with this advice, for in the following years he composed his now-classic *Dialogue Concerning the Two Chief World Systems*, which examined in detail the evidence and arguments on both sides of the debate, although he clearly favored Copernicanism in the process. When this book was published in 1632, it was strongly criticized in some church circles as being a violation of the widely known decree of 1616 against Copernicanism. A special commission was appointed by the pope to evaluate this question. In the process of its investigation the special commission found in the secret files of the Holy Office another document that stated that in 1616 Galileo had been served an injunction by Cardinal Robert Bellarmine in the name of the Holy Office to the effect that he should not "teach, hold, or defend it [Copernicanism] in any way whatsoever, verbally or in writing."

It should be noted that both the precise meaning and the legal status of whatever injunction may have been served on Galileo are matters of continuing dispute. The reason for this is that there are two conflicting accounts of the key meeting between Galileo and Cardinal Bellarmine on 26 February 1616, at which the injunction apparently was served. This conflict is not likely to be resolved unless additional, previously unknown documents are unexpectedly uncovered. The first account, in the 1616 memorandum later found in the files of the Holy Office in 1632, implies that Galileo either resisted, or more likely had not yet replied to, Bellarmine's admonition that he abandon Copernicanism when "immediately thereafter" (it would have been a violation of Pope Pius V's instructions to Bellarmine if Galileo had not been given an opportunity to reply) the blanket injunction just quoted was imposed on Galileo by the commissary-general Michelangelo Seghizzi, who was present at the meeting as the Holy Office's top legal official. This document, which is not properly signed or notarized as would have been legally required, is not the injunction itself (which has not been found), but a clerical memo of some sort summarizing the gist of the meeting. Examination of the paper, ink, and handwriting has put to rest an earlier view that the memo was forged in either 1616 or 1632 to entrap Galileo.

The second account points to quite a different picture. Three months after the fateful meeting, in an effort to dispel rumors that he had been chastised in some way by his church, Galileo requested and received from Bellarmine a letter, dated 26 May 1616, that was intended to state the results of their meeting. In that letter Bellarmine explicitly stated that Galileo had not denied any of his views, and that the only thing that had happened was that Galileo had been informed of the impending announcement of the Congregation of the Index, which was formally published on 5 March, that Copernicanism "is contrary to the Holy Scripture and therefore cannot be defended or held." This is considerably less sweeping than the admonition quoted earlier from the Holy Office's memo, as Galileo himself was to point out later at his trial. Also, Bellarmine's letter does not mention an injunction.

Galileo, of course, had no way of ever seeing the relevant memo in the secret files of the Holy Office, and the officials of the Holy Office did not know about Bellarmine's letter to Galileo. Both documents surfaced in 1633 in the middle of Galileo's trial; both sides were quite surprised by the other side's document; the legal dilemma was apparent. The one person whose authoritative voice could have settled the matter, Cardinal Bellarmine, had died in 1621. Seghizzi had died in 1625. The net result of all this is the most unfortunate situation that the Galileo trial, which in many ways has remained the defining episode for the relations between science and religion ever since, took place in a context in which two of the key documents are ambiguous and conflicting, now as well as then.

Be that as it may, when Urban VIII, who had not previously known of this injunction, first learned about it in 1632, his friendship for Galileo permanently turned into hostility. He must have felt that Galileo had deliberately misled him by not informing him about the injunction during their private conversations. At any rate a trial, which occurred in the next spring, became unavoidable. The primary legal issue at the trial was whether Galileo had violated the terms of the injunction allegedly issued seventeen years earlier. He was ultimately convicted of "vehement suspicion of heresy," a judgment passed on him ironically by a former good friend and fellow intellectual. It is interesting to note that Cardinal Francesco Barberini supported and defended Galileo vigorously throughout the trial, although without avail of course, even to the point of refusing to sign the court's judgment. Galileo, who was then already approaching seventy, spent the remainder of his days under what we would now call house arrest at his villa at Arcetri, near Florence, where he continued his work and writing on theoretical issues in mechanics rather than anything more on the forbidden topics in astronomy.

The damage caused to the Catholic church from this episode has been immense. The shadow of being opposed to freedom of thought still darkens the Catholic church to some degree. Relations between science and religion are still strained. During Urban VIII's papacy the opportunity of beginning an integration of science into a reexamined Christian tradition (which had happened with Aristotelian science and philosophy in the thirteenth century) was lost, perhaps for good. Unfortunately, Urban VIII is probably still best known today as the pope who condemned Galileo.

SELECTED BIBLIOGRAPHY

Biagioli, Mario. *Galileo, Courtier: The Practice of Science in the Culture of Absolutism*. Chicago: University of Chicago Press, 1993.

Blackwell, Richard J. *Galileo, Bellarmine, and the Bible*. Notre Dame, Ind.: University of Notre Dame Press, 1991.

Drake, Stillman. *Galileo at Work: His Scientific Biography*. Chicago: University of Chicago Press, 1978.

Fantoli, Annibale. *Galileo: For Copernicanism and for the Church*. Trans. George V. Coyne. Vatican City: Vatican Observatory Publications, 1994.

Grisar, Josef. "Päpstliche Finanzen, Nepotismus, and Kirchenrecht unter Urban VIII." *Miscellanea historiae pontificiae* 7 (1943): 203–365.

Hook, Judith. "Urban VIII: The Paradox of a Spiritual Monarchy." In *The Courts of Europe: Politics, Patronage, and Royalty, 1400–1800*. Ed. A.G. Dickens. New York: McGraw-Hill, 1977, 213–31.

Langford, Jerome J. *Galileo, Science, and the Church*. Ann Arbor: University of Michigan Press, third edition, 1992.

Lavin, Marilyn Aronberg. *Seventeenth-Century Barberini Documents and Inventories of Art*. New York: New York University Press, 1975.

Nussdorfer, Laurie. *Civic Politics in the Rome of Urban VIII*. Princeton: Princeton University Press, 1992.

Pastor, Ludwig Freiherr von. *The History of the Popes from the Close of the Middle Ages*. Vols. 28 and 29. Trans. Dom Ernest Graf. St. Louis: Herder, 1955.

Pecchiai, Pio. *I Barberini*. Rome: Biblioteca d'Arte Editrice, 1959.

Pieralisi, Sante. *Urbano VIII e Galileo Galilei*. Rome: Poliglotta, 1875.

Redondi, Pietro. *Galileo Heretic*. Trans. Raymond Rosenthal. Princeton: Princeton University Press, 1987.

Santillana, Giorgio de. *The Crime of Galileo*. Chicago: University of Chicago Press, 1955.

Scott, John B. *Images of Nepotism: The Painted Ceilings of Palazzo Barberini*. Princeton: Princeton University Press, 1991.

Westfall, Richard S. *Essays on the Trial of Galileo*. Vatican City: Vatican Observatory Publications, 1989.

INNOCENT XI (1676–89): DEFENDER OF CHRISTENDOM

Francesco C. Cesareo

On 19 May 1611 a son was born to Livio Odescalchi and Paola Castelli in the city of Como who was destined to ascend the throne of St. Peter as Innocent XI. Benedetto Odescalchi was born into a noble family with a reputation for piety and Christian living whose commercial and banking interests provided a comfortable life for Benedetto and his siblings. While the Odescalchi family had gained wealth through mercantile successes, they did not neglect those less fortunate in their society. The family was known for its charity and regular almsgiving, which Benedetto would continue throughout his life. Benedetto's formal education began in the local parish school. Having completed his rudimentary education, Benedetto continued his studies at the local Jesuit college, where he received instruction in grammar, literature, and rhetoric. In 1626, at the age of fifteen, Benedetto left school and went to Genoa, where he was introduced into the affairs of the business world by his uncle Papirio, who directed the mercantile house known as the Società Odescalchi. For the next few years Benedetto gained practical experience in the administration of the family business.

At the time of Benedetto's return to Como in 1632, the governor of the state of Milan, Cardinal Gil de Albornoz, had instituted two urban militias and was organizing a rural militia to protect the city of Como and its suburbs. At the suggestion of one of his relatives, Benedetto was chosen to lead one of these militias on 20 October 1635, an honorific post that was usually conferred on a noble at that time. In 1636 Benedetto left Como and went to Rome, an event that marks a turning point in his life. Cardinal

Alfonso della Cueva counseled Benedetto to resume his studies, suggesting that he pursue law, since this would allow him to embark on a career in either civil or ecclesiastical life. Heeding this advice, Benedetto enrolled in the University of Rome in the fall of 1636, where he studied canon and civil law. In 1638 Benedetto transferred to Naples and received his degree in November 1639. Benedetto gradually decided to enter the clerical state and received the tonsure on 18 February 1640.

Benedetto returned to Rome in 1643 with the intention of living a private clerical life, applying himself to acts of piety, charity, study, and the affairs of his patrimony. His brother Carlo, however, had other plans for him. Cardinal della Cueva introduced Benedetto to Cardinals Francesco Barberini, the nephew of the reigning pope, Urban VIII, and Giovanni Pamphili, the future Innocent X. The Barberini quickly sought to place Benedetto in their service. Through the insistence of his brother, along with members of the college of cardinals, Benedetto was persuaded to accept several ecclesiastical posts that had been procured for him. On 16 December 1643 Benedetto was offered an appointment as special apostolic commissioner for taxes in the papal territory of the Marches. In quick succession he was appointed protonotary apostolic, president of the Camera Apostolica chamber, governor of Macerata, and clerk of the apostolic chamber. On 6 March 1645 Pope Innocent X elevated Benedetto to the rank of cardinal, despite the fact that he lacked even minor orders. In conformity with the constitutions of Sixtus V, Benedetto was ordained a deacon. The special esteem in which Benedetto was held by Pope Innocent X is evident in his appointment as papal legate to Ferrara on 16 June 1648. Benedetto sought to decline the pope's appointment. Innocent X's insistence, however, led Benedetto to accept. As legate, Benedetto struggled to provide for the needs of the citizens and strove to improve their religious and moral life through his own example. His efforts on behalf of the citizens led them to confer on Benedetto the title "father of the poor."

In March 1650 Pope Innocent X appointed Benedetto bishop of the diocese of Novara. He received ordination to the priesthood in the chapel of the archbishop's palace in Ferrara in late November 1650 and episcopal consecration in the cathedral of Ferrara on 30 January 1651. As bishop, he exercised constant pastoral concern for the spiritual and temporal well-being of the faithful. Benedetto paid special attention to the preparation of clerics who would serve the people of the diocese, enforcing discipline and proper intellectual and spiritual formation among them. He sponsored increased instruction in Christian doctrine for adults and children. He also diligently defended the rights of the church against the intrusions of civil authorities in the ecclesiastical realm. Above all, he became well known for his generous alms to the poor of his diocese. He governed his diocese carefully according to the Tridentine ideal for resident bishops, conducting a visitation of the parishes and promoting a regional religious revival.

After the death of Pope Innocent X at the beginning of January 1655, Benedetto participated in the conclave to elect a successor. The new pope, Alexander VII, did not permit Benedetto to leave Rome since he intended to employ him in the curia. Benedetto reluctantly submitted his resignation as bishop of Novara, and during the next two decades he held a variety of curial positions. He was a member of several congregations and served as camerlengo and diplomatic counselor to Popes Alexander VII, Clement IX, and Clement X. When Pope Clement X died in 1676, Benedetto entered the conclave as a potential successor. Possible opposition to his election from Louis XIV was defused by the French ambassador, François Annibal d'Estrées. On 21 September 1676 Benedetto was elected pope, but he accepted only after the cardinals subscribed to a series of articles that he had drawn up outlining his plans for reform of the church. Benedetto took the name Innocent in memory of Innocent X, who had elevated him to the college of cardinals.

Pope Innocent XI. (The Art Archive/Dagli Orti)

Innocent XI intended to live a life of great simplicity and to promote changes in curial administration. He reduced court ceremonies to a minimum and restricted disbursements for his personal needs. He introduced new vigor and discipline among the Roman curia, the hierarchy, the clergy, and the laity by requiring strict application of the guidelines of the Council of Trent. He also addressed the financial problems depleting the papal treasury through his policy of stringent economy, tax reform, and efficient bookkeeping. As pope, Innocent continued to perform the works of charity characteristic of his earlier life. He provided both spiritual and material assistance to the sick, the poor, beggars, the retired, and older unmarried women. He established schools in Rome for the upbringing of destitute girls and continued to be a generous benefactor of the Hospice of St. Galla to rehabilitate the sick, the poor, and the homeless.

Innocent presided over a pontificate marked by constant political struggles with Louis XIV of France. They battled in defining the proper relationship between their rival temporal and spiritual authorities on a host of particular issues: arrangements for diplomatic appointments to bishoprics, disputes over territory, and the traditional Gallican rights of the French church. Despite Louis XIV's efforts to undermine Innocent's plans, the pope led a long, successful war against the Ottoman Turks between 1683 and 1689.

For Innocent, the propagation and defense of the Catholic faith was among the highest priorities. Shortly after his election he established new dioceses in South America plus Dominican universities in the Philippines and in Guatemala. He desired to bring Christianity to all regions of the world and was convinced that this was his duty as a good pastor. In addition, Innocent strove to defend the faith in Europe against the encroachments of Protestantism and new theological currents that threatened the unity of Catholicism, especially Jansenism and Quietism. Innocent XI's thirteen-year pontificate came to an end with his death on 12 August 1689. His reputation for holiness led to the initiation of a canonization process in 1714. In 1956 he was beatified by Pope Pius XII.

Innocent XI assumed the papal office with a clear understanding of the needs of his age. Consequently, from the outset he embarked on a concrete program of action with three objectives: implementing a program of reform within the church, assuring the safety of Christian Europe, and defending the freedom and rights of the church. It is in these areas that the significance of Innocent XI's pontificate lies. Soon after his election Innocent inaugurated a practical program designed to meet the pastoral needs of the laity. Concerned with the state of the faith among the people, Innocent emphasized instruction in Christian doctrine. Parents were admonished, under pain of excommunication, to send their children to catechism classes. Innocent insisted that Christian doctrine be taught not only to the children, but to young adults, soldiers, and all the faithful. He placed this responsibility not only on the ordinary clergy, but on the cardinals as well, who were often seen teaching doctrine to the young. Parish priests were also directed to use preaching as a means of instructing the faithful. Innocent insisted, moreover, that they must preach in simple, practical fashion.

Innocent XI emphasized the importance of the church's sacramental life. He encouraged the faithful to participate in the sacraments on a regular basis, in line with both the devotional movements and the doctrinal directives of the era. As part of his program for reform within the church, Innocent struck out against the practice of nepotism. He was the first pope to refrain from seeking the support of his closest kin, never allowing his family to enrich themselves in any way at the church's expense. While many within the college of cardinals opposed Innocent's efforts in this area, he drew up a bull designed to eliminate this abuse once and for all. When the bull was sent to the cardinals, it met so much resistance that Innocent backed down. Nevertheless, his own refusal to engage in nepotistic practices marked the first steps toward abolition of the problem.

Innocent reaffirmed the decrees of the Council of Trent applying to bishops, particularly those concerning residency. He established a congregation of cardinals to examine the fitness of episcopal candidates in Italy, and on occasion Innocent himself would examine the bishops. In the selection of cardinals Innocent proceeded cautiously, elevating only worthy nominees. He sought information on the candidate's moral and practical qualifications, and these weighed heavily in his decision. Innocent sought to curtail the elaborate lifestyles of the cardinals and bishops, reminding them how far they had drifted from the example of Christ and the apostles and how detrimental this was for the faithful. Innocent attached great importance to the reform of religious orders, which he regarded as "centers of light for the church." Referring to the vows of poverty, chastity, and obedience, Innocent emphasized the need for purity of faith and morals, education, and discipline. He directed special attention to female congregations, similarly urging discipline and spiritual renewal.

Innocent XI even attempted to effect moral regeneration of the city of Rome. Bringing to the papacy a rigid asceticism, he sought to improve the customs of the city's inhabitants. To implement his plans, Innocent distributed a booklet that instructed parish youth on Christian modesty in their attire and habits. He issued edicts prohibiting public recitals, theater, carnivals, and jousts, as well as certain forms of music and song. He hoped to make Rome an example of righteous Christian living for the whole world, satisfying his duties as pastor in the process.

At the time of Innocent XI's election much of southeastern Europe and adjoining regions were on the brink of falling to the Ottoman Turks. In Innocent's mind there was but one political question that he needed to concern himself with, namely, averting this peril. In 1683 the Turks were making their way west toward Vienna in hope of conquering the city. Innocent believed that if Vienna fell to the Turks, they would then move toward Rome. Innocent encouraged the rulers of Europe to settle or at least put aside their differences so that a united opposition could thwart the Turkish advance. He worked to unite the Christian princes in a defensive league under the leadership of Emperor Leopold against this common enemy and sent vast sums of money to aid the Christian cause. While Innocent was never able to convince Louis XIV to join the efforts against the Turks, eventually a combined imperial force under Charles, the duke of Lorraine, and King John III Sobieski of Poland launched a successful counterattack, liberated Vienna, and saved the Christian countries of the West. In 1684 Innocent united Emperor Leopold I, King John III Sobieski, and Marcantonio Giustiniani of Venice in a holy league against the Ottoman Empire still entrenched in the Balkans and parts of Hungary. Victory at Pest in 1684 and the liberation of Buda in 1686 led to the reconquest of the remainder of Hungary and eventually Belgrade. This broke the expansive power of the Ottoman Empire.

Historians acknowledge that Innocent was the driving force behind Europe's efforts against the Turkish threat. Without a doubt, Innocent XI's success against the Turks marks the most significant moment of his pontificate. The records of his beatification process put it this way: "No matter how great the merits of Pope Innocent XI with regard to the Catholic faith and the customs, nonetheless this great merit would have been a vain success, if he had not been at the same time the true, although unarmed, victor at Vienna and Buda against the Ottoman Turks. It can be said that in those victories consists his greatest merit" (Miccinelli, 103).

Besides the war against Ottoman expansion, Innocent's pontificate was marked by a constant conflict with Louis XIV. The struggle between the French monarch and the pope revolved around French governmental encroachments on the liberties of the church, which often showed a disregard for papal authority. Among the issues that strained relations between the king and the pope was that of the *regale*. The kings of France had claimed the right of disposing the revenues of a bishopric when it was vacant and of nominating individuals to all their dependent benefices. This right was not applicable to all the dioceses of the realm, nor was it extended to other dioceses by the Second Council of Lyons (1274). Louis XIV did not accept the restriction and was determined to extend the *regale* to all parts of the kingdom. All but two French bishops accepted Louis's decision without opposition.

Innocent supported the opposing bishops and addressed two briefs to Louis XIV admonishing him to respect the prerogatives of the church. To demonstrate to the pope that the French church took its orders from Paris rather than from Rome, Louis convened an assembly of the clergy asking it to advise him regarding the *regale*. The assembly showed overwhelming support for the actions of the king and issued the declaration of the clergy of France (March 1682) outlining the principles of Gallicanism. Innocent responded to the declaration by promulgating a brief abrogating everything the assembly had done. Furthermore, he refused to grant canonical institution to priests who had been nominated by the Crown to vacant bishoprics if they had participated in the assembly or subscribed to the declaration, on the grounds that their doctrine was unsound. This resulted in over forty vacant bishoprics at the time of Innocent XI's death.

In an attempt to divert the pope's attention from his encroachments on ecclesiastical rights, Louis XIV sought to demonstrate his great zeal for orthodoxy. Desiring to unite the realm under one religious faith, Louis sought to convert the Huguenots to Catholicism. While Innocent was pleased with the king's intentions, he did not approve of the campaign for conversions that the king had inaugurated. Innocent disapproved of the use of force and persecution as a means of suppressing heresy. Furthermore, Innocent rejected Louis XIV's proselytizing campaign when attempts were made to modify the customary method of obtaining converts to the church. Louis permitted the Huguenots to be received into the Catholic church without explicitly forswearing their former beliefs or submitting to the declaration of faith drawn up by the Council of Trent. Innocent made it clear that he was unwilling to tolerate the dilution of Tridentine teachings for the sake of making conversions among the French Protestants.

The climax of Louis's campaign against Protestantism came on 18 October 1685 when he abrogated the Edict of Nantes, bringing an end to religious freedom in France. While the pope endorsed and approved of the abrogation itself, he did not condone the widespread persecutions that resulted subsequently. While Louis hoped that this event would settle his differences with the pope, no concessions came from Rome, and relations between France and the papacy grew worse. Throughout his pontificate Innocent remained unshaken in his defense of the church's prerogatives and rights in France, even in the face of a threatened armed invasion of the Papal States by French troops.

Historians of the papacy acknowledge Innocent XI as one of the outstanding popes of the seventeenth century. The significant achievements of the pontificate of Innocent XI were undoubtedly the liberation of Europe from the Ottoman Turks, the reassertion of the church's authority, and the reaffirmation of personal spirituality and dedication to service. The esteem in which Innocent XI was held in Rome even after his death is attested in the journal of Jean Dumont, who wrote: "From the day of his election, 21 September 1676, to that of his death, he was ever seen exclusively bent on fulfilling the duties of his office, removing abuses, visiting hospitals, relieving the poor. No sooner had he assumed the tiara than he took a step such as no previous pope had dared to attempt, namely the suppression of nepotism. Parsimonious, nay miserly, where his own person was concerned, he was liberal for the common good. To the emperor and to Venice he gave his wholehearted support against the Turks. To him the emperor owed it that Vienna kept up its resistance and was eventually relieved. He defended the rights and privileges of the church with a vigor which by itself alone gives him a claim to the admiration of all" (Jean Dumont, *Voyage en Rome en Italie*, 1699, quoted in Pastor, *History* 32: 531).

SELECTED BIBLIOGRAPHY

Colombo, Giuseppe. *Notizie biografiche e lettere di Papa Innocenzo XI*. Torino: Tipografia S. Giuseppe, 1878.

Epistolario Innocenziano: Lettere del Card. Benedetto Odescalchi e di Papa Innocenzo XI Papa. Ed. Pietro Gini. Como: Società Storica Comense, 1977.

Magnuson, Torgil. *Rome in the Age of Bernini*, 2 vols. N.J.: Humanities Press, 1986.

Maras, Raymond J. *Innocent XI: Pope of Christian Unity*. Notre Dame, Ind.: Cross Roads Books, 1984.

Miccinelli, Carlo. *Il Beato Innocenzo XI: Cenni Biografici*. Rome: Tipografia Poliglotta Vaticana, 1956.

O'Brien, Louis. *Innocent XI and the Revocation of the Edict of Nantes*. Berkeley: University of California Press, 1934.

Pastor, Ludwig Freiherr von. *The History of the Popes from the Close of the Middle Ages*. Vol. 32. Trans. Dom Ernest Graf. St. Louis: Herder, 1957.

Pius XII, Pope. "Come limpido astro." *The Pope Speaks* 4 (1957–58): 51–67.

Ranke, Leopold von. *History of the Popes: Their Church and State*. London: George Bell & Sons, 1896.

Roper, Abel. *The Life and Reign of Innocent XI, Late Pope of Rome*. London: n.p., 1690.

Torriani, Edoardo. "Alcuni documenti riguardanti il papa Innocenzo undecimo, prima Benedetto Odescalchi di Como." *Revue d'histoire ecclésiastique suisse* 9 (1915): 35–46, 134–49.

INNOCENT XII
(1691–1700)

BRENDAN DOOLEY

When Neapolitan nobleman Antonio Pignatelli assumed the papacy as Innocent XII after an agonizing five-month consistory deadlocked by the great-power factionalism that was soon to develop into military struggles involving Rome and the rest of Europe, the Venetian ambassador Domenico Contarini expressed the high hopes of the most astute observers: "If he could operate by himself, he would surpass the best popes of the church. . . . he is enriched with all the most desirable features of a head of the church" (*Relazioni degli stati europei*, 437). Indeed, with some of the leading contemporary cultural figures in his retinue, including embryologist and physician Marcello Malpighi, architect Carlo Fontana, and Giovanni Giusto Ciampini, cofounder of Italian scientific journalism, Innocent XII clearly had the potential to make his papacy a significant part of the 1690s revival fostered by the newly established Accademia degli Arcadi in Rome that gave a name to the entire period. While change was in the air in other fields, his abolition of nepotism and restrictions on the venality of offices amounted to nothing less than a revolution in public and ecclesiastical administration. However, with the seventeenth-century style of papacy in decline, the qualities necessary for success no longer corresponded necessarily to those required for cultural leadership; and the position of the pope as a predominantly spiritual leader was not yet consolidated. Not surprisingly, Innocent XII raised more expectations than he was able to satisfy in a brief nine-year rule.

Born in Basilicata in 1615, Pignatelli obtained the doctorate in both civil and canon law from the Collegio Romano, and he followed the other well-recommended and well-born clerics in Rome to the highest reaches of the ecclesiastical *cursus honorum*. A prelacy under Urban VIII led to a vice-legate position to Urbino. Under Innocent X he became inquisitor in Malta (1646) and three years later governor of Viterbo. After gaining the archbishopric of Larissa in 1652, he was sent as nuncio to Florence, where he remained until he was sent as nuncio first to Poland (1660) and then to Vienna (1668); but his refusal to declare affiliation to the French or Spanish parties in the curia impeded his progress to a cardinalship under Clement IX. Under Clement X, whose admiration he enjoyed, he accumulated honors with particular rapidity. By this time already bishop of Lecce, he now became a member of the Congregation of Bishops and Regulars in 1673, maestro di camera in 1675, and cardinal and bishop of Faenza in 1681. After a brief period as legate to Bologna, he was sent as archbishop of Naples in 1685.

As archbishop of Naples, Pignatelli showed the spirit of compromise that made him an undependable ally for any cultural revival. Indeed, he was spared the necessity to defend the Neapolitan professionals in the liberal arts against whose influence on the Neapolitan cultural scene local Jesuits had been engaging the powers of the local Inquisition off and on since the days of the controversial Accademia degli Investiganti, the hotbed of scientific innovation in the south of Italy. But when the Neapolitan Inquisition once more sprang into action in the beginning of his pontificate, he refused to accede to a popular petition by the city government, on behalf of the professionals, for the abolition of the local Inquisition, and he reprimanded city officials for exiling the inquisitor. All he would concede was that heresy trials could be held by the archbishop, traditionally a local subject, rather than by the far more rigorous inquisitor sent from Rome. When the petitioners tried to extend the debate into questions like the right of asylum in churches and the conferring of benefices upon foreign candidates, he stood firm.

Among Innocent's first actions as pope were ones regarding nepotism and the venality of ecclesiastical offices. The time was right. By 1691, Pastor notes, the Borghese were known to have accumulated some 260,000 scudi by means of the papacy of Paul V, the Pamphili 1,400,000 by Innocent X, the Chigi 900,000 by Alexander VII, the Altieri 1,200,000 by Clement X, and the Ottoboni 800,000 by Alexander VIII—not counting incomes directly deriving from the Datary and from vacated offices. Reforms had been attempted without success in 1681 and 1686. Opposition to change was based at least to some extent upon doubts about the wisdom of exchanging a long-standing and workable system for a new and untried one. Papal finances depended increasingly upon taxes from the Papal States rather than on spiritual incomes from elsewhere in Christendom. Administering these taxes demanded the best efficiency and bureaucratic expertise that current practices could muster. With the increasing centralization of papal power and the decline of the consistory as a real governing body since Sixtus V, venal offices and nepotism had assured the pope of a dependable cadre of patrimonial bureaucrats entirely faithful to their patron. Indeed, jurist Giambattista De Luca, one of the most original legal minds of the day, praised their effectiveness as well as their propriety. Venal positions, he pointed out, were not in reality a form of simony, since ecclesiastical and political matters were by now impossible to distinguish and since the price paid for the office was really a compensation for the money lost by the alienation of the income it provided. Papal nephews had become veritable first ministers, not unlike the first ministers created by the Spanish and French monarchies, with the added advantage that they could be trusted to sustain the interests of the current papacy rather than those of the various factions within the curia.

Tomb of Pope Innocent XII. (The Art Archive/San Gennaro Cathedral Naples/Dagli Orti)

The abolition of nepotism (22 June 1692) and the restrictions on venal offices pushed papal administration abruptly into the next stage of maturity, with all the growing pains imaginable from such a transition. From now on, the circle of candidates was to be widened, and merit was to be a significant criterion for advancement. Even cardinals were to be named at least in part to reward actual accomplishments rather than, as before, to accommodate the most powerful princes in Europe and to liberate, by promotion, high curial offices that could be resold. But before new sources of income could be identified to replace the incomes previously derived from nepotistic appointments and from the sale of offices, Innocent could count on much fewer resources to keep his administration going. This meant a radical program of austerity. In fact, Pastor points out that the 78,000 scudi per year that Innocent spent to maintain the court amounted to less than what Leo X had spent on his table alone.

The new austerity program naturally affected Innocent's building projects, reducing the rate of construction to relatively modest proportions compared to a papacy like that of Innocent X. However, architecture and good rulership still went hand in hand. Apart from the tomb Innocent commissioned for himself and the one he encouraged for Arcadian Academy patron Queen Christina of Sweden, both in St. Peter's, and the sumptuous altar dedicated to St. Ignatius in the Church of the Gesù, all done by Carlo Fontana, most constructions were of a practical nature. He had Francesco Fontana and Matteo de' Rossi complete new customs buildings. He had a new granary built near Borgo Santo Spirito and a newly widened street, later dubbed Via delle Tre Pile after his coat of arms, to direct traffic away from the Campidoglio. He had an aqueduct conducted to Civitavecchia. Most ambitious of all, he had Carlo Fontana complete the Montecitorio Palace begun and quickly abandoned forty years previously by Gian Lorenzo Bernini, organizing the square in front of it with a fountain. He envisioned the new building, called the Curia Innocenziana, as a single centralized location for the legal tribunals, giving topographical reality to the de facto centralization of the papal bureaucracy in much the some way as Giorgio Vasari's Uffizi Palace, completed more than a hundred years before in Florence.

Alarming increases in the poverty rate in Rome demanded incisive solutions for which the diversion of considerable resources for direct handouts did not seem sufficient. Since the plague of 1656 the population had continued to rise, and of the 10,000 new inhabitants recorded among the 131,000 total reported in 1693 with respect to ten years previously, many had come in from the countryside looking for better prospects than those offered by sharecropping or day labor. The vast majority of these new entrants did not succeed in finding suitable situations in the city, and a good proportion of them ended up in jail. Indeed, in the last decades of the century some 72 percent of the prison population came from outside Rome, including 63 percent from the Papal States. Following the contemporary trend that viewed poverty as mainly a problem of public order, Innocent embarked on one of the most ambitious programs in Italy for the enclosure of mendicants and vagabonds. Those unable to work he had rounded up in the Lateran Palace, which could hold as many as five thousand. The rest he had placed in the Hospice of S. Michele a Ripa, expanded to ten times its previous capacity by Carlo Fontana, including a textile factory on the premises for vocational training. Placing the new hospice along with other existing institutions under a new commission of cardinals, he made it the nucleus for the vast complex of assistential and correctional facilities completed under Clement XI.

Rather than cultural or artistic leadership, what Innocent desired above all was to reinforce the church's spiritual leadership. Again, according to the Venetian ambassador, the pope's qualities were ideal: "He has integrity, a good conscience, is entirely disinterested, separated from his relatives, and full of infinite charity toward the poor" (*Relazioni degli stati europei*, 437). True, some of his initiatives in this direction may well have been more specifically directed at improving public relations—for instance, the long audiences granted to the poor and needy every week, and the resuscitated viaticum to the houses of the sick and the dying, appropriately celebrated in a propaganda pamphlet by Giuseppe Solimeno. Other initiatives struck merely at superficial aspects of Catholic life in order to increase control over behavior. The prohibition of theater in Rome (1697), which, like similar prohibitions in England a half-century earlier, occurred when theater was achieving unprecedented popularity as a form of cultural expression, aimed to eliminate a venue in which criticism of the regime often masqueraded as innocent comedy.

Insistence upon appropriate dress of clerics was meant to improve the church's image and increase respect for ecclesiastical institutions. However, the insistence upon observance of proper clerical dress was also part of a much wider-ranging initiative aimed at enforcing ecclesiastical discipline, following up the famous report by Mariano Sozzini that had first moved Innocent XI into action. Also during Innocent XI's reign Giuseppe Crispino, later bishop of Amelia, authored an important treatise on episcopal visitations in harmony with the efforts of a whole group of contemporary reforming bishops, from Gregorio Barbarigo in Padua to Innico Caracciolo in Naples. The situation confronted by these efforts was that of a lower clergy out of control of local bishops, often in the thrall of local ruling elites, and increasingly unable to provide for the needs of an increasingly demanding flock. Thus in 1696 Innocent XII set up the so-called Congregation on Ecclesiastical Discipline aimed at rigorously enforcing rules regarding celibacy and at providing assurances of clerical education, proper ordination, and, to prevent the temptation of venality, adequate incomes.

Defending the position of the papacy as the protector of doctrinal purity called for political acumen as well as spiritual qualities. The upper clergy in France and Holland subscribed increasingly to the austere theses of Jansenism, regarded by many in the curia as being of questionable orthodoxy. In France these tendencies were stoutly defended in the name of Gallicanism, that is the right of the Crown and clergy to local jurisdiction. Innocent XII reopened the question for the first time since the so-called Clementine Peace of 1669, forcing Louis XIV into backing down on the validity of a 1682 assembly of pro-Gallican clergy. The issue was far from concluded at the death of the pope.

On doctrinal issues Innocent followed a line, also supported by his palace preacher, Jesuit luminary Paolo Segneri, aimed at providing missionaries with the greatest freedom to maneuver. Probabilism, for instance, was a moral doctrine that, simply put, justified any actions that in all probability, according to whatever information the actor possessed at the moment, could be viewed as sinless. In the missionary field Segneri and others found this doctrine highly useful as a working basis for providing the tender consciences of the faithful with the assurances necessary for bringing them back to frequent partaking of the sacraments. Innocent thus tolerated it in spite of the opposition of Jesuit general Tirso Gonzales as well as of influential prelate Jacques-Benigne Bossuet, whose position harmonized with the tendencies toward greater moral rigor among the French upper clergy.

Quietism, on the other hand, which had become among the most effective gathering points for the faithful in recent times, seemed to make missionary work more difficult. As the contemplative methods of the mystics gradually spread out from the confines of the cloisters, popular enthusiasm had welcomed the appearance of a new source of spiritual justification. In some of their extreme forms these methods called for the achievement of "quiet"—the opening of the soul to God described by St. John of the Cross—through a total abandonment of the person's will to God's. Occasionally they placed so much stress on the justification attainable in this fashion that they left no room for sacraments or clergy. In spite of support for Quietism by influential prelates like Cardinal Pier Matteo Petrucci, sixty-eight propositions from the works of the leader of the movement, Rome-based Spanish cleric Miguel de Molinos, had been condemned in 1687. When François de Salignac de La Mothe-Fénelon openly expressed his support for the celebrated French Quietist mystic and prophetess Jeanne Marie Bouvier de La Motte-Guyon, Innocent XII agreed with Bossuet, Louis XIV, and Segneri in sending down another condemnation.

As peacemaker of Christendom, Innocent fared far less well than in other aspects of his role. Called upon abruptly and urgently toward the end of his papacy, he fell for the current fashion of viewing Louis XIV as the key to European unity. As arbiter of the Peace of Rijswick that closed the War of the League of Augsburg in 1697, he approved of articles, later condemned by, among others, German philosopher Gottfried Wilhelm Leibniz, preventing religious changes in newly acquired or ceded territories. Pastor has suggested that he thus unwittingly played into the desire of Louis XIV to foment discontent in Protestant states where proselytizing zeal was ablaze, thereby seeking to enkindle another religious civil war in which France might be able to win further territory. Later he put up no opposition when the Spanish council of state, in order to gain French support against further divisions of the Spanish empire, decided to offer the succession of Charles II, the last Spanish Habsburg, to the lateral branch represented by Philip of Bourbon, nephew of Louis XIV, perfectly preparing the scenario of the War of the Spanish Succession that rocked Italy and Europe from 1700, the year of Innocent XII's death.

SELECTED BIBLIOGRAPHY

Balzani, Alberto. *L'ospizio apostolico dei poveri invalidi detto "Il S. Michele" dal 1693 al 1718*. Rome: Istituto di studi romani, 1969.

Campello, Gian Battista. "Diario." *Studi e documenti di storia e diritto*. 8 (1887):

167–98; 9 (1888): 57–90; 10 (1889): 185–206, 449–64; 11 (1890): 379–91; 14 (1893): 79–89.

Carvale, Mario, and Alberto Caracciolo. *Lo Stato pontificio da Martino V a Pio IX*. Turin: Unione Tipografico–Editrice Torinese, 1978.

Chiaberge, Giuseppe Ignazio. *Orationes P. Josephi Ignatii Chiaberge, Societatis Jesu: Et carmen genethliacum ejusdem auctoris*. Taurini: Typographia Joannis Francisci Mairesse, 1724.

Chiarotti, Laura. "Populazione del carcere nuovo nella seconda metà del XVII secolo." *Archivio della società romana di storia patria* 115 (1992): 147–80.

Donati, Claudio. "La chiesa di Roma tra antico regime e riforme settecentesche." In *Storia d' Italia: Annali IX: La Chiesa e il potere politico dal Medioevo all'età contemporanea*. Ed. Giorgio Chittolini and Giovanni Miccoli. Turin: Einaudi, 1986, 721–68.

Fatica, Michele. "La reclusione dei poveri a Roma durante il pontificato di Innocenzo XII (1691–1700)." *Ricerche per la storia religiosa di Roma* 3 (1979): 133–80.

Galasso, Giuseppe. *Napoli spagnola dopo Masaniello*. Florence: Sansoni, 1982.

Pastor, Ludwig Freiherr von. *The History of the Popes from the Close of the Middle Ages*. Vol. 32. Trans. Dom Ernest Graf. St. Louis: Herder, 1957.

Pellegrino, Bruno, ed. *Riforme, religione, e politica durante il pontificato di Innocenzo XII, 1691–1700: Atti del convegno di studio*. Galatina: Congedo, 1994.

Petrocchi, Massimo. *Il Quietismo italiano del Seicento*. Rome: Edizioni di Storia e Letteratura, 1948.

Prodi, Paolo. *The Papal Prince: One Body and Two Souls: The Papal Monarchy in Early Modern Europe*. Trans. Susan Haskins. New York: Cambridge University Press, 1987.

Relazioni degli stati europei lette al Senato dagli ambasciatori veneti nel secolo decimosettimo, ser. 3, *Relazioni di Roma*, vol. 2. Ed. Nicolò Barozzi and Guglielmo Berchet. Venice: Naratovich, 1878.

Turrini, Miriam. "La riforma del clero secolare durante il pontificato di Innocenzo XII." *Cristianesimo nella storia* 13 (1992): 329–61.

BENEDICT XIV (1740–58): "THIRD-PARTY" POPE

John B. Guarino

Born of a Bolognese noble but not "illustrious" family on 31 March 1675, Prospero Lambertini was educated in Rome at the Clementina College and at La Sapienza as a canon lawyer. He pursued a traditional curial career helped along by a fellow Bolognese, Alessandro Caprara, an auditor of the Rota, and by the attention given to his intellectual abilities by Popes Innocent XII and Clement XI. Thus, after graduation in 1694, he rose from assistant (advocate) at the Rota to consistorial advocate (1701). With this experience he became "devil's advocate" (*promotor fidei*) at the Congregation of Rites (1708). There he acquired the knowledge that would serve as the basis for his book *On the Beatification and Canonization of the Servants of God* (1734–38). He soon was loaded with other curial offices, notably secretary of the Congregation of the Council (1718). Nevertheless, he found time for an active social and intellectual life and made long-term friendships with Abbot Jean Bouget and Pierre Guerin de Tencin as well as many acquaintances, like the Maurist Bernard de Montfaucon, who were in contact with leading French and Italian intellectual circles. Interestingly enough, Lambertini delayed his ordination to the priesthood until 1724, when he was nearly fifty years old. Now a career in the hierarchy was open to him.

Pope Benedict XIII valued Lambertini's advice on political and ecclesiastical matters and made him a cardinal *in pectore* (in secret) (1726) and then bishop of Ancona (1727). His elevation to the cardinalate was made public in 1728. Pope Clement XII sent him home to Bologna as archbishop in 1731. In both cities Lambertini conducted himself as a pastor in the

Tridentine spirit, combining features of Carlo Borromeo's and Gabriele Paleotti's approaches. He carried out visitations in parishes and convents, encouraged preaching, and fostered both clerical and secular education. These experiences provided the basis for his other famous book, *The Diocesan Synod* (1748). However, there is no evidence that he actually held diocesan synods at Ancona or Bologna.

At the death of Clement XII, in the longest conclave since the Middle Ages, Lambertini was elected pope on 17 August 1740. He chose the name Benedict XIV in honor of Benedict XIII, who had made him a cardinal. The conclave had been prolonged by the factional struggles of the cardinal nephews: the "old" cardinals created by Clement XI and led by Annibale Albani and the "new" cardinals created by Clement XII and led by Neri Corsini. The former were supported by the Spanish and Neapolitan crowns, and the latter were supported by the French and Austrian crowns. Lambertini emerged as a compromise candidate representing cardinals created during the "middle" pontificate of Benedict XIII. Indeed, this was to be symbolic of the moderation that characterized Benedict XIV throughout his pontificate. His election marked the end of the era of "illustrious" families on the papal throne. To the extent that his predecessors had come to concentrate on the means (ostentation and jurisdiction) rather than the ends (spiritual regeneration) of reform, Benedict's pontificate also signified in some measure a break with the era of the Counter-Reformation. Benedict may be considered an "enlightened Catholic" pontiff in that he was aware of and conciliatory toward the tendencies of his century. He has been called a "third-party" member in the sense of being a reformer who was neither Molinist nor Jansenist.

Both contemporaries and later historians point out that Benedict, unlike his predecessor (Clement XII) and his successor (Clement XIII), was not a nepotist. Neither was he complacent about the traditional limitations on his appointments. Thus he indicated to Tencin, by now a cardinal, his serious personnel problems. Men inherited from Clement XII had to be retained or, worse, promoted to the cardinalate given the traditional career paths of the curia. It was apparently to some of these incumbents that Benedict was alluding when he wrote to Tencin in 1743 that several prelates in the Roman curia followed lifestyles unbecoming to ecclesiastics. Furthermore, he regretted that because of the length of their services and the offices they held, he had to give some of them cardinal's hats. However, he would provide them low incomes to discourage this sort of living. Once he promoted such persons and got them out of the way, Benedict was free to place in these offices men with whom he was satisfied. For example, he made Vincenzo Malvezzi master of the Camera Apostolica and later cardinal (1753) and praised him for excellent morals.

It had become established that for the major Catholic countries, the so-called great crowns, the promotion to the cardinalate of the nuncios to their respective courts, was a matter of prestige when these nuncios were concluding their terms of service at the respective nunciatures. Customarily, these former nuncio cardinals were then made cardinal-legates. In 1743 Benedict complained to Tencin that most of the nuncios "actually in place" in the major Catholic countries (appointed by Clement XII) were not worthy of becoming cardinals or legates. Only reluctantly did he make these promotions in response to foreign pressure. Writing to Tencin about this, Benedict sarcastically remarked that the "great crowns" were always calling upon the popes to appoint only worthy men as cardinals, but when

it was a matter of the nuncios to their courts, the "great crowns" always cried for "honor" and "equal treatment." Marcello Crescenzi, nuncio in Paris, was to be made cardinal-legate at Ferrara (1743); Benedict regarded him as a mediocre spendthrift and was not impressed with either his intellect or with his commitment as a spiritual leader. Indeed, Benedict refused Crescenzi's request (1743–46) to be both legate and archbishop of Ferrara for the sake of the double income that the two jobs would provide. Benedict's reasons were his low opinion of Crescenzi's capacity and the reluctance of the people of the area to see civil and religious powers united in one individual. This was a problem of which he was well aware, given the temporal and spiritual aspects of his own position as "pope-king" in the Papal States.

Painting of Pope Benedict XIV by G.M. Crespi. (The Art Archive)

Benedict XIV encountered even greater traditional limitations on his choices of the so-called crown cardinals. The pope could at least choose who would be his nuncios to the "great crowns" (once those chosen by his predecessor had left the scene), but the tradition had become established that the rulers of nearly all the Catholic countries nominated persons to be cardinals representing the interests of their nations in the sacred college. Also, the "great crowns" demanded parity among themselves at every promotion of cardinals. Benedict XIV disliked this system, especially the nomination by a ruler of a person who was not of the ruler's own country. Benedict had little use for a crown cardinal of 1747, namely, Giovanni Francesco Albani, the nominee of Saxony-Poland. Benedict apparently felt that he was too young to be a cardinal: Albani was twenty-seven when he received the cardinal's hat. Benedict, with obvious enjoyment, repeated to Tencin the Roman "pasquinade" that labeled Albani as "Albanischi" in mockery of his nomination by Saxony-Poland, a nomination that Benedict attributed to the efforts of his uncles, Cardinals Annibale and Alessandro Albani, for whom Benedict had little regard.

Clearly, Benedict XIV realized that these influences and conditions hindered his attempts to achieve reform in the papal administration; often he was unable to appoint people of his own stamp. Perhaps Benedict failed to bring the college of cardinals up to its full complement of members because he was faced with all these limiting factors. They contributed to making the image of the sacred college one that was not his own even though his pontificate was longer than that of any other pope in the period from 1721 to 1774. Among the standards that Benedict applied in evaluating potential candidates for the cardinalate and other offices were experience, loyalty to the Holy See, impartiality, moderation, diligence, good morals, thrift, and in some cases learning and "sound," "reasonable" theology and philosophy. These characteristics, which contemporaries saw in Benedict himself, are revealed in his reforms of the curia and the Papal States.

Benedict XIV had the will to reform the papal government. As the pope lamented to Tencin, he inherited the Papal States from Clement XII in a state of decay and deficit. The economy was characterized by diverse local customs, privileges, and immunities in various provinces and cities, underdeveloped and poorly regulated industry and commerce, a weak middle class and underemployed populace, and periodic shortages of sound money and food. To alleviate the deficit left to him by his predecessor, Benedict undertook a policy of austerity and financial reform. He cut the military, reduced stipends, and did not renew loans (*monti vacabili*). He began an accounting of income and expenditures for the Papal States; he required both the Datary and the communes to adhere to this procedure. However, his tax policy was contradictory, inconsistent, and incomplete. As contemporaries pointed out, the papal administration did not raise sufficient revenues because the tax system was in need of thorough overhaul. Furthermore, although he replenished the treasure of Sixtus V in the Castel Sant'Angelo, he failed to invest the money.

With the assistance of Secretary of State Cardinal Silvio Valenti-Gonzaga and papal auditor Cardinal Clement Argenvilliers as well as the enlightened banker and investor Marchese Girolamo Belloni, Benedict undertook a commercial policy that sought to develop industry and trade in the Papal States, especially after 1748 (Peace of Aachen ending the War of the Austrian Succession). Belloni, the author of several works on commercial liberalization dedicated to Benedict XIV, was also administrator general of the customs. Benedict formally declared the "free circulation" of grain and all other foods and movable goods internally throughout the northern and central provinces of the Papal States. This meant that such goods could be moved from city to city, province to province, and legation to legation. The bull of 1748 excluded Rome and the provinces around it from these provisions. This and later decrees ended many monopolies of the sale and purchase of certain goods (rags, tobacco, and so on) but did not end the internal duties and tolls or the external tariffs that hindered the free trade of goods within the Papal States and with foreign countries.

In 1753–54 the pope entrusted the Congregation of Buongoverno with the task of developing and implementing a general plan for the elimination of all internal and external duties, tariffs, and tolls. Buongoverno was also to inquire into the methods of improving agriculture and artisan industry, to solicit information from the citizenry, and to compile data on the existing structures. Conflicting interests and time-consuming inquiries and petitions contributed to the contradictory and sporadic tax and tariff policies of Benedict XIV. The pope was unable to develop and implement his overall plan for the abolition of all tolls and all barriers to the free circulation of goods throughout all of the Papal States. Nevertheless, Benedict did establish the free movement of goods in the northern and central legations and provinces, which were the richest sections of the Papal States; this was the first step in liberalization of trade.

In addition, Benedict sought to improve the papal ports at Anzio and Ancona; he confirmed Civitavecchia in its privileges as a free port. These projects were designed to encourage exports from the Papal States, an objective in Belloni's plan. Somewhat successful in these efforts, Benedict was less successful in his efforts to repair the roads and to encourage the spirit of industry in the idle youth of his capital and states. Unfortunately, as Benedict wrote to Tencin, the War of the Austrian Succession (1740–48), which saw troops of Spain, Naples, and Austria on the soil of the neutral Papal States, hindered his reforms, increased the deficit that he had tried to end, and brought hardships and shortages to the people themselves. Despite this "martyrdom" of the Papal States, as Benedict called it, he strove to maintain neutrality during the war by acknowledging Maria Theresa's right to inherit her father's domains while recognizing Charles VII's election as emperor. After Charles's death the pope recognized the election of Maria Theresa's husband Francis as emperor (1745). To the extent that Benedict could, he insisted on the historic prerogatives of the papacy in international affairs, notably at the Peace of Aachen, where he secured that Spain should not seek investiture for Parma and Piacenza from the emperor since these duchies were under papal suzerainty.

Benedict was anxious to avoid an open break with the sovereigns. Therefore, he was willing to accommodate to a significant degree the regalist and jurisdictionalist tendencies of the crowns. He developed a conciliatory concordatial policy with Naples (1741), Sardinia-Piedmont (1742), and Spain (1753) with the help of Cardinal Valenti-Gonzaga, Datary Cardinal Pompeo Aldrovandi, and his successor at the Datary (1743), Cardinal Gian Giacomo Millo. These agreements made substantial concessions to the crowns in the areas of royal patronage and jurisdiction over church personnel and property as well as the royal *placet* or *exequatur* (acceptance of papal documents). Thus in Spain, for example, almost all benefices were no longer to be filled through the Datary but rather were left to royal nomination or presentation. This enabled Benedict to eliminate much lobbying and trafficking at the Datary in regard to such benefices and other ecclesiastical properties or goods, especially advance payment and security for benefices. In order to bring an end to protracted negotiations, Benedict resorted to personal diplomacy and key confidants while circumventing the royal ambassadors and papal nuncios. This flexible policy aroused curial displeasure, as did the reduction of curial revenues that these concordats entailed. Nevertheless, Benedict was adamant in renewing previous pontiffs' condemnation of the enslavement of the Indians in the colonies (1741), albeit with little success.

A similar inclination to moderation is apparent in Benedict's handling of the controversy in France between Jansenists and Zelanti over the refusal of the sacraments to those who "appealed" against Clement XI's bull *Unigenitus* (1713), which condemned Jansenism. After unsuccessfully attempting to silence both sides because of agitation in the Parlement of Paris (1752–54) and after a split vote in the assembly of the clergy (1755), King Louis XV sought Benedict's judgment through Stainville (Choiseul), the French ambassador in Rome. The pope had recourse to six cardinal consultors, including Valenti-Gonzaga and the Jansenist sympathizer Domenico Passionei. Among the consultors, Benedict particularly relied on Antonio Andrea Galli and Fortunato Tamburini. When Benedict had appointed them cardinals, he had referred to them as "sound" and "reasonable" theologians. In effect, for Benedict, the controversial points of the doctrines of grace and free will were perhaps insoluble; at any rate, they were dangerously divisive, so the "reasonable" course of action was not to press the issue.

Benedict believed that all three schools (Augustinian, Thomist, and Molinist) should be tolerated and that freedom of discussion on the matter should be allowed by the bishops and the inquisitors. Let the French speak French and the Italians speak Italian, he said to Tencin. He admitted that he had his own favorites as a "private doctor"; apparently St. Thomas, whom he declared "free of error" (1752), and Pope St. Leo I, whom he made doctor of the church (1754), were prominent among them. Therefore, it is not surprising that his encyclical *Ex omnibus* (1756) did not characterize *Unigenitus* as a "rule of faith" and authorized refusal of the sacraments only to those who publicly and notoriously rejected the bull. This moderation did not bring peace to the church in France, where the king tried to impose the settlement in his declaration and *lit de justice*.

Meanwhile, in Italy Benedict condemned a Jesuit attack on the encyclical and commissioned Constantino Ruggieri to write a defense of *Ex omnibus*.

Benedict was not hostile to the Society of Jesus itself, but he expressed his resentment to Tencin about the society's tendency to rally in support of insubordinate members, for example, those who resisted the papal condemnation of ancestor veneration in the Chinese Rites controversy (1742). In moral matters Benedict inclined toward the "third-party" position of probabiliorism, which holds that one is to follow the opinion that is most probable; he opposed probabilism, which holds that one is permitted to follow any opinion that is simply probable and which was associated with the Jesuits. However, when in his last year he commissioned Cardinal Francisco de Saldanha da Cama to investigate alleged Jesuit irregularities in the Portuguese dominions, he insisted that the inquiry proceed with due deliberation (1758). Moderation and liberalization characterized Benedict's encyclical *Vix pervenit* (1745) on usury. If the sum loaned would have paid off a legitimate debt or could have been used profitably elsewhere in a productive enterprise, he allowed the creditor to assess interest. Indeed, Benedict called for Scipione Maffei and Daniele Concina to lower the volume of their debate on the issue.

Benedict's desire for simplification was shown in his reluctance to authorize devotion to the Sacred Heart and in his reduction of feast days, as Lodovico Antonio Muratori advocated. Benedict corresponded with and protected Muratori as well as a variety of other enlightened, "third-party," Jansenist and philo-Jansenist writers. He modified ecclesiastical discipline by guaranteeing to Catholic authors the right to defend themselves before the Congregation of the Index prior to the condemnation of their books. Benedict warned that if charges of heresy are exchanged, always listen to both the accuser and the accused since they may change places. He believed in personal leniency toward individual intellectuals like Voltaire, for perhaps then they would not be so alienated from the church. Nevertheless, he clearly realized that enlightened ideas were a great danger to the church and that the struggle against them was "more important" than the endless controversies over grace, predestination, and free will that obsessed the Jansenists and their opponents. Hence Benedict condemned Freemasonry (1751) and placed works by Montesquieu and Voltaire on the Index (1751 and 1752).

With a mixture of Tridentine spirit and enlightened Catholicism, Benedict sought the improvement of clerical education and scientific studies both as cardinal and as pope. In Bologna he encouraged the Istituto delle Scienze, providing laboratory equipment and setting up an anatomical museum. He established the Academia Benedettina in Bologna to foster presentation of research on the sciences by eminent scholars, including the famous scientist Laura Bassi. Indeed, Benedict encouraged her and the mathematician Maria Gaetana Agnesi in their study, teaching, and publication. At the University of Bologna, in which Benedict had a long-standing interest, he established a school of surgery and promoted dissection as a basis for practical anatomical and medical study. Finally, Benedict left his own magnificent library to the Istituto (1754–56).

In Rome Benedict undertook organizational reforms at La Sapienza with the cooperation of Cardinals Valenti-Gonzaga and Argenvilliers. He created chairs of mathematics, chemistry, and physics. Benedict reduced support for law to make way for science, but science enrollment did not go up and law enrollment stayed high since a law degree paved the way for a curial career. Benedict founded four scholarly academies that were devoted to church councils, church history, liturgy, and ancient history. These he developed along Maurist lines of scientific history that he had long admired. On the advice of the Jesuit astronomer Ruggero Boscovitch, he ended the general ban on Copernican works (1757–58).

Among the pope's confidants was the Jansenist Giovanni Gaetano Bottari, who was secret chaplain to the pope and who participated in Benedict's evening discussion groups along with the pope's longtime friend Bouget, now his domestic prelate. The pope nominated Bottari as an academic in several of the newly created academies of history as well as an advisor to the Congregations of the Index and the Holy Office. Through his own circle, the Archetto at the Palazzo Corsini, Bottari was the connection among the anti-Jesuit, "enlightened Catholic," and Jansenist intellectual currents flourishing in Rome in the open atmosphere fostered by Benedict XIV, the "philosopher king," as Renée Haynes calls him. Benedict extended the Capitoline and Vatican museums and contributed to the promotion of art by his Academy of Nude Painting (1754). He renovated the basilicas of Santa Maria Maggiore and Santa Croce, among other churches, but he seemed to be more concerned that in general churches be clean rather than elaborate, that services be appropriate (no operatic music), and that the clothing of the clergy not be extravagant.

An early riser, Benedict worked long hours, wrote much, and, when he could, walked all over Rome talking to whomever he met. Possessed of a sometimes-vulgar wit and good humor, he repented profusely when he had occasional bursts of temper. A devoted friend, he did much of the work for his terminally ill secretary of state Valenti-Gonzaga. After the latter's death in 1756, Benedict placed another moderate, Cardinal Alberico Archinto, in the job. Benedict's longtime correspondent Cardinal Tencin died in March 1758, and he himself succumbed to gout and pneumonia on 3 May 1758 at the age of eighty-three after a pontificate of almost eighteen years. Benedict XIV was regarded highly by "enlightened Catholics" (Muratori), respected by Protestants (Horace Walpole), and honored by philosophes (Voltaire). The organic themes of moderation, simplification, and liberalization embodied in his policies, however limited and incomplete, all seem to reflect the "enlightened Catholic," Muratorian, and "third-party" spirit present within the eighteenth-century church. That spirit was respectful of the historical past but open to change and new ideas. As Benedict indicated to the secretary of cipher Antonio Rota, something is better than nothing.

SELECTED BIBLIOGRAPHY

Allen, David F. "Upholding Tradition: Benedict XIV and the Hospitaller Order of St. John of Jerusalem at Malta, 1740–1758." *Catholic Historical Review* 80 (1994): 18–35.

Andrieux, Maurice. *Daily Life in Papal Rome in the Eighteenth Century.* Trans. Mary Fitton. London: George Allen & Unwin, 1968.

Appolis, Emile. *Le "tiers parti" catholique au XVIII siècle.* Paris: Editions A. et J. Picard & Co., 1960.

Benedict XIV. *Opera omnia Benedicti XIV Pont. Max. in tomos XVII distributa.* Prati: Aldina, 1836–1847.

Bertone, Tarcisio. *Il governo della chiesa nel pensiero di Benedetto XIV, 1740–1758.* Rome: Libreria Ateneo Salesiano, 1977.

Boutry, Maurice. *Choiseul à Rome, 1754–1757, Lettres et Mémoires inédites.* Paris: Calmann Lévy, 1895.

Bullarium Sanctissimi domini nostri Benedicti Papae XIV. 4 vols. Rome: Hieronymus Mainardi, 1760–62; Venice: Typografia J. Gatti, 1778.

Caraccioli, Louis-Antoine. *La Vie du Pape Benoît XIV Prospero Lambertini.* Paris: Hôtel Serpente, 1783.

Caravale, Mario, and Alberto Caracciolo. *Lo stato pontificio da Martino V a Pio IX.* Turin: Unione Tipografico–Editrice Torinese, 1978.

Carlen, Claudia, ed. *The Papal Encyclicals, 1740–1878.* Vol. 1. Ann Arbor, Mich.: Pierian Press, 1990.

Cecchelli, Marco, ed. *Benedetto XIV (Prospero Lambertini).* 2 vols. Cento: Centro Studi "Girolamo Baruffaldi," 1981–82.

Cinque, Giovanni Paolo de, and Raphaele Fabrinio. *Vitae et res gestae summorum pontificium.* Rome: Typografia Cracas, 1787.

Codignola, Ernesto. *Illuministi, giansenisti, e giacobini nell'Italia del settecento.* Florence: La Nuova Italia Editrice, 1947.

Dal Pane, Luigi. *Lo stato pontificio e il movimento riformatore del settecento.* Milan: Dott. A. Giuffrè Editore, 1959.

Dammig, Enrico. *Il movimento giansenista a Roma nella seconda metà del sécolo XVIII.* Vatican City: Biblioteca Apostolica Vaticana, 1945.

Gelmi, Josef. *La segreteria di stato sotto Benedetto XIV (1740–1758).* Trent: Pontificia Università Gregoriana, 1975.

Giuntella, Vittorio E. *Roma nel settecento.* Bologna: L. Cappelli Editore, 1971.

Gross, Hanns. *Rome in the Age of Enlightenment.* Cambridge: Cambridge University Press, 1990.

Haynes, Renée. *Philosopher King: The Humanist Pope Benedict XIV.* London: Weidenfeld & Nicolson, 1970.

Heeckeren, Emile de. *Correspondance de Benoît XIV.* 2 vols. Paris: Plon-Nourrit et Cie., 1912.

Jemolo, Arturo. *Il giansenismo in Italia prima della rivoluzione*. Bari: Laterza, 1928.

Morelli, Emilia, ed. *Le Lettere di Benedetto XIV al Cardinale de Tencin*. 3 Vols. Rome: Edizioni di Storia e Letteratura, 1955, 1965, 1984.

———. *Tre Profili: Benedetto XIV, Pasquale Stanislao Mancini, Pietro Roselli*. Rome: Edizioni dell'Ateneo, 1955.

Nau, Paul. "A l'origine des encycliques modernes: Un épisode de la lutte des évêques et des Parlements, 1755–1756." *Revue historique de droit français et étranger* 34 (1956): 225–67.

Pastor, Ludwig Freiherr von. *The History of the Popes from the Close of the Middle Ages*. Vols. 35 and 36. Trans. E.F. Peeler. St. Louis: Herder, 1950.

Raybaud, L.-P. *Papauté et pouvoir temporel sous les pontificats de Clément XII et Benoît XIV, 1730–1758*. Paris: Librairie Philosophique J. Vrin, 1963.

Rosa, Mario. *Riformatori e ribelli nel 700 religioso italiano*. Bari: Dedalo Libri, 1969.

Venturi, Franco. *Settecento riformatore*. Vol. 1, *Da Muratori a Beccaria*. Turin: Giulio Einaudi, 1969.

CLEMENT XIII
(1758–69)

HANNS GROSS

The pontificate of the Rezzonico pope Clement XIII marks the abandonment of any reform attempt within the framework of the Catholic enlightenment both within the Papal States and the Catholic church as a whole.
It is true that his predecessor Benedict XIV had already begun to reverse
the process during the last third of his reign, once he realized the threat
it could pose to papal power, yet the clear repudiation only became apparent during the early years of Clement XIII's papacy. In some respects
he can be seen as the last of the Tridentine popes born out of season.

Carlo Rezzonico was born in Venice on 7 March 1693, the son of Giambattista Rezzonico and Vittoria Barbarigo. The family originated in Como.
The paternal branch moved to Venice in 1640, where it acquired wealth
through commerce, to the extent that it was admitted into the Libro d'oro
of the Venetian nobility at the cost of the considerable sum of 100,000
ducats. At the age of ten Carlo was sent to study at the Jesuit Collegio di
San Francesco Saverio in Bologna. He stayed there for eight years. On
returning to his native Venice, he studied dogmatic theology and canon
law at the University of Padua for two years, graduating with a doctorate
in utroque iure on 30 September 1713. In the same year he refused the
offer of a canonry at Padua from Bishop Giorgio Cornelio and moved
instead to Rome to pursue a curial career. There he entered the so-called
ecclesiastical academy (Accademia ecclesiastica), the prerequisite gateway
to high office in the church, reserved to scions of noble families.

On 28 May 1716 Rezzonico entered curial service as referendary to the
Signatura or apostolic protonotary. After being ordained priest the same

year, he was appointed by Pope Clement XI governor of Rieti. In 1721 he was moved to Fano in the same capacity, a post he held until Pope Innocent XIII recalled him to Rome in 1723 to become a *ponente* (presiding judge) in the sacred consulta. Five years later, on the death of Federico Cornelio, he began a stint as auditor at the Rota on behalf of his native Venice. At the behest of the Republic, Pope Clement XII admitted him to the sacred college of cardinals on 20 December 1737. As cardinal, he was a member of various congregations but was never a figure of prime importance in the curia. Six years later, on 11 March 1743, when Rezzonico was fifty, Benedict XIV appointed him to the see of Padua.

Padua was an important and very extensive diocese, with a distinguished university and many monasteries and religious institutions. It lay close to the heart of Cardinal Rezzonico as bishop to raise the intellectual and spiritual level of his diocesan clergy. Among his role models he claimed Carlo Borromeo, the paragon of Catholic reform bishops. In his first pastoral letter he outlined his program. He announced a thorough pastoral visit and declared his intention of preparing a set of ecclesiastical dispositions for his see in line with the Tridentine spirit. He counseled his parish priests to read patristic works and not to practice lax casuistry. On 10 March 1744 Rezzonico started his pastoral visit, which lasted two years. At the close he held a diocesan synod that concerned itself, among other matters, with the rebuilding of the seminary at Padua. Rezzonico devoted a great part of his personal fortune to the project, so much so that Benedict XIV considered Carlo Rezzonico the most worthy prelate in Italy.

Throughout the fifteen years of his episcopacy Rezzonico resided in his diocese, except for the period from the close of 1749 to the summer of 1751, which he spent in Rome negotiating the intricate question of the patriarchate of Aquileia, the cause of a long-drawn-out conflict between Venice and the Holy Roman Empire. The Lambertini pope, Benedict XIV, died on 3 May 1758. The conclave opened twelve days later. After an initially divided assembly, Neri Corsini, the nephew of the late Pope Clement XII, put forward the candidature of Carlo Rezzonico. On 29 June the official representative of the Habsburgs, Cardinal Rodt, archbishop of Constance, threw his weight behind the Venetian, for Rezzonico proved acceptable to Austria because of his role in solving the Aquileia question. Thus in the face of continued French opposition he was elected on 6 July 1758 with thirty-one votes out of forty-four. His coronation took place on 16 July.

Reflecting his pastoral concerns, one of the first acts of Clement XIII was to address the encyclical *A quo die* (14 September 1758) to all the bishops, reminding them of their charges. In it he outlined the characteristics of the ideal pastor: charity, holiness, humility, generosity, good will, a spirit of prayer, concern for souls, prudence and watchfulness in government, the duty of residence, and teaching. He closed with an appeal for apostolic courage, a quality of which he would be in great need, for two topics had already overshadowed the proceedings in the conclave. One was a rejection of the policy of Benedict XIV, which many thought had yielded too much to the jurisdictional claims of the Catholic powers. The other was a preoccupation with recent developments in Portugal concerning the Jesuit question. At the beginning of his reign both Cardinals Giuseppe Spinelli and Alberico Archinto, who was confirmed by him as secretary of state, exerted considerable influence over him. Neither was favorably inclined toward the Society of Jesus. But Cardinal Archinto died suddenly on 30 September. By the middle of October the position was entrusted to Cardinal Luigi Torrigiani, a friend of the Jesuits and opponent of the Jansenists, thus initiating a reversal of policy.

For some years the marquis of Pombal's program of transforming Portugal into an absolute state, which involved, among other projects, the establishment of large privileged commercial companies, had come into direct collision with the economic interests of the great religious orders, especially the Jesuits. The rift with the latter went back to the revolt of the Amerindians of the Reductions in Paraguay during the rectification of the border between Spain and Portugal. In 1757 the Jesuit confessors were removed from the Portuguese court, and on 1 April 1758, about a month before his death, Benedict XIV appointed the Portuguese cardinal Francisco de Saldanha da Cama visitor of the society in order to investigate any alleged abuses. Saldanha, strictly tied to Pombal, exceeded his powers and declared all Portuguese Jesuits guilty of indulging in trade contrary to canon law. A few days later the patriarch of Lisbon, Cardinal Jose Manuel d'Atalaya, suspended all Jesuits from exercising pastoral functions. On 3 September 1758 an attempt was made to murder King Joseph I of Portugal. The Jesuits were accused of complicity in the deed.

Painting of Pope Clement XIII by Raphael Mengs. (Courtesy of the Vatican Library)

On 13 December all seven Jesuit establishments in the country were surrounded by soldiers, who refused to admit anyone. A month later ten Jesuits were arrested and without being examined were tried; three of them were sentenced to death, which was then followed by the confiscation of all Jesuit property. Pombal compelled the Portuguese bishops to issue pastoral letters explaining the government's action. At this point Clement XIII stepped in and in a letter to Joseph I came to the defense of the Jesuits, only to be repulsed in the king's reply. Subsequently 133 Jesuits were compelled to leave the port of Lisbon on 17 September 1759 and landed at the Roman port of Civitavecchia on 24 October. While the transport was still at sea, a royal decree was published on 5 October, backdated to 3 September, that condemned all Jesuits to banishment as rebels and traitors. The episode concluded with a series of royal decrees in 1760 that brought a complete breach with the curia. Despite efforts by Clement XIII in 1763 and 1767, there was to be no peace with Portugal during his lifetime.

Although the first impetus toward the suppression of the Jesuits was given by Portugal, the Jesuit position was not seriously threatened until France took the field in opposition to the society. It set the tone for all Europe, and nowhere perhaps was Ignatius of Loyola's institution more influential. In France the demand for the suppression of the Jesuits was raised by the parlements, the stronghold of Gallican doctrine, in their struggle against the royal power. It was intensified by the disputes between the Jesuits and the Jansenists and was fed by the hostile attacks of the philosophes. The anti-Jesuit attitude of the parlements was first clearly demonstrated on the occasion of Robert-François Damiens's attempted murder of Louis XV on 5 January 1757. Damiens, it was rumored, had been a servant in a Jesuit college. In order to avert worse consequences, the Jesuits responded by agreeing to teach the four Gallican articles of 1682, including the rubric that claimed the complete independence of the secular princes. The conflict was brought to a head by the dubious commercial activities and subsequent bankruptcy in 1761 of the Jesuit Antoine Lavallette on the island of Martinique, where he accumulated a debt of four and a half million livres. Taking advantage of the situation, the Parlement of Paris launched an organized offensive against the Jesuits, which was soon imitated by the provincial parlements. It started with an examination of the constitution of the society to check whether it was compatible with the laws of the state. At the conclusion it issued a series of decrees that condemned such implied Jesuit doctrines as tyrannicide and anti-Gallicanism and prohibited the Jesuits from accepting novices.

Urged by Clement XIII to intervene in the defense of the Society of Jesus, Louis XV attempted mediation by temporarily suspending the execution of the decrees by the parlement and appointing a special commission of his own to examine the society's constitution. He also convoked an assembly of French bishops, who in the majority favored the Jesuit position. What is more, the king gained the support of an important segment of the French Jesuits, who signed two declarations, one condemning tyrannicide and the doctrine of indirect papal power over temporal matters and the other adhering to the four Gallican principles. In Rome, however, this effort at mediation did not meet with approval. Lorenzo Ricci, the Jesuit general, vehemently criticized the action of the French Jesuits, considering it a useless surrender and an act of disobedience. Pope Clement

XIII, who had hitherto made little attempt to intervene in the affairs of the French clergy except to condemn François Phillipe Mesenguy's *Exposition de la doctrine chrétienne*, the widely read pro-Jansenist catechism, and had thereby incurred criticism for failing to support the Jesuits, in January 1762 rejected the proposal of the royal commission to appoint a vicar-general for the French assistancy of the order, which would have separated it from the rest of the society.

Subsequently Louis XV made another effort at mediation, conferring by an edict (March 1762) on the five French provincials the powers normally exercised by the general of the society. The Parlement of Paris refused to register the decree. On 6 August the Parlement of Paris enacted the dissolution of the Society of Jesus within its jurisdiction. Its action was followed by that of several of the provincial parlements. Clement, in a special consistory held on 3 September, declared the resolution null and void. Nonetheless, the fate of the Society of Jesus in France was finally sealed at a plenary session of the chambers of parlement held on 1 December 1764, when a decree was read in which Louis XV declared that in virtue of his supreme authority the order was henceforth to cease its existence in France. In reply Clement XIII issued the bull *Apostolicum pascendi munus* on 7 January 1765, which stated that the Holy See could not allow restrictions to be placed on the execution of its supreme pastoral duty by any human consideration. A month later the Parlement of Paris banned the bull.

France was the leader among the Bourbon powers in the campaign against the Jesuits. In Spain they were never as popular and influential as in France. Still, there was particularly strong opposition to the society among the regular clergy. The Augustinians bore them a grudge for their attack on their greatest scholar, Cardinal Enrico Noris. Great harm was done to the relations between the Spanish government and the Jesuits by the disturbances in Paraguay, in particular the resistance of the Indians to the Treaty of Limits between Spain and Portugal. The man in charge of Spain's foreign policy, Richard Wall, considered the Amerindians' opposition to be an obstacle to his Anglophile policy and, despite their protestations of innocence, was angry with the Jesuits as the supposed authors of the insurrection. Accordingly, the conditions in Paraguay supplied ample material for a flood of abusive writings against the society, in which the Reductions were represented as a state within a state.

Shortly after Clement XIII's election, Ferdinand VI died, and on 6 December 1759 Charles III, the former king of the Two Sicilies, quietly entered Madrid. He was under the influence of his former tutor and later Neapolitan chief minister, Bernardo Tanucci, who, although he was no friend of the Jansenists as a party, shared their dislike of Rome, which he declared a hotbed of atheism, where hypocrisy, the Datary, and the Jesuits held sway. He dismissed Clement XIII as a simpleton. The death of the pro-Jesuit Queen Mother Elizabeth Farnese and the ascendancy of ministers such as the count of Aranda and Pedro Rodríguez de Campomanes gave a renewed impetus to the reform policy. In March 1766 violent risings broke out in Madrid and other cities against high prices and the forced introduction of French fashions. A commission chaired by Aranda and organized by Campomanes, meeting for several months, accused the Jesuits of fomenting the revolt and, even more, of casting doubt upon the legitimacy of Charles III by spreading scurrilous rumors that he was the son of Julio Alberoni in order to replace him with his brother Don Luigi. Charles decided in secret upon the expulsion of the Jesuits. On 27 February 1767 they were banned by royal decree from Spain and its dominions. In the brief *Inter acerbissima* of 16 April Clement XIII besought the king to suspend the provision, but to no avail. After consulting with an extraordinary congregation of cardinals, the pope refused to accede to the Spanish request to admit the expelled Jesuits into the Papal States. Repulsed there, they eventually found a precarious refuge in Corsica.

Naples followed Spain's example. The most active forces of the Italian Catholic reform movement rallied around Tanucci to participate in the battle against Rome, thereby creating a broad consensus so that the struggle against the Jesuits did not appear, as in Portugal and Spain, one provoked by the will of the state. In October 1767 Tanucci, after many urgings, succeeded in persuading Charles III to order his son, who had assumed the Neapolitan throne, to expel the Jesuits. On 24 November they were discharged on papal territory. Clement XIII reacted with a strong note of protest. Although relations between Naples and the papacy became very strained, Tanucci tried to avoid a complete break, promising himself greater political results from a condition of constant tension.

The high point of the struggle with the Bourbon powers was reached in the conflict with Parma. The Holy See claimed this small Italian state as a fief, and as such, it was chosen by Clement XIII as the most convenient state over which to assert papal authority. Still, the influence of the Spanish anti-Jesuit policy made itself felt in this small state. Its chief minister, the French-born Guillaume-Leon du Tillot, an enlightened reformer, published a decree prohibiting mortmain in 1764 after negotiations on the matter with Rome had failed, followed the next year by one subjecting ecclesiastical land to taxation. But it was his claim to exercise the *imprimatur*, or approval, for decrees of the Inquisition on behalf of the Parmesan government and his prohibiting recourse to foreign law courts, especially to Rome, that unleashed a violent reaction from Clement XIII.

On 30 January 1768 Clement issued a brief known as *Monitorio di Parma* with a vehemence never used before, quashing the whole of Tillot's legislation and excommunicating its author and supporters. All Europe was struck with surprise by this move, in which the pope hoped to break the weakest link in the anticurialist front. The immediate response of Parma was the expulsion of the Jesuits on the night between 7 and 8 February

1768. Clement's move was generally regarded as a grave mistake that played into the hands of his enemies. The very legitimacy of the temporal power was being questioned, as in Voltaire's *Les droits des hommes et les usurpations des autres*. Predictably the Bourbons rallied around the duke of Parma. They decided to halt the crisis before it got out of hand by asking Clement XIII, in a concerted act, to revoke the *Monitorio* and threatening that if they received a negative reply, they might proceed with the occupation of Avignon in France and Pontecorvo and Benevento in the Kingdom of Naples. But Clement remained adamant, and so the Bourbon powers proceeded with the threatened occupation.

When further negotiations failed, the three principal Bourbon powers pressed in January 1769 for the dissolution of the Society of Jesus. Maria Theresa had already assured the Bourbons of her neutrality. Clement called a consistory for 3 February to reply to their notes, but, smitten by apoplexy, he died during the night of 2 February 1769. He was buried in St. Peter's, where his nephew, the Roman senator Prince Abondio Rezzonico, had a funeral monument erected for him. In Rome the rumor spread, fed among others by Cardinal Domenico Orsini, the Neapolitan envoy, that Clement XIII had been poisoned by the Jesuits because he had decided to dissolve the society. The rumor was without foundation.

Clement XIII's relationship with Austria was very good, thanks to the support he received at the conclave. In fact, it augured well to rectify the French bias of the papacy that dated back to Clement XI's support for the candidacy of the duke of Anjou during the War of the Spanish Succession. Shortly after his election the pope granted Maria Theresa the title of "Apostolic Majesty." More significantly, he authorized the levying of an extraordinary tax on the clergy to finance the Seven Years' War. However, differences were to emerge without breaking out into open conflict as Maria Theresa appointed to influential posts those whose ecclesiastical policy was aimed at secularizing schools and institutions of higher learning and at diminishing clerical privileges. One of these was Gerhard van Swieten, of Dutch Catholic parentage. He was regarded by Maria Theresa as a model of religion. She failed to see that his Dutch Catholicism was deeply imbued with Jansenism. His goal was to loosen the ties between the university and ecclesiastical circles, particularly the Jesuits. Of more importance still was Count Wenzel Anton von Kaunitz, who assumed the conduct of foreign affairs in 1753 and later presided over the council of state. He was strongly influenced by the writings of Voltaire.

While Austria would remain substantially neutral in the Jesuit question, jurisdictional disputes arose. The first disaffection was provoked by Rome's action when in 1760 it refused to recognize Maria Theresa's right to propose a list of candidates for episcopal appointments in Lombardy. This privilege was, in fact, based on a custom that had never been formalized in a treaty, and because of this Rome considered itself justified in ignoring it. In subsequent years Vienna took important steps to limit mortmain and to reform the commission of censorship, withdrawing it from ecclesiastical control. An ordinance by the council of state on 1 October 1768 made papal excommunications subject to the state's *placet*, in effect abolishing the church's authority to excommunicate. In 1769 the ecclesiastical right of asylum was abolished.

In Germany, apart from some preoccupation with the mooted secularization of the ecclesiastical principalities, the greatest problem for the Holy See was to counter the effects of a book entitled *De statu Ecclesiae*, written by the auxiliary bishop of Trier, Johann Nikolaus von Hontheim, under the pseudonym of Febronius. It resurrected the episcopalist theory and became an important instrument for jurisdictionalist policy. Although the book was put on the Index on 27 February 1764, many German bishops were sympathetic to it. Therefore Clement XIII followed up this step with a letter to all the bishops instructing them to attack the book with vigor. The letter was not received in the manner desired by Rome. Subsequently, as a result of the personal intervention of the nuncio Niccolo Oddi, Archbishop Emmerich Josef von Breidenbach, who was the Elector of Mainz, ordered the book destroyed in May 1764. His action was followed by others. But the elector of Trier, Prince Clement Wenzeslaus of Saxony, protected Hontheim, confirming him in 1768 in his post of vicar-general *in spiritualibus* (of spiritual matters).

Giuseppe Garampi, the distinguished prefect of the Papal Archives, was sent on a diplomatic mission to Germany in 1761. There he was surprised by the interest with which well-written historical works were read on the other side of the Alps and by the way Protestants and some Catholics used history to oppose the papacy. On the other hand, he noted that there was a lack of Catholic literature that met the demands of the times. He therefore proposed the formation in Rome of a republic of scholars from every nation, whose task it should be to refute the modern errors with the instruments of its foes, in an objective, scientific way. This plan was not acted upon.

Within the Papal States Clement XIII faced his greatest challenge during the distressing years of famine in 1763–64 and again in 1765–67. Rome had experienced grain shortages intermittently before, but none could compare to the serious situation that confronted the pope in 1763–64, when a great drought hit all of Italy and especially the central and southern region. It was this calamity that bared the defects of the whole agrarian structure, not only of Rome and the Papal States, but of their neighbors in Naples and Tuscany, and was to test the traditional institution of the *annona*, the authority charged with overseeing the grain supply for Rome and for providing cheap bread.

From all parts of the Papal States, and also from Tuscany and Naples, the hungry rushed into the city. The number of "foreigners" may have grown to as many as 26,000 in spite of the increased surveillance at the city gates. Only with the greatest reluctance did the papal authorities have recourse to the international market when it became clear that the internal process of supply and the mechanism of the *annona* had come to a halt. Continuous flood-producing rain marked the start of the famine of 1765–67, which for the Papal States was worse than that of 1764. By the end of July 1766 the weight of a loaf of bread had been so much reduced and its quality so debased that a group of women shouted protests at the pope. At the close of the summer, however, grain from Apulia and northern Europe arrived to alleviate the situation. But the cost of this disaster was high. At the height of the crisis on 9 April 1764, Clement authorized the withdrawal of half a million scudi from the *erario sanziore*, the "sacred treasure," deposited by Sixtus V at the Castel Sant'Angelo for dire emergencies, but a part of the curia objected, so that only about half the sum, 287,000 gold scudi, was released. To make up the loss, the *erario sanziore* was to be assigned the yield of a tax imposed on real estate and capital. The new tax provoked resistance in a city traditionally spared such everyday irritants. Unfortunately, the government had no alternative but to take out another 1,352,532.79 scudi, without provision for repayment. The treasure at the Castel Sant'Angelo was never to recover thereafter.

From that moment on, Clement XIII and his successors had to have recourse to larger quantities of paper notes or *cedole* to meet the demands of the budget. While these measures met the immediate emergency, they provoked future difficulties. Even more serious was the disarray in which the *annona* found itself. The logic of the system required that it cover its deficits from the profits of the previous financial years. This equilibrium was thrown out of gear in the 1760s. Until the crisis of 1763 the *annona* had been successful in maintaining a surplus of about 400,000 scudi. From then on its balance sheets were in the red by about 700,000 to 800,000 scudi. The fatal stroke was that the great landowners in the Roman Agro, both aristocratic and religious, who until then had renounced much of their profits to support the system, now refused to cooperate with the *annona*. From 1763 only a third (32.7 percent) of the cultivable area was used for grain because the purchase price the *annona* offered was too low. Clement XIII sought to compel the landed proprietors in the Roman Campagna to undertake more intensive cultivation of grain, but the great economic and social power and the large network of clientele that these great families and ecclesiastical institutions commanded made any attempt to expropriate the land of recalcitrants a dubious prospect.

The plan for financial reform of the treasurer-general Giovanni Angelo Braschi, who assumed office in 1766, did not meet with any great success. He proposed to restore the finances of the state not by such simple expedients as reducing expenses and raising new taxes, as had been done hitherto, but by radically restructuring the system, particularly the tariff policy. The first steps toward realization were, in fact, completed by the close of 1768, but the death of Clement soon afterwards put an end to that initiative.

SELECTED BIBLIOGRAPHY

Bellinati, Claudio. *Attività pastorale del Card. Carlo Rezzonico, vescovo di Padova, poi Clemente XIII (1743–1758)*. Padua: Tipografia Antoniana, 1969.

Cajani, Luigi, and Anna Foa. "Clemente XIII." *Dizionario biografico degli italiani* 26 (1982): 328–43.

Cordora, Giulio Cesare. *De suis ac suorum rebus aliisque suorum temporum usque ad occasum Societatis Iesu commentarii. Miscellanea di storia italiana*, seri. 22 (1993): 189–382.

Crétineau-Joly, Jacques. *Histoire religieuse, politique, et littéraire de la Compagnie de Jésus*. Vol. 5, 114–248. Paris: P. Mellier, 1846.

Dörer, F. "Der Schriftenverkehr zwischen dem päpstlichen Staatssekretariat und der apostolischen Nuntiatur Wien in der zweiten Hälfte des 18. Jahrhunderts." *Römische historische Mitteilungen* 4 (1960–61): 63–246.

Giuntella, Vittorio Emanuele. *Roma nel settecento*. Bologna: Licinio Cappelli, 1971.

Gross, Hanns. *Rome in the Age of Enlightenment: The Post-Tridentine Syndrome and the Ancien Regime*. Cambridge: Cambridge University Press, 1990.

Herr, Richard. *The Eighteenth-Century Revolution in Spain*. Princeton: Princeton University Press, 1958.

Holzwarth, F.J. *Die Verschwörung der katholischen Höfe gegen Clemens XIII*. Mainz: F. Kirchheim, 1872.

Lynch, John. *Bourbon Spain, 1700–1808*. Oxford: Basil Blackwell, 1989.

Montor, Alexis François Artaud de. *Histoire des souverains pontifes romains*. Vol. 8, 116–209. Paris: F. Didot, 1847.

Pastor, Ludwig Freiherr von. *The History of the Popes from the Close of the Middle Ages*. Vol. 36 and 37. Trans. E.F. Peeler. St. Louis: Herder, 1950.

Piccialuti, Maura. *La carità come metodo di governo: Instituzioni caritative a Roma dal pontificato di Innocenzo XII a quello di Benedetto XIV*. Turin: G. Giappichelli, 1994.

Picot, Michel Pierre. *Mémoires pour servir à l'histoire ecclésiastique pendant le dix-huitième siècle*. Paris: A. Le Clere, 1806.

Ravignan, Gustave François Xavier de Lacroix de, and Julien Lanier. *Clément XIII et Clément XIV*. Paris: Julien & Lanier, 1854.

Reinhardt, Volker. *Überleben in der frühneuzeitlichen Stadt: Annona und Getreideversorgung in Rom, 1563–1797*. Tübingen: Max Niemeyer, 1991.

Theiner, Augustin. *Histoire du pontificat de Clément XIV*. Paris: Firmin Didot Frères, 1852.

Van Kley, Dale K. *The Damiens Affair and the Unraveling of the Ancient Régime, 1750–1770*. Princeton: Princeton University Press, 1984.

———. *The Jansenists and the Expulsion of the Jesuits from France, 1757–1765*. New Haven: Yale University Press, 1975.

Venturi, Franco. *Settecento riformatore: La chiesa e la repubblica dentro i loro limiti, 1758–1774*. Turin: Giulio Einaudi, 1976.

Woolf, Stuart. *A History of Italy, 1700–1860: The Social Constraints of Political Change*. London: Methuen & Co., 1979.

BIBLIOGRAPHIC NOTE

Basic biographical sources on early modern popes in English, as on most pontiffs prior to the very recent ones, are decidedly limited. For those who want to know more, the very best place to begin is with Ludwig von Pastor's *The History of the Popes from the Close of the Middle Ages* (38 volumes), edited and translated by Frederick Ignatius Antrobus and others, (St. Louis: Herder, 1938–53). Volumes 17 through 37 cover the early modern period. There are dozens of brief overviews of the history of the papacy, and one of the most recent is one of the very best: Eamon Duffy's *Saints and Sinners: A History of the Popes* (New Haven, Conn.: Yale University Press, 1997). Duffy's work is a one-piece narrative that readers will find engaging. Another overview, but one broken up into brief biographical articles, is J.N.D. Kelly's *The Oxford Dictionary of Popes* (Oxford: Oxford University Press, 1986). Other brief biographies of many of the popes in this part can be located in the recent and, for English readers, authoritative *Oxford Encyclopedia of the Reformation*, 4 vols., ed. Hans J. Hillerbrand et al. (Oxford: Oxford University Press, 1996). Some of the best brief biographies can be found in the magisterial *Dizionario biografico degli italiani* (Rome: Istituto dell'enciclopedia italiana, 1958–), a collection that is still decades from completion.

Readers seeking background on the context in which early modern popes lived and worked have at their disposal many scholarly works, especially if they read Italian. Among the better ones are Mario Caravale and Alberto Caracciolo, *Lo stato pontificio da Martino V a Pio X* (Turin: Unione Tipografico-Editrice Torinese, 1978); Giorgio Chittolini and Giovanni Miccoli, eds., *Storia d'Italia, Annali IX: La chiesa e il potere politico dal Medioevo all'età moderna* (Torino: Einaudi, 1986); Paolo Prodi, *The Papal Prince: One Body and Two Souls: The Papal Monarchy in Early Modern Europe*, trans. Susan Haskins (New York: Cambridge University Press, 1987); and Hanns Gross, *Rome in the Age of Enlightenment* (Cambridge: Cambridge University Press, 1990). There are also two pertinent volumes in the Longman History of Italy series: Eric Cochrane, *Italy, 1530–1630*, ed. Julius Kirshner (New York: Longman, 1988); and Dino Carpanetto and Giuseppe Ricuperati, *Italy in the Age of Reason, 1685–1789* (New York: Longman, 1987).

For each individual pope examined in this part, there are a few sources to which readers might turn to begin additional research. Full-scale English biographies of specific popes in this era, aside from the pertinent volumes in Pastor, tend to be few and of inconsistent quality. Other works provide information on one or another aspect of the administration of each pope. On Pius V, see, for example, Joseph Mendham, *The Life and Pontificate of Saint Pius the Fifth* (London: J. Duncan, 1832). The inquisitorial activities of Pius are carefully analyzed in Massimo Firpo and Dario Marcatto's magisterial edition of the documents related to the trial of Cardinal Giovanni Morone, *Il processo inquisitoriale del cardinale Giovanni Morone*, 6 vol. (Rome: Istituto storico italiano, 1981–89). Two collections of articles on Pius V are also helpful. See Aniceto Fernandez, ed., *San Pio V e la problematica del suo tempo* (Alessandria: Cassa di Risparmio di Alessandria, 1972); and Carlenrica Spantigati and Giulio Ieni, eds., *Pio V e Santa Croce di Bosco: Aspetti di una committenza papale* (Alessandria: Edizioni dell'Orso, 1985). On Gregory XIII, there are simply no recent biographies whatsoever, but there are recent works examining his activity as a proponent of calendar reform, as a supporter of new architecture, and as a generous benefactor of both the Society of Jesus and its educational initiatives. See Nicola Courtright, "Gregory XII's Tower of the Winds in the Vatican" (Ph.D. diss., New York University, 1990); Philip Caraman, *University of the Nations: The Story of the Gregorian University with Its Associated Institutes, the Biblical and the Oriental* (New York: Paulist Press, 1981); and John W. O'Malley, *The First Jesuits* (Cambridge, Mass.: Harvard University Press, 1993). Sixtus V also lacks any extended recent biography, although his politics, his urban reorganization and public building projects, and his patronage of art and culture have received considerable recent attention. See, for example, René Schiffmann, *Roma felix: Aspekte der städtebaulichen Gestaltung Roms unter Papst Sixtus V* (Bern: Peter Lang, 1985); Helge Gamrath, *Roma Sancta renovata: Studi sull'urbanistica di Roma nella seconda metà del sec. XVI secolo con particolare riferimento al pontificato di Sisto V (1585–1590)* (Rome: "L'Erma" di Bretschneider, 1987); Giorgio Simoncini, *"Roma restaurata" Rinnovamento urbano al tempo di Sisto V* (Florence: Olschki, 1990); Maria Luisa Madonna and Mario Bevilacqua, eds., *Roma di Sisto V: Arti, architettura, e città fra Rinascimento e Barocco* (Rome: Edizioni de Luca, 1993); and I. Polverini Fosi, "Justice and Its Image: Political Propaganda and Judicial Reality in the Pontificate of Sixtus V," *Sixteenth Century Journal* 24 (1993): 75–95.

Clement VIII, the last of the sixteenth-century popes discussed in this part, has been the subject of many specialized studies but no comprehensive biography. A very well-developed entry on Clement by Agostino Borromeo appeared in a biographical dictionary, but at almost twenty-five densely packed pages, it is much more than a sketch. See his "Clemente VIII," *Dizionario biografico degli italiani* 26 (1982): 259–83. Consideration of Clement's artistic patronage can begin with Morton Colp Abromson, *Painting in Rome during the Papacy of Clement VIII (1592–1605): A Documented Study* (New York: Garland Publishing, 1981), and should include the study of the Clementine transept of the Lateran Basilica found in Jack Freiberg's *The Lateran in 1600: Christian Concord in Counter-Reformation Rome* (Cambridge: Cambridge University Press, 1995). For Clement's religious activities, especially those with political and literary ramifications, see William J. Bouwsma, *Venice and the Defense of Republican Liberty: Renaissance Values in the Age of the Counter-Reformation* (Berkeley: University of California Press, 1968); and Paul F. Grendler, *The Roman Inquisition and the Venetian Press, 1540–1605* (Princeton: Princeton University Press, 1977). Clement's multifaceted foreign policy can be studied in local and regional histories like, among others, A. Enzo Baldini, *Puntigli spagnoleschi e intrighi politici nella Roma di Clemente VIII: Girolamo Frachetta e la sua relazione del 1603 sui cardinali* (Milan: Franco Angeli, 1981); Charles A. Frazee, *Catholics and Sultans: The Church and the Ottoman Empire, 1453–1923* (New York: Cambridge University Press, 1983); and Klaus Jaitner, ed., *Die Hauptinstruktionen Clemens VII für die Nuntien und Legaten an den Europäischen Fürstenhöfen, 1592–1605*, 2 vols. (Tübingen: Max Niemeyer, 1984).

Seventeenth-century popes treated in this part similarly are the subject of inconsistent scholarly attention. For Paul V, readers must mine information from general works on the period or on topics related to the age and to his administration. On his governmental administration, see Nicole Reinhardt, *Macht und Ohnmacht der Verflechtung: Rom und Bologna unter Paul V* (Tübingen: Bibliotheca Academica Verlag, 2000); Enrico Stumpo, *Il capitale finanziario a Roma fra cinque e seicento: Contributo alla storia della fiscalità pontificia in età moderna, 1570–1660* (Milan: A. Giuffrè, 1985); and Wolfgang Reinhard, *Papstfinanz und Nepotismus unter Paul V (1605–1621)* (Stuttgart: A. Hiersemann, 1974); plus the large number of works analyzing his interaction with the Republic of Venice, including Francis Oakley, "Complexities of Context: Gerson, Bellarmine, Sarpi, Richer, and the Venetian Interdict of 1606–1607," *Catholic Historical Review* 82 (1996): 369–96; and Pietro Pirri, *L'interdetto di Venezia del 1606 e Gesuiti* (Rome:

Institutum Historicum Societatis Iesu, 1959). For Paul's patronage of art, see Anna Maria Corbo and Massimo Pomponi, eds., *Fonti per la storia artistica Romana al tempo di Paolo V* (Rome: Ministero per i beni culturali e ambientali, 1995); and Steven F. Ostrow, *Art and Spirituality in Counter-Reformation Rome: The Sistine and Pauline Chapels in S. Maria Maggiore* (New York: Cambridge University Press, 1996).

Urban VIII is probably best known because of the trial of Galileo that occurred under his watch. For the best recent works on this matter, see Annibale Fantoli, *Galileo: For Copernicanism and for the Church*, 2nd ed., trans. by George V. Coyne (Vatican City: Libreria editrice vaticana, 1996); Richard S. Westfall, *Essays on the Trial of Galileo* (Vatican City: Vatican Observatory Publications, 1989); and Mario Biagioli, *Galileo, Courtier: The Practice of Science in the Culture of Absolutism* (Chicago: University of Chicago Press, 1993). On Innocent XI, there are two book-length English treatments, although Pastor's account is better than either one: Raymond J. Maras, *Innocent XI: Pope of Christian Unity* (Notre Dame, Ind.: Crossroad Books, 1984); and Abel Roper, *The Life and Reign of Innocent XI, Late Pope of Rome* (London, 1690). One historian in the 1930s, Louis O'Brien, devoted considerable effort to describing the relationship of Innocent XI with France. See his *Innocent XI and the Revocation of the Edict of Nantes* (Berkeley: University of California Press, 1934). The reform activity and religious policies of the last seventeenth-century pope, Innocent XII, are the subject of a good deal of recent, high-quality scholarship. See Bruno Pellegrino, ed., *Riforme, religione, e politica durante il pontificato di Innocenzo XII, 1691–1700: Atti del convegno di studio* (Galatina: Congedo, 1994); Miriam Turrini, "La riforma del clero secolare durante il pontificato di Innocenzo XII," *Cristianesimo nella storia* 13 (1992): 329–61; and Michele Fatica, "La reclusione dei poveri a Roma durante il pontificato di Innocenzo XII (1691–1700)," *Ricerche per la storia religiosa di Roma* 3 (1979): 133–80. There is no general study of Innocent XII, however, that surpasses Pastor's treatment of this pope.

The early modern part ends with two popes from the eighteenth century who also have received relatively scant scholarly attention. There are more biographical works devoted to Benedict XIV, that reformer and prolific author, than to that rather impotent Enlightenment politician Clement XIII. See, for example, Louis-Antoine Caraccioli, *La vie du Pape Benoît XIV Prospero Lambertini* (Paris: Hôtel Serpente, 1783); and Renée Haynes, *Philosopher King: The Humanist Pope Benedict XIV* (London: Weidenfeld & Nicolson, 1970). One of the better works on Benedict is a collection of papers from an international historical conference that covers his life fairly comprehensively: Marco Cecchelli, ed., *Benedetto XIV (Prospero Lambertini)*, 2 vols. (Cento: Centro Studi "Girolamo Baruffaldi," 1981–82). Consideration of Benedict within the broader context of the institutions and developments of his time can be found in Enrico Dammig, *Il movimento giansenista a Roma nella seconda metà del secolo XVIII* (Vatican City: Biblioteca Apostolica Vaticana, 1968); Mario Rosa, *Riformatori e ribelli nel 700 religioso italiano* (Bari: Dedalo Libri, 1969); Ernesto Codignola, *Illuministi, giansenisti, e giacobini nell'Italia del settecento* (Florence: "La Nuova Italia" Editrice, 1947); Hanns Gross, *Rome in the Age of Enlightenment* (Cambridge: Cambridge University Press, 1990); Franco Venturi, *Settecento riformatore, vol. 1, da Muratori a Beccaria* (Torino: Giulio Einaudi, 1969); Tarcisio Bertone, *Il governo della chiesa nel pensiero di Benedetto XIV, 1740–1758* (Rome: Libreria Ateneo Salesiano, 1977); and David F. Allen, "Upholding Tradition: Benedict XIV and the Hospitaller Order of St. John of Jerusalem at Malta, 1740–1758," *Catholic Historical Review* 80 (1994): 18–35.

For Clement XIII, readers are best advised to begin with Pastor's account of his life. The fullest recent biographical treatment is by Luigi Cajani and Anna Foa, "Clemente XIII," *Dizionario biografico degli italiani* 26 (1982): 328–343. For his ecclesiastical career and papal administration, see Augustin Theiner, *Histoire du pontificat de Clément XIV* (Paris: Firmin Didot Frères, 1852); Claudio Bellinati, *Attività pastorale del card. Carlo Rezzonico, vescovo di Padova, poi Clemente XIII (1743–1758)* (Padua: Tipografia Antoniana, 1969); and Maura Piccialuti, *La carità come metodo di governo: Istituzioni caritative a Roma dal pontificato di Innocenzo XII a quello di Benedetto XIV* (Turin: G. Giappichelli, 1994). Despite the title of the latter, it includes material on Clement. For the political aspects of Clement's administration, readers will have to rely on more general works like Dale K. Van Kley, *The Jansenists and the Expulsion of the Jesuits from France, 1757–1765* (New Haven, Conn.: Yale University Press, 1975); John Lynch, *Bourbon Spain, 1700–1808* (Oxford: Basil Blackwell, 1989); Franco Venturi, *Settecento riformatori: La chiesa e la repubblica dentro i loro limiti, 1758–1774* (Turin: Giulio Einaudi, 1976); Hanns Gross, *Rome in the Age of Enlightenment.* (Cambridge: Cambridge University Press, 1990); and Dale K. Van Kley, *The Damiens Affair and the Unraveling of the Ancien Régime, 1750–1770* (Princeton: Princeton University Press, 1984).

Primary sources deriving from the lives of early modern popes and specialized works tracing specific elements in their work are legion and cannot be summarized briefly. Suffice it to say that any of the popes described in this part would make a fine, long-term biographical project. To understand what primary materials an aspiring biographer should plan to consult in such a project, one must begin with an examination of the list of archival sources in the pertinent Pastor volumes. To these lists must be added the new, excellent guide to the principal repository of documentation on the papacy, the Archivio Segreto Vaticano: Francis X. Blouin general ed., *Vatican Archives: An Inventory and Guide to Historical Documents of the Holy See* (New York: Oxford University Press, 1998). The authors of entries included in this part of *The Great Popes through History* have provided excellent bibliographies that include some published primary source collections.

It is worth noting also that the most recent English collection of papal encyclical letters begins chronologically in 1740, that is, with the pontificate of Benedict XIV: see Claudia Carlen, ed., *The Papal Encyclicals*, 5 vols. (Wilmington, N.C.: McGrath Publishing Co., 1981; Ann Arbor, Mich.: Pierian Press, 1990).

PART V

THE MODERN PAPACY

INTRODUCTION

Frank J. Coppa

The papacy's role in the modern era has long been recognized, praised, and criticized. At the opening of the nineteenth century Napoleon deemed it "one of the greatest offices of the world" and a "lever of opinion," whose military equivalence he compared to a "corps of 200,000 men" (Mc-Manners, 141). Nevertheless, Bonaparte, like many of his contemporaries, charged that the papacy confused spiritual authority and political aims. This complaint prevailed throughout most of the nineteenth century and has persisted to the twenty-first. It was especially prevalent prior to 1870, fueled by the fact that until the Italian seizure of Rome that year, the popes exercised political as well as religious power, governing a large slice of central Italy. So long as the popes ruled over their own state and were temporal rulers as well as spiritual sovereigns, some confusion and considerable criticism existed about their political and religious aims. However, the loss of their territory and temporal power during the course of the Risorgimento, the movement for Italian unification, did not silence Rome's enemies. Subsequent developments encouraged these critics to raise their voices in opposition. Criticism of the modern papacy continues both from within and outside the church. One purportedly Catholic writer denounced the institution as bolstered by structures of deceit and deception. In a more moderate vein, the archbishop of San Francisco, John R. Quinn, in a 1996 speech, called for the reform of the Roman curia as well as the manner in which papal primacy is exercised.

The papacy remained neither silent nor passive in the face of the spirited offensive launched against it, mounting an energetic counteroffensive. The communication revolution, which triumphed in the Vatican when Guglielmo Marconi established Vatican Radio in 1931, made it possible for Rome to remain in touch with the hierarchy and faithful worldwide in a matter of moments, rendering its control all the more feasible and formidable. Not all appreciated this development, and some joined the long-established chorus of papal opponents. In the eighteenth and nineteenth centuries there were those who loudly decried papal primacy. Even after the loss of the temporal power there were those who feared the power of the popes, but others believed that the "beast" had been defanged following the loss of the papal state. Thus when Pierre Laval pleaded with Stalin to conciliate the pope, the Soviet dictator dismissively inquired how many divisions the pontiff directed. Although the pope possessed no military divisions and, after the Lateran Accords of 1929 creating Vatican City, was restricted to a scant 44-hectare or 108-acre state with some 500 subjects, others recognized that the papacy continued to wield a tremendous moral influence.

Undoubtedly the authority of the papacy was to be challenged by the mania for modernization and the rush toward renovation unleashed by developments at the end of the eighteenth century. The papal monarchy no less than the other crowns of the continent was threatened by the transition from the *ancien régime* to the revolutionary age. Skeptics readily rejected the message of Jesus, the role of the church, which aimed to nourish it, and the authority of the papacy, which sought to guide it. Rome sought to retaliate against this policy of rejection. Already in 1775 Pius VI condemned attacks on orthodoxy by the "monstrous desire of innovation." Nonetheless, throughout much of the eighteenth century dechristianization and secularization proceeded apace in society as human thought shifted from religious and philosophic speculation to political, social, and economic considerations.

The fifteen popes from Pius VI (1775–99) to John Paul II (1978–   ) have had to confront the momentous events and innumerable crises of the last two centuries that rocked the modern world. Five of these popes, Pius VI, Pius VII (1800–1823), Pius IX (1846–78), Leo XIII (1878–1903), and John Paul II, have pontificated for more than two decades, providing almost half of the list of the twelve longest-reigning popes in the institution's two-thousand-year history. Pius IX convoked an ecumenical council to confront the modern world (Vatican Council I, 1869–70), while John XXIII convoked another (Vatican Council II, 1962–65) to reach an accommodation with it. Ten of these central figures in the modern church are examined in detail in the biographical entries that follow, concentrating on those popes who have at once shaped the papacy and influenced the course of world events.

The outbreak of the American and French revolutions, paralleled by the takeoff of the Industrial Revolution in Great Britain, contributed to the transformation of Europe and the world, ushering in the modern age. As the discovery of the steam engine and the new puddling furnace created profound social and economic changes, the American, French, and Napoleonic revolutions provoked extraordinary political upheavals in the Western world and the vast reaches of Asia and Africa upon which it impinged. Together, these developments launched far-reaching philosophical, political, territorial, economic, and social as well as religious revisions in the nineteenth century, dominating events in the twentieth. The currents unleashed by these revolutions challenged the traditional political order and the prevailing religious establishment. The emergence of liberalism, constitutionalism, nationalism, republicanism, and laissez-faire economics and later Darwinism, democracy, socialism, and secularism presented a potential threat to the Catholic community and its temporal and spiritual leadership, the papacy. The popes who have been selected for their response to nineteenth-century developments include Pius VII, Pius IX, and Leo XIII. The pontificate of the last continued into the twentieth century.

In the twentieth century the crisis provoked by modernization continued with the development of Americanism, modernism, racism, fascism, communism, and totalitarianism. Feminism, the sexual revolution, the population explosion, the increasing intrusion of the scientific mind into realms long under religious scrutiny, environmental hazards, and even the threat of a nuclear holocaust challenged the papacy. In the third millennium the papacy continues to confront the challenges of the technological revolution and new moral dilemmas, such as those posed by genetic engineering, stem-cell research, and cloning. Those popes selected for their responses to these twentieth-century developments include Pius X, Benedict XV, Pius XI, Pius XII, John XXIII, Paul VI, and John Paul II. During this time of rapid transition Rome had to adjust to the new world order where science challenged revealed religion and where orthodoxy was denounced as a repressive check upon progress. Although Rome confronted the consequences of modernization during the course of the nineteenth and twentieth centuries and faces the challenges of the twenty-first century, the roots of the crisis of the modern papacy can be traced to both the Enlightenment and enlightened despotism, which worked together to undermine the autonomy of the church and the power of the popes.

In France state intervention took the form of Gallicanism, in Germany, Febronianism, in Austria and Lombardy, Josephism, and in Tuscany, Jansenism. Indeed, in 1740 the Catholic powers contested the very office of the papacy as their rivalry delayed the election of a new pope for half a year, the longest conclave of the century. In Germany the thought and work of Bishop Johann Nikolaus von Hontheim, auxiliary of the bishop of Trier, in his *De statu Ecclesiae* (The state of the church) (1763) published under the pseudonym of Justinus Febronius branded the authority of the papacy a usurpation that provoked most of the problems plaguing the church. Joseph II, who succeeded Maria Theresa in 1780, boasting that his "trade is to be royalist," concurred with much of the Febronian program limiting papal power. Upon assuming power he ended all direct communication between the bishops and the pope, insisting that all papal pronouncements and documents receive his *placet* or approval before publication in his dominions. Joseph did not hesitate to interject the state into the education of clerics, confiscate the property of the secular and regular clergy, abolish ecclesiastical laws, and reorganize the dioceses and parishes of his lands without papal consultation. To convince the clergy of the wisdom of his course and principles, Joseph instituted new imperial seminaries at Vienna, Budapest, Louvain, Pavia, and Freiburg, while suppressing many diocesan seminaries.

The 1773 dissolution of the fanatically loyal Society of Jesus, at the behest of the Bourbon powers of France, Spain, and Naples, represented but one of the many difficulties endured by Rome during the age of reason as it witnessed skepticism, indifferentism, and hostility toward the traditional faith. The church, and especially the papacy, were mercilessly ridiculed by philosophes in France, Portugal, Spain, and Naples who saw Christianity and its hierarchy as an implacable enemy of progress, rationality, and humanity. Attached to the cult of science, the philosophes discredited mysteries, miracles, and, above all, papal prophecies. The orthodox precepts of the faith were branded ignorance and stupidity by the encyclopedists who cataloged human knowledge, deriding the assertions of Rome while seeking the secularization of society. The Enlightenment thus proved painful for the papacy. The perils it planted for the church and its guardians blossomed during the course of the revolutionary age that followed.

It is true that the revolt of the American colonies (1775–78), justified by the broad precepts of the Enlightenment, did not prove detrimental to the Catholic church or its head. In fact, the Catholic minority in the colonies, no more than 20,000, rallied to the national cause, as did Catholic France and Spain. In 1780 the assembly of the French clergy contributed 30,000,000 livres to support the revolutionaries. George Washington, appreciative of Catholic support, admonished his soldiers not to participate in anti-Catholic manifestations, which he deemed "immature and childish." Benjamin Franklin, in turn, let the papal nuncio in Paris, Prince Doria Pamphili, know of the American determination to assure liberty of conscience. This materialized in the First Amendment to the Constitution.

The consequences of the French Revolution, however, proved more detrimental than the American Revolution to the church and the papacy. Beginning with the confiscation of church property in 1789, followed by the Civil Constitution of the Clergy shortly thereafter, the ensuing years witnessed a determined, often-violent assault against the temporal and spiritual authority of the papacy that culminated in the spiriting of Pius VI (1775–1799) from the Eternal City and the proclamation of a republic in Rome. The worship of reason and the cult of the supreme being were proclaimed in France as rivals and alternatives to the traditional faith. Napoleon, who became first consul in 1799, questioned the prudence of this policy and sought some reconciliation with Rome. In 1801 he concluded a concordat with the Holy See. The agreement did not prevent the emperor from occupying the Papal States in 1808 nor its annexation in 1809. Pius VII, like his predecessor, was dragged into exile by the French. As Napoleon's domination spread throughout Europe, the papacy once again appeared to be on the verge of collapse. The threat dissipated with the dissolution of Napoleon's legions in the steppes of Russia and the emperor's exile to St. Helena. Alan Reinerman, in his entry on Pius VII (1800–1823), reveals how this pope, ably assisted by his secretary of state, Cardinal Ercole Consalvi, survived the Napoleonic ordeal and returned to Rome as spiritual ruler of the church and sovereign of his state.

The settlement of 1815 saw a reconstitution of the Papal States, the restoration of the Jesuits, and a renewed appreciation for the union of throne and alter. The monarchs who adhered to the Holy Alliance, the product of the religious fervor of Tsar Alexander of Russia, promised to conduct their foreign relations in accordance with the precepts of holy religion. Writers such as Edmund Burke, Joseph de Maistre, Louis de Bonald, and Father Gioacchino Ventura, who borrowed freely from Burke, de Maistre, and de Bonald, saw a close nexus between religion and society. While their message found resonance in the romantic movement of the period, not all justified papal absolutism.

Franz von Baader's pamphlet "Concerning the Separability or Inseparability of the Papacy from Catholicism" (1838) denounced spiritual bondage as no less burdensome than its secular variant. Furthermore, the revolutions of 1820 and 1830 and even those of 1848 were directed against the religious order that critics charged bolstered the prevailing power structure. The revolutions of 1830 encouraged the appearance of a liberal Catholic movement that sought to disassociate the church and the papacy from the moribund monarchical structure, giving rise to Felicité Robert de Lammenais's Avenir movement, which invoked a separation of church and state. At the same time the outbreak of revolution in the Papal States, suppressed only by Austrian intervention, prompted the 1831 Memorandum of the Powers (France, Great Britain, Russia, Austria and Prussia) urging the pope to make reforms in his government. Pope Gregory XVI (1831–46) condemned the Avenir movement (1832) and shelved the reformist suggestions of the powers.

The pontificate of Pius IX (1846–78), examined by Frank J. Coppa, remains the longest in the history of the church. It opened on an optimistic note as the new pope, affectionately called Pio Nono, was hailed as the liberator who would reconcile liberty and Catholicism and unite the Italian peninsula. The dream disappeared amid the debris of the revolutionary upheaval of 1848, during which Pius IX determined that the revolutionaries sought to undermine Catholicism rather than being the instruments of divine intervention to topple the remnants of Josephism. Advised by Cardinal Giacomo Antonelli, he fled from his own subjects and witnessed the proclamation of a Roman republic guided by Mazzini and defended by Garibaldi. The pope, who was restored to power by the Catholic states, Austria, France, Spain, and Naples, judged that his position as supreme pontiff was jeopardized by his brief flirtation with constitutionalism. Following his restoration in Rome, Pius focused on his position as head of the faith, leaving the execution of political matters in the hands of his astute secretary of state, Antonelli.

Within the church Pope Pius IX favored centralization by imposing the Roman liturgy, by seeking to reduce the autonomy of the bishops of the Eastern churches united with Rome while extending the scope of Roman jurisdiction, by increasingly granting the Roman title of *monsignore*, and by prompting the bishops to make periodic *ad limina* visits to Rome. Pius refused to reconcile himself to the loss of the bulk of his territory that was incorporated into the Kingdom of Italy proclaimed in 1861, responding to the call for accommodation with the new currents by issuing the encyclical *Quanta cura*, to which was appended the Syllabus of Errors, in 1864, which critics charged put the papacy in conflict with the modern world. Mobilizing the forces of the church to bolster the position of the papacy, he convoked the Vatican Council in 1869, which in the following year proclaimed the primacy and infallibility of the pope. Opponents such as the Bavarian theologian Ignaz von Döllinger charged that the proclamation lacked antiquity, universality, and consent.

The combative Pius refused to sanction the loss of Rome during the Franco-Prussian War, which ended the oldest sovereignty in Europe, or accept the conditions imposed by the Italians in the Law of Papal Guarantees of 13 May 1871, thus provoking the Roman Question, which persisted until 1929. He was followed in this course by all of his successors until Pius XI negotiated the Lateran Accords (1929) with Mussolini's Italy. Pius IX was no more accommodating or willing to submit to the *Kulturkampf* in Bismarck's Germany or the Los von Rom movement in Austria, which sought freedom from Rome. Critics such as the archbishop of Rheims spoke of the "idolatry of the papacy," citing the need for some accommodation with the modern world. Pius, a crusader in a secular age, was not prepared to do so; his successor would make an attempt.

At the turn of the century, Pope Leo XIII (1878–1903), examined by Emiliana P. Noether, sought to heal the rift between Rome and democratic governments such as existed in Republican France (the *Ralliement*). He also sought a solution to the tribulations of the working classes in the industrial age, citing the weaknesses of laissez-faire social indifferentism, on the one hand, but condemning Marxism as a cure worse than the disease (*Rerum novarum*, 15 May 1891). In *Graves de communi* (18 January 1901) Leo expressed his position on Christian democracy, emphasizing its moral rather than its political role. His diplomatic initiatives led him to arbitrate the dispute between Spain and Germany over the Caroline Islands and to secure the opening of a Russian embassy to the Vatican while instituting diplomatic relations with imperial Japan. As Noether reveals, Leo's pontificate was perceived by some as a movement away from the intransigence of Gregory XVI and Pius IX, marking the first attempt of the papacy to reach an accommodation of sorts with the modern world. Nonetheless, Leo would not condone Americanism, which allegedly sought to reorganize the church along more democratic lines and impose the ideals of the United States upon Catholicism worldwide.

Leo's successor Pius X (1903–14), examined in the entry by William Roberts, proved even less open to contemporary thought and developments. He condemned both Americanism and modernism, considering pernicious the doctrine that would transform the laity into a force for "progress" in the church. As Roberts reveals, Pius X's intransigent defense of papal prerogatives contributed to the separation of church and state in France in 1905 and in Portugal in 1911, while neglecting the diplomatic role of the universal church. The next pope, Benedict XV (1914–22), examined in this volume by Joseph Biesinger, belonged to the diplomatic school of Leo rather than the pastoral one championed by his immediate predecessor. Nonetheless, Benedict proved unable to bring World War I, which found Catholics on opposing sides of the conflict, to a speedy conclusion. Benedict's peace proposal of 1917 earned him the suspicion of the Central Powers, on the one hand, and the Allies, on the other. Although he was vehemently opposed to communism, during the famine of 1921 this pope organized a major relief program on behalf of the Russians. Benedict's successor, Cardinal Achille Ratti, who assumed the name of Pius XI (1922–39), is examined in the entry by Peter C. Kent. Kent explores both the diplomatic and intransigent sides of this pope. During the International Congress of Genoa of 1922 Pius XI had his representative make contact with those of the Soviet Union, upsetting those on the right for the attempt to reconcile that regime with the Vatican and those on the left for his failure to do so.

A number of opponents of papal power pointed to the Vatican's affinity with the far right, with some even suggesting that Catholicism had a fascist form of government, resting on the leadership principle with an infallible pope in supreme command. Kent shows that Pius XI's conclusion of the Lateran Accords with Mussolini's Italy in 1929, followed by the concordat with Hitler's Germany in 1933, did little to quiet this criticism. Likewise, the papacy's tacit support of the authoritarian Engelbert. Dollfuss in Austria and the Falangist Francisco Franco in Spain, while displaying a consistent hostility and uncompromising opposition to communism, led some to equate Catholicism with fascism. Nonetheless, Pius XI refused to remain silent in the face of Fascist abuses and Nazi racism and in 1938 commissioned the Jesuit John La Farge to draft an encyclical explicitly condemning racism and anti-Semitism.

His successor, Pope Pius XII, however, proved less willing to publicly confront the fascist regimes and shelved his predecessor's projected encyclical, which was never officially published by the church. The neutrality of Pius XII (1939–58) during World War II and his supposed silence in the face of the Holocaust were decried in Rolf Hochhuth's play *The Deputy*. This and other aspects of this controversial pope and pontificate are explored by Charles Delzell. There were those who found it symptomatic and predictive that on 8 December 1954 the conservative Pius XII signed the decree for the opening of the apostolic process for the beatification of Pius IX, who had papal infallibility proclaimed. The controversy continues, with some seeking to canonize Pius XII while others are equally determined to demonize him.

The election of the seventy-seven-year-old Angelo Roncalli as Pope John XXIII (1958–63) provoked an attempt at *aggiornamento*, or bringing the church up to date. This and other aspects of this crucial pontificate are explored by Patrick Granfield. Pope John called some 2,500 bishops to Rome to modernize the church. Not surprisingly, the four sessions of the Second Vatican Council from 1962 to 1965—John lived only to see the first—brought the Catholic church and the papacy to the forefront of world opinion. Conservatives charged that John, who openly endorsed democracy and championed workers' rights to form trade unions, virtually turned the church upside down while undermining the papacy. The Vatican Council, which stressed the powers of the bishops, especially in the schema *De Ecclesia*, supposedly made the bishops cogovernors with the pope of the church, redressing the balance of power between them. Paul VI (1963–78), according to some, continued John's reforms, while others believe that he slammed the door on future change. Richard Wolff in his entry proves essentially sympathetic to Paul VI, whom he describes as Catholicism's bridge to the modern world. Wolff acknowledges that Paul has been criticized as well as eulogized, but on balance he is convinced that his accomplishments outweighed his mistakes. Although evaluations of Paul's contribution vary, he abolished the Index of Prohibited Books and moderated the anti-Communist crusade of the papacy, receiving the Soviet foreign minister Andrey Gromyko in 1966 and the president of the "evil empire" Nikolai Podgorny the following year. He also traveled widely, paving the way for John Paul II, who would become the most traveled pope in history.

During the summer of 1978 the church lost two popes, Paul VI and his successor John Paul I, bringing forth a Polish cardinal as John Paul II (1978–), terminating the Italian domination of the papacy from 1523 to 1978, almost half a millennium. John Paul II's pontificate is examined in the entry by Roy Domenico. Pope John Paul II, in his first encyclical, *The Redeemer of Man*, articulated a plan to prepare the church and the papacy for the twenty-first century. He is not only the first Polish pope and the first from Eastern Europe, but also the first pope to enter Canterbury Cathedral, the first to preach in a Lutheran church, and the first to enter a synagogue and a mosque. The first and only of the modern popes to be shot, he survived the assassination attempt in St. Peter's Square in May 1981. He resumed his hectic schedule, making some one hundred voyages outside Italy since 1978. Early in 1998 he made a momentous visit to Castro's Cuba, and he marked the new millennium by a trip to the Holy Land and offering an apology to Jews for centuries of anti-Judaism within the church.

In 1982 the pope met President Ronald Reagan of the United States, who had likewise survived an assassination attempt in 1981, and the two apparently experienced a meeting of minds. By 1984 William Wilson, who had been the president's special representative to the pope, was appointed ambassador to the Vatican. It has been claimed that the pope and the American president not only conspired in a "holy alliance" to support the outlawed Solidarity movement after the martial-law crackdown of 1981 in Poland, but sought to precipitate the end of Soviet domination of the whole of Eastern Europe. Both were to see their vision fulfilled, as well as the collapse of communism in the Soviet Union itself.

During the height of the Vatican's crusade against communism, the papacy confronted criticism of its leadership within the church. The Jesuits, long the bulwark of papal primacy, no longer saw the ultimate leadership of the Roman church in the papacy and its worldwide hierarchy but in the "people of God." The more radical voices even called for a new theology to emerge from the masses below to replace the one imposed from above, reviving notions put forward by Lamennais during the pontificate of Gregory XVI and by the Americanists condemned by Leo XIII. In South and Central America a number of prominent figures in the order have called upon the church to exercise a "preferential option" for the poor and oppressed, proposing a Christian-Marxist alliance to forge a new socialist society to replace the decadent capitalist one. The Jesuit onslaught on the capitalist establishment is enshrined in the theology of liberation. This extraordinary train of events has pitted the "white pope," the Holy Father, against the "black pope," the superior-general of the Jesuits, so called because of his black cassock.

While class and social issues troubled the church in Latin America and other parts of the third world, the church in Western Europe and North America found itself under fire for its alleged gender bias and homophobia, as well as clerical domination and the papacy's position on such issues as priestly celibacy, birth control, and abortion. There are those who have boasted that the popes have changed little, taking as their motto *Semper Idem* (always the same), despite the tradition of electing these leaders. There has been a remarkable continuity from one pope to another, yet each has emerged as a distinct figure, and each has promoted a degree of change as the papacy has adjusted to the political, social, and economic structures of the surrounding world. Pope Pius XII, in his address to the Tenth International Congress of Historians in Rome in 1955, tried to bridge the gap between the church's unchangeability and its need to adapt itself to the changing environment.

Within the last two centuries the pontificates of Leo XIII and John XXIII have been praised for their reformism, while those of Gregory XVI, Pius IX, and Pius X have been denounced for their attempts to halt social progress, rejecting the liberty, equality, and fraternity of the revolutionary age while fighting a rear-guard action against the contemporary world. Perhaps it is no coincidence that one pope from the former group, John XXIII, and one from the latter, Pius IX, are both scheduled for canonization. Despite the controversy surrounding papal policy, there is a consensus that it has involved the church in world affairs, functioning both as a spiritual center and political organization that exchanges political representatives. One measure of its continuing influence can be gleaned from the fact that more than one hundred governments maintain diplomatic relations with the Holy See, which has formal diplomatic relations with most countries and informal relations with the rest. The Holy See's objectives, which provide for the defense not only of the rights of the papacy and the church but of the populations of the various countries, are attained not only through the network of formal diplomatic relations but also by means of the local bishops who provide another mechanism for communication.

During the course of the twentieth century the ravages of two world wars and the persistence of a plethora of global problems exposed the weakness of excessive national sovereignty, leading to the development of mechanisms of international cooperation and collaboration. During these decades the Catholic church, the traditional translational organization, under the leadership of the popes, resumed an active role in international affairs. Although many of the solemn principles advocated first by the League of Nations and later adopted by the United Nations mirrored positions of the Catholic church and centuries-old Christian traditions, there were obstacles to the church's participation in an international community organized on the basis of independent sovereign states. The creation of Vatican City provided the Holy See with the claim to enter the concert of powers, altering in the eyes of some the weaker position it had endured at the time of the formation of the League of Nations.

The papacy, however, pointed out that some confused the Holy See with Vatican City, attributing to Vatican City recognition as a sovereign body in the concert of states, juridically equal to other states, despite its small territory and population and the peculiarities of its organization and action. The church, on the other hand, insisted on the attribution of sovereignty to the Holy See as the supreme organ of government of the Catholic church. This difference in perception has influenced the Holy See's attitude toward the League of Nations, the United Nations, and its position vis-à-vis individual countries.

The higher clergy has been convoked in council twenty-one times during the life of the church, and only twice in the last two centuries covered in this part of this volume on the great popes: Vatican I, convoked by Pope Pius IX, which assumed a confrontational response to modernization, and Vatican II, convoked by Pope John XXIII and brought to completion by Pope Paul VI, which sought some accommodation with contemporary developments. This part focuses on the papal response to the modern world and its influence and impact on developments from the outbreak of the French Revolution to the collapse of communism in Eastern Europe and Russia. In the ten entries that follow, the authors have sought to determine not only the forces that impinged on the beleaguered popes but how they responded, delving into their motivation while exploring the consequences of their attitudes and actions.

Within these entries one will find the popes' reactions to the French Revolution and the Napoleonic imperium, their response to the revolutionary upheaval that troubled Europe from 1820 to 1848, and the papal reactions to liberal Catholicism, Italian and German unification, and the *Kulturkampf*. This part also traces the papacy's support of missionary efforts in the vast reaches of the third world beyond Europe and the Americas, its relationship to colonialism and the new imperialism, its role in World War I, and the Vatican's relationship to the democracies and the dictatorships in the interwar period, 1919–1939, as well as its role during World War II, including the so-called silence of Pope Pius XII during the Holocaust. In addition, these entries examine the papacy's attitude toward internationalism, communism, the reconstruction of the post–World War II world, the crisis of authority that has troubled the church since the late 1950s, the convocation of the First World Congress of the Lay Apostolate in 1951, and the attempted accommodation with the modern world initiated by the Second Vatican Council.

These biographical studies of the notable popes of the modern age examine these ten key popes within the broader framework of religious, cultural, political, social, and economic events. The Holy See has had to face internal and external opposition, including the undermining of traditional forms of authority in the church as well as the society at large. Rejecting the ethics of a secular society, including the collectivism of communism and the selfish individualism of economic liberalism, the Vatican has sought its own *via media* or third path. The modern papacy has delved into the morality of the marketplace and the limits to be placed on capitalism, the rights of the individual versus those of the community, and the rights and responsibilities of the working classes as well as those of their employers. Among other things, these entries trace how the papacy moved from the notion of a "just war" to "war no more," and how it came to appreciate the need for an international world order to preserve the peace as well as the environment. Finally, this part explores the modern papacy's need to balance the welfare of the rich and the poor, the West against the third world, and the interaction between science and religion, as well as the changing relationship between church and state.

PIUS VII (1800–1823)

ALAN J. REINERMAN

When Pius VII became pope in 1800, the papacy had reached its lowest ebb in centuries. For over a century the prestige of the papacy and the hold of Catholicism on society had been withering under the attacks of the intellectuals of the Enlightenment, while in most Catholic lands absolute monarchs had undermined papal authority by establishing state churches under their effective control rather than Rome's. Still greater disasters had followed the French Revolution: the rejection of papal authority and the persecution and prohibition of Catholicism in France, the occupation of the Papal States and proclamation of the end of the temporal power, and the expulsion of Pius VI from Rome. When, at the death of that pope in French captivity in 1799, the leaders of the French republic proclaimed that the end of the papacy was at hand, many were prepared to believe them. Few would have predicted that under Pius VII a revival of Catholicism would begin that within a few decades would bring the papacy greater prestige and more effective authority than it had had for centuries.

The future pope was born Barnabas Chiaramonte on 14 August 1742 in Cesena in the Papal States, the son of Count Scipio Chiaramonte and Marchionesse Giovanna Chini, both of the high aristocracy. In 1758 he entered the Benedictine order, where he devoted himself to the study of theology. After completing his studies, he was ordained to the priesthood and was appointed a lecturer in theology at the Abbey of St. John in Parma (1766–75). Subsequently he taught at the Abbey of St. Anselm in Rome (1775–81), where he met and won the respect of Pope Pius VI. In 1781

Pius VI appointed him bishop of Tivoli and in 1785 transferred him to the more important bishopric of Imola and named him a cardinal. His first decade at Imola was quietly successful, but his tranquillity, like that of all Italy, was shattered by the invasion of the armies of the French Revolution in 1796.

In 1797 Napoleon conquered the Legations, the papal territory that included Imola, and demanded that its bishops express their support for the revolution. Most refused, considering the revolution fundamentally hostile to Catholicism and hoping for the victory of the conservative powers. Chiaramonte, however, in contrast to most Catholic leaders of his time, realized that the Catholic church had to come to terms with the revolution and its consequences, for they were in the long run irresistible; moreover, he believed that such a reconciliation was possible, for he saw no essential conflict between the principles of the revolution and those of Catholicism. For the rest of his life he worked to reconcile the church to the new world that had sprung from the revolution, firmly defending the essential principles of the church, but willing to compromise everything else when necessary. The first public statement of his willingness to accept the new forces sweeping over Europe was the homily that he gave, in response to Napoleon's demand, on Christmas in 1797, a key document in the development of liberal Catholicism. At a time when most Catholic leaders were denouncing the revolution as satanic, he declared that not only were the revolutionary ideals of liberty, equality, and fraternity fully compatible with Christian principles, but that they would endure only if they were based on Christianity.

This homily won him the good will of Napoleon; it also attracted the attention of those Catholic leaders who saw that the church must come to terms with the new revolutionary order. Among the latter was Ercole Consalvi, secretary of the conclave that met in Venice in 1799–1800 to choose a successor to Pius VI. Convinced that the church needed an open-minded leader who could lead its adaption to the postrevolutionary world, Consalvi remembered the homily and secured Chiaramonte's election as pope Pius VII. The new pope appointed Consalvi as his secretary of state, and henceforth they worked closely together.

Pius VII's first major step toward adapting the Catholic church to the modern world was the concordat of 1801 with Napoleon. Bonaparte let Pius know shortly after his election that he wished to negotiate a settlement of the church-state quarrel that had divided France and driven Catholicism there underground. There was strong opposition at Rome to negotiations with a leader sprung from the revolution that had done the church so much harm, and many cardinals preferred to put their trust in the conservative powers. Pius, however, realized that to cling to the dying old regime would be fatal for the church, which had to come to terms with the new political order, and he directed Consalvi to negotiate a concordat. The negotiations were long and difficult, for Napoleon wished to bring the church as far as possible under his control, while Pius VII was determined to preserve its essential independence. In the end, Pius VII made many concessions to reach a settlement: in particular, he abandoned the traditional claim that Catholicism was the state religion of France, accepted religious toleration for all, recognized the loss of the church property confiscated during the revolution, and agreed to allow Napoleon considerable influence on the appointment of clergy. But he abandoned nothing that had not already been lost in practice, and in return he recovered legal existence for the church and freedom of public worship in France, and recognition of the pope's supreme religious authority.

Freed from persecution and no longer handicapped by identification with the old regime, the church began a rapid revival in France. Moreover, papal authority was given an unexpected increase, ironically at Napoleon's insistence. Distrusting the bishops appointed under the monarchy, Napoleon demanded that the pope remove them all and replace them. No pope had ever taken so drastic an action— popes had the theoretical authority to do so, but in practice the power of kings and national hierarchies under the old regime would have made such a move very dangerous. When Pius VII enforced the resignation of the entire French hierarchy, he demonstrated beyond all doubt the supremacy of papal authority over the French church. Conservatives bitterly criticized Pius VII for the concessions he had made in the concordat. Moreover, in 1801 Napoleon slyly issued "organic articles" supposedly interpreting the concordat, but in practice increasing his control over the church. Nonetheless, Pius VII, though he issued a protest, refused to abrogate the concordat, for he knew the advantages it had brought to the church. Indeed, in 1803 he proceeded to negotiate a similar concordat with the satellite kingdom Napoleon had set up in northern Italy.

Painting of Pope Pius VII by David. (Courtesy of the Vatican Library)

Pius VII had shown his conciliatory side in negotiating the concordat, but he soon demonstrated that where principle and the essential independence of the papacy were concerned, he could be unyielding. He firmly resisted Napoleon's continuing efforts after 1802 to extend his control further over the church, and relations began to deteriorate. In 1804 Napoleon invited Pius to come to Paris to preside at his coronation. Pius VII agreed: it was politically inexpedient to alienate the all-powerful Napoleon, and he hoped that his journey might lead to better relations. He also hoped that he might be able to work out a satisfactory settlement of religious affairs in Germany, now also under Napoleon's domination. Consequently, he was not put off by warnings that Napoleon planned to crown himself so as to avoid the appearance of owing his crown to Rome, on the contrary, Pius VII himself was happy to be able to avoid the appearance of giving a crown to a revolutionary adventurer whose power might prove transitory. His hopes were disappointed: no settlement of German religious affairs could be reached, and better relations with Napoleon proved elusive. After his coronation the emperor became steadily more imperious in his demands on Rome as his European power grew, and he increased his efforts to dominate the papacy and convert it into a useful tool. Matters came to a head after 1806 when Napoleon, seeking to undermine England's economy by banning its trade from the continent, demanded that the Papal States close its ports to British ships and trade. This Pius could not do, for compliance would have meant joining Napoleon in his war with England, and he was firmly convinced that the papacy's spiritual character compelled it to remain neutral in all wars unless attacked.

Napoleon, infuriated by Pius's refusal, brought increasing pressure to bear upon the pope by such measures as interfering with the exercise of papal authority over the French clergy, confiscating church property, and sending troops to occupy the ports of the Papal States. When these measures had no effect, he forced Pius to dismiss Consalvi, whom he blamed for papal resistance, and then presented his demands to the new secretary of state, Cardinal Bartolome Pacca, who at Pius's orders proved equally adamant. Finally, in 1808 he sent troops to occupy Rome, warning that the occupation would become permanent unless the pope yielded. Pius VII still refused Napoleon's demands, which now included both formal papal participation in the war with England and greater state control over the French church, and he excommunicated those responsible for the occupation, though without naming Napoleon. Determined to break his resistance, Napoleon had Pius VII arrested in 1809 and annexed the Papal States to France. The pope remained in prison for five years, first at Savona, then at Fontainebleau, cut off from all contact with the outside world. These years saw Pius VII firmly resist constant pressure by Napoleon directly or by French clergy subservient to him to yield to the emperor's demands. His steadfast courage became an inspiration to those in Europe who still resisted Napoleon, from the popular resistance movements in Spain and Italy to normally anti-Catholic England. Only once did he waver. In 1813 Napoleon, eager to settle with the pope after his Russian disaster of the previous year, came in person to talk with him. He persuaded Pius VII, then in ill health, to sign what he presented as the preliminary basis for a concordat whose details would be worked out in further negotiations. The emperor proceeded to publish this document as a formal "concordat of Fontainebleau." Pius VII at once repudiated it and refused to engage in further negotiations.

Upon the collapse of Napoleon's power in 1814, Pius VII was released and returned to Rome in triumph, to the enthusiastic welcome of his people. The applause was well deserved. His determined resistance had defeated Napoleon's effort to make a tool of the papacy, preserving the freedom of action and reputation for impartiality that were essential for the performance of its spiritual mission. Moreover, he had raised the prestige of the papacy to its highest point in centuries, for his resistance and long imprisonment had made him a hero and martyr in the eyes of Europe. The remaining years of his pontificate were less dramatic, though still significant. In poor health after his captivity, Pius VII delegated political affairs to Consalvi, to whom he gave staunch support against the cardinals who opposed many of his policies. It was the prestige that Pius had won for Rome that enabled Consalvi to regain the Papal States at the Congress of Vienna (1814–1815), despite the attempts of various powers to annex part or all of them. Thereafter, Pius VII supported Consalvi's plans to reform and modernize the restored Papal States, which both realized were essential if it was to win the support of a generation that years of French rule had accustomed to modern ideas and efficient government. Their reforms had sufficient success that during the Italian revolutions of 1820–1821 the Papal States remained quiet. Unfortunately, this success was temporary: the reforms were sabotaged by the opposition of the Zelanti or "Zealots," the reactionary party that was dominant among the cardinals and prelates at Rome, so that they never went fully into effect and were repealed after Pius VII's death. As a result, the chance to place the papal regime on a solid base of popular support was missed, it became increasingly unpopular, and its ultimate downfall in 1870 became inevitable.

Pius VII played a more active role in religious policy, where he wished to undo the damage inflicted on the church during the revolution and to continue its adaptation to the modern world. Continuing his earlier policy, he negotiated concordats with Naples and Bavaria and less formal agreements with a dozen other states, including such non-Catholic states as Prussia, which placed church-state relations on a more modern basis and allowed Catholicism to flourish again. These agreements were generally favorable to Rome, partly because of Consalvi's diplomatic skill, but also because of the enhanced prestige Pius had won for the papacy. Pius VII hoped to reach an agreement with the Austrian Empire that would reduce the extensive state controls over the church introduced by its rulers in the eighteenth century, but despite long negotiations, he was able to secure only slight reductions during his lifetime, though the improvement in the Austrian attitude toward Rome brought about by his efforts contributed to the concordat reached long after his death. With Russia, long hostile to Catholicism, he was unable to secure any improvement in relations, but in England the respect won by his resistance to Napoleon set the stage for eventual Catholic emancipation in 1829. He at first felt unable to deal with the Latin American republics that had revolted against Spain for fear of alienating that power, but in 1823 he decided, with his usual realism, that the new states would endure, and he organized a diplomatic mission that led eventually to a reconciliation with them after his death.

Another way in which he sought to strengthen the church was by encouraging the religious orders, which had suffered greatly during the revolutionary era. His first and most important move was to revive the Jesuits (the Society of Jesus) in 1814. In the eighteenth century Rome had been forced by pressure from the Bourbon powers of France, Spain, and Naples to suppress the Jesuits, though they were the most loyal and effective of the orders; in 1814, though the powers still disapproved, such pressure was unthinkable, so great had been the revival of papal authority under Pius VII.

After a long period of declining health, which had never recovered from his ordeal under Napoleon, Pius was seriously injured in a fall on 6 July 1823 and died on 20 August. He is buried in St. Peter's in Rome, under a monument designed by Consalvi. Evaluations of this pope and his pontificate began almost immediately. Pius VII must be considered one of the most important and most successful of modern popes. He successfully resisted Napoleon's attempt to dominate and instrumentalize the papacy, which if successful would surely have been fatal to its authority, and he revived papal prestige and authority after its decline in the eighteenth century, raising it to a level unmatched for centuries. For many, his greatest contribution was to break with the dying old regime and begin the vital task of modernizing the Catholic church so as to adapt it to the postrevolutionary world.

SELECTED BIBLIOGRAPHY

Barberi, Andrea, ed. *Bullarii Romani Continutio*. 19 vols. Rome: Camera Apostolica, 1835–57.

Boulay de la Meurth, Alfred. *Documents sur la négotiation du Concordat et sur les autres rapports de la France avec le Saint Siège en 1800–1801*. Paris: Leroux, 1891–1905.

Carlen, Claudia, ed. *The Papal Encyclicals, 1740–1981*. 5 vols. Wilmington, N.C., McGrath Publishing Co., 1981.

Chadwick, Owen. *The Popes and European Revolution*. New York: Oxford University Press, 1981.

Consalvi, Ercole. *Memorie*. Ed. Mario Nasalli Rocca di Corneliano. Rome: Signorelli, 1950.

Ellis, John Tracy. *Cardinal Consalvi and Anglo-Papal Relations, 1814–1824*. Washington, D.C.: Catholic University of America Press, 1942.

Engel-Janosi, Friedrich, ed. *Die politische Korrespondenz der Päpste mit den österrei-chischen Kaisern, 1801–1918*. Vienna: Herold, 1964.

Hales, E.E.Y. *The Emperor and the Pope*. Garden City, N.Y.: Doubleday, 1961.

Haussonville, Comte d'. *L'Eglise romanie et le premier Empire (1800–1814)*. 5 vols. Paris: Lévy, 1868–70.

Koenig, Leo. *Pius VII. Die Sakularisation, und das Reichskonkordat*. Innsbruck: Wagner, 1904.

Latreille, André. *Napoléon et le Saint-Siège (1801–1808)*. Paris: Alcan, 1935.

Leflon, Jean. *Pie VII: Des abbayes bénédictines à la papauté*. Paris: Plon, 1958.

Mayol de Lupe, Comte de. *La Captivité de Pie VII*. Paris: Émile-Paul, 1912.

Montor, Alexis François Artaud de. *Histoire du Pape Pie VII*. Paris: Lecler, 1836.

O'Dwyer, Margaret M. *The Papacy in the Age of Napoleon and the Restoration: Pius VII 1800–1823*. Lanham, Md.: University Press of America, 1985.

Olszamowska-Skowronska, Sophie, ed. *La correspondance des papes et des empereurs de Russie (1814–1878)*. Rome: Pontificia Università Gregoriana, 1970.

Pacca, Bartolomeo. *Historical Memoirs*. Trans. George Head. London: Longmans, 1850.

Petrocchi, Massimo. *La restaurazione, il Cardinale Consalvi, e la riforma del 1816*. Florence: Le Monnier, 1941.

———. *La restaurazione romana, 1815–1823*. Florence: Le Monnier, 1943.

Reinerman, Alan J. *Austria and the Papacy in the Age of Metternich*. Vol. 1, *Between Conflict and Co-operation, 1809–1830*. Washington, D.C.: Catholic University of America Press, 1979.

Rinieri, Ilario. *La diplomazia pontificia nel XIX secolo*. 5 vols. Turin: Unione Tipografico, 1901–06.

Schmidlin, Josef. *Papstgeschichte der neuesten Zeit*. Vol. 1, *Pius VII*. Munich: Herder Kösel-Pustet, 1933.

Walsh, Henry H. *The Concordat of 1801*. New York: Columbia University Press, 1933.

PIUS IX (1846–78): THE LAST "POPE-KING"

FRANK J. COPPA

Pius IX is the longest-reigning pope, in the modern age one of the most memorable and controversial, and one of the central figures of the nineteenth century. He is known not only for his reorganization of the papacy and orientation of the church, but also for his profound political impact in Europe and the world beyond in the nineteenth and twentieth centuries. More than any other figure, Pius IX shaped the character of the Catholic church and the papacy prior to the convocation of the Second Vatican Council (1962–65). Ruler of the Papal States until their disappearance in 1870 and head of the church from 1846 to 1878, he influenced both the Risorgimento, the movement for Italian unification, and the counter-Risorgimento, the intransigent papal opposition to the unification of the peninsula. This pope wholeheartedly championed ultramontanism, marked by a centralization of authority in Rome and the papacy. Among other things, he defined the Immaculate Conception of Mary as born without original sin (1854), condemned the ideologies of liberalism, naturalism, nationalism, socialism, and communism (1864), convoked the First Vatican Council (1869–70), and encouraged it to proclaim papal infallibility (18 July 1890).

Waging war against secular practices and policies he deplored in the modern world, Pius lost the Papal States, but responded by increasing centralization in the church, championing ultramontanism, and creating the structure of the modern papacy. Pius refused to accept the loss of his territory, declaring himself a prisoner in the Vatican, where he remained until his death on 7 February 1878, thus creating the Roman Question, which was not resolved until 1929. Subsequent popes followed his course until the establishment of Vatican City by the Lateran Accords of 1929, concluded between the Vatican of Pius XI and Mussolini's Italy. He likewise refused to bow to the anti-Catholic measures unleashed by Bismarck and his liberal allies in the *Kulturkampf* in the newly created German Empire.

Born in Senigallia, a small city in the Marches, not far from Ancona, he was the ninth child and fourth son of Count Girolamo Mastai-Ferretti and the former Caterina Solazzi. The family was noble but not wealthy, and the young Giovanni-Maria received his early education from his mother, who was devoted to Mary. In 1803, at the age of eleven, he was sent to St. Michael's School in Tuscany, administered by the Scolopi Fathers. In October 1809 his studies were interrupted by an attack of epilepsy which constrained the seventeen-year-old student to return home. Later he resumed his studies at the Roman College and at the end of 1815 decided to enter the priesthood. He was ordained in 1819 by special dispensation of Pius VII (1800–1823) because of his malady. Initiated into Jesuit spirituality from 1819 to 1821, he did not join the order, but acquired a deep appreciation of their mission and work. His first assignment was at the Roman orphanage of Tata Giovanni, where he remained until 1823. Subsequently, from 1823 to 1825 he took part in a papal mission to Chile and Peru to explore the prospect of Rome establishing relations with the former Spanish colonies and thus became the first to occupy the chair of Peter who had visited America. Upon his return to Rome he became the director of the Hospice of San Michele (1825–27). He served as archbishop of Spoleto from 1827 to 1832, was appointed bishop of Imola in 1832, and was granted the red hat by Gregory XVI in 1840. He was elected pope during the conclave of 1846 and assumed the name Pius in honor of Pius VII, who had also been bishop of Imola and who had provided Mastai-Ferretti with the dispensation that made his ordination possible.

The new pope understood the need for change in his states, where poverty was endemic, and workers and peasants confronted a deterioration in their pathetically low standard of living. Recognizing that the curia faced a revolution of discontent, he championed a limited reformism to prevent the outbreak of revolution. Although he was not a revolutionary or even a liberal and was ultraorthodox in religious matters, Pius was critical of the slow and ponderous Roman administration that provoked a constant round of conspiracy, revolt, and repression. He believed that the condition of the Papal States could be improved by infusing a bit of common sense and Christian justice into the government, calling for it to be better attuned to the aspiration of its people. Deploring the plight of the thousands of Jews who found their home in his state, he abolished some of the humiliating constrictions upon them and removed the restrictions that kept them locked in the ghetto. Pius also assisted the Jews of Rome with a sum of 300 scudi for the damage they sustained by the flood of the Tiber (1846–47) and allowed them to share the benefits of public charity.

Pius did not understand the opposition of Gregory XVI's government to the introduction of railways, the illumination of major streets, gas installations, the construction of suspension bridges, and the participation of Roman citizens in scientific congresses. He had cataloged his reformist program in a work entitled *Thoughts on the Administration of the Papal States*, in which he called for some collegiate body to advise and coordinate its administration. Many of its specifics were borrowed from the Memorandum of the Powers of 1831, in which France, Great Britain, Austria, Prussia, and Russia had suggested reforms to the Rome government. Pius promised to implement the changes that Gregory had resolutely rejected when he shelved the Memorandum of the Powers.

Italians responded to Pius IX's reformism by identifying him with the pope-liberator prophesied by Vincenzo Gioberti in his *Primato morale e civile degli Italiani* (On the civil and moral primacy of the Italians, 1843). This notion was confirmed by his appointment of Cardinal Pasquale Gizzi, considered a leading liberal, as his secretary of state, and his amnesty of 16 July 1846 of political prisoners. The July amnesty proved to be the spark that set Italy aflame, upsetting Metternich, who quipped that God pardons but does not grant amnesties. A new press law of 1846 permitted the publication of liberal and national sentiments and widely broadcast the startling changes introduced by the new pope. In 1847 Pius announced the formation of a consultative chamber or Consulta to advise him on administrative and political matters, and he instituted a council of ministers, which was permitted to discuss crucial state issues. Pius IX's reforms were enthusiastically received in the Papal States and throughout Italy, provoking demonstrations of public gratitude before the papal residence, the Quirinale Palace. Seduced by the public adulation, the pope did not perceive any danger in the fact that the Romans applauded their prince, who was also head of the

Pope Pius IX. (Courtesy of the Library of Congress)

church. Austria did not share his optimism. In Vienna Metternich worried that the adulation might lead the pope to introduce concessions that would weaken his government and pave the way for revolution.

Pius, in fact, recognized the need to limit his reformism, torn as he was between his obligation to protect the church and his desire to please his people and avert a revolution. Thus he had reservations about creating a civil guard, granting his people a constitution, and establishing a political league in Italy, but he reconsidered all three positions at the beginning of 1848, when the threat of revolution loomed over Italy and Europe. The guard was created, a constitution was drafted for the Papal States, and talks were opened with the other Italian princes for the formation of a political league. He agreed to the constitution only after a committee of ecclesiastics assured him that this was not only theologically permissible, but eminently practical and necessary. A virtual revolution was being waged in the pope's name, much to Pius IX's alarm.

While Pius reluctantly made these concessions, he could not control the consequences. For this, among other reasons, Pius refused to secularize his administration, introduce constitutionalism into the church, accord political rights to all inhabitants of his state, regardless of their religion, or wage war upon Catholic Austria. It proved difficult, if not impossible, to remain within these prescribed limits. The call for papal participation in the national crusade proved crucial, revealing the rift in his dual role as prince and priest. Pius felt constrained to favor the latter at the expense of the former. As an Italian, and perhaps even as a prince, Pius welcomed the national resurgence, but as head of the universal church, his first priority remained the preservation of its independence. Thus even though his cabinet urged him as prince to enter the war of national liberation, Pius followed the warning of the theologians, who judged such participation inadmissible for the pope. As predicted by his political advisors, the papal refusal to join the war of national liberation, announced in an allocution of 19 April 1848, provoked a revolution in Rome and led the pope to flee from his subjects to the Kingdom of Naples at the end of November 1848.

The explosive events of 1848 turned the pope, who would brook no interference with his spiritual power and resented limitations upon his temporal authority, against constitutionalism. Subconsciously he deemed his prerevolutionary flirtation with liberalism partly responsible for the violent outbreak of 1848 in Italy and warned of the grave consequences risked by ecclesiastics who sought the adulation of the masses. Pius admitted that initially he had been deceived by the call for legitimate change, but when he had granted more than was wise, his subjects had demanded more. The cycle had come to an end when the revolutionaries wanted him to wage an aggressive war, and his refusal had culminated in revolution and flight. During his exile, after long prayer, he had realized the incompatibility between constitutionalism and the governance of the church. Freedom of the press and liberty of association he likewise deemed suspect, fearing that they would lead to religious incredulity and social dissolution. His government abandoned other liberal concessions of the prerevolutionary period, restoring the restrictions upon the Jews, who could no longer leave their "usual residence" without a permit from the Holy Office. Preserving his commitment to the values of a vanishing world, Pius refused to adhere to the new national faith. In this fashion the reformist pope of 1846–48 turned into the conservative of the Second Restoration following the revolutionary upheaval of 1848–49.

Once Pius IX returned to Rome in 1850, the chastened pope concentrated on directing the affairs of the church while preserving papal authority. Refusing to return to the Quirinale, where he had been more of a prince, he opted instead to reside in the Vatican, leaving much of the political responsibility to his secretary of state and chief minister, Cardinal Giacomo Antonelli. Convinced that the church was menaced by the pernicious secularism of the age and the flagrant immorality associated with the modern philosophies, Pius sought solace in divine Scripture and the consolation of religion. As part of his counteroffensive, the curia was transformed as laymen and the more worldly clergy were removed. Asserting greater control over the bishops worldwide, this pope also favored centralization and uniformity in liturgical matters. In fact, by the time of his death in 1878, the Roman liturgy was all but universal. Unquestionably, Pius assured dogmatic unity in the church, but some questioned the price paid to do so. The seizure of most of his territory in 1859–60 and the loss of Rome a decade later he perceived as an integral part of the broader attack upon the church and its principles. He therefore proved unwilling to negotiate on the issue of the temporal power or accept its absorption into a united Italy because he considered it essential for the preservation of the church.

In the dozen years between the Restoration (1849) and the proclamation of the Kingdom of Italy (1861), Pius IX issued numerous condemnations of Cavour and his colleagues, responsible for Italian unification and the seizure of most of the Papal States. In 1864 he issued the encyclical *Quanta cura*, to which was appended the Syllabus of Errors, which rejected the notion that the temporal power should be abolished while denouncing liberalism, socialism, communism, nationalism, secret societies, and the separation of church and state. Pius was seen to align the papacy and the church against contemporary developments. The papal counteroffensive was continued by the convocation of the Vatican Council that culminated in the declaration of papal infallibility, even as the Italians seized Rome and made it their capital. Pius, who perceived the Holy See as the center of unity and symbol of order in the church, played an important role in the council and its proclamation of infallibility. In July 1871 the pope charged that some sought to distort the meaning and impact of infallibility in the attempt to turn princes and governments against the church and undermine religion.

In the eyes of some, Pius IX, heralded at his accession as a reformer who would reconcile liberty and religion, closed his pontificate as a reactionary and the "high priest of illiberalism." His broad and vocal condemnations ranged the church not only against the Risorgimento and Italian unification, but against much of the prevailing culture of the century. Furthermore, his opposition did not prevent Italian unification, did not stop the march of liberalism and nationalism, and put the church on a collision course with the modern world. His refusal in 1858 to return the Jewish boy Edgardo Levi Mortara, who had been secretly baptized by a Christian servant and seized by papal forces, to his parents scandalized Europe. The Mortara affair outraged public opinion in Europe and America, alienated Napoleon III, who served as protector of the pope, and thus worked to undermine the Papal States, which was condemned as medieval and out of touch with the modern world. Rejecting the national faith of the age, his conflict with liberalism and nationalism contributed to the Roman Question in Italy and the *Kulturkampf* in Germany.

Losing his state, Pius clearly failed as a prince. On the other hand, this pope always considered himself a priest first and a prince second, and his ecclesiastical accomplishments were more substantial. During his thirty-two-year pontificate he founded over two hundred new dioceses and erected thirty-three apostolic vicariates along with fifteen prefectures. He restored the Latin patriarchate in Jerusalem in 1847 and reestablished the hierarchy in England in 1850 and in the Netherlands in 1853. Devotion to the Blessed Virgin, to whom his mother had consecrated him as an infant, led Pius to favor the proclamation of the Immaculate Conception on 8 December 1854. This provided encouragement to the strong Marian movement in the nineteenth century and the development of Marian devotion in the twentieth.

Pius set up a special department within the Congregation of the Propagation of the Faith to deal with the Eastern-rite churches, even as he favored Thomism and centralization within the Latin church. His fervor for the missions led him to establish a special seminary for the training of missionary priests, under the Propagation, and to encourage missionary activity in the second half of the nineteenth and the early twentieth centuries. Following his death, there was talk of his beatification, and his cause was formally opened in 1954 by Pius XII. In 1985 John Paul II opened his cause for sainthood. Both decisions engendered controversy. The contentious debate was rekindled in the new millennium when word spread that Pius IX was soon to be proclaimed a saint alongside John XXIII, allegedly to balance this more liberal pontiff. At the beginning of September 2000, John Paul II beatified both Piux IX and John XXIII, the last formal step before canonization and sainthood. Ironically, the popes who had somewhat different visions of the church, and who respectively convoked Vatican Council I and Vatican Council II to implement their positions, were honored simultaneously.

Controversy is also found in the historiography on Pius IX, with some writers continuing their "vendetta" against the pope perceived to be the "enemy of the Italian people" and the opponent of the "liberal movement within the church," while others have extolled Pius IX as the "Saint of God." Thus one might do well to consider the archival and primary sources on this controversial pope before delving into the more polemical secondary sources.

SELECTED BIBLIOGRAPHY

Acta Sanctae Sedis. Rome: Ex Typographia Polyglotta, 1865–1908.

Andreotti, Giulio. *La sciarada di Papa Mastai.* Milan: Rizzoli, 1967.

Atti del Sommo Pontefice Pio IX, felicemente regnante: Parte seconda che comprende i motu-proprii, chirografi editti, notificazioni, ec. per lo stato pontificio. Rome: Tipografia delle Belle Arti, 1857.

Aubert, Roger. *Le pontificat de Pie IX (1846–1878).* Paris: Bloud & Gay, 1952.

Barberi, Andrea. *Bullarii romani continuatio.* 19 vols. Rome: Camera Apostolica, 1835–57.

Bonghi, Ruggero. *Pio IX e il papa futuro.* Milan: Treves, 1877.

Brennan, Richard. *A Popular Life of Our Holy Father Pope Pius the Ninth.* New York: Benziger, 1877.

Brown-Olf, Lillian. *Their Name Is Pius: Portraits of Five Great Modern Popes.* Milwaukee: Bruce, 1941.

Butler, Cuthbert. *The Vatican Council: The Story Told from Inside in Bishop Ullathorne's Letters.* New York: Longmans, Green & Co., 1930.

Carlen, Claudia, ed. *The Papal Encyclicals, I: 1740–1878.* Wilmington, N.C.: McGrath Publishing, 1981.

Castelli, Michelangelo. *Ricordi di Michelangelo Castelli (1847–1875).* Ed. Luigi Chiala. Turin: Roux, 1888.

Chadwick, Owen. *A History of the Popes, 1830–1914.* Oxford: Clarendon Press, 1998.

———. *The Popes and European Revolution.* Oxford: Clarendon Press, 1981.

Coppa, Frank J. *Cardinal Giacomo Antonelli and Papal Politics in European Affairs.* Albany: State University of New York Press, 1990.

———. "Pessimism and Traditionalism in the Personality and Policies of Pio Nono." *Journal of Italian History* 2 (Autumn 1979): 209–17.

———. *Pope Pius IX: Crusader in a Secular Age.* Boston: Twayne Publishers, 1979.

Corrigan, Raymond. *The Church and the Nineteenth Century.* Milwaukee: Bruce Publishing Company, 1938.

Crispolti, Filippo. *Pio IX, Leone XIII, Pio X, Benedetto XV: Ricordi personali.* Milan: Treves, 1932.

De Cesare, Raffaele. *The Last Days of Papal Rome, 1850–1870*. Trans. Helen Zimmern. London: Constable & Co., 1909.

De Franciscis, Pasquale, ed. *Discorsi del sommo pontefice Pio LX pronunziati in Vaticano ai fedeli di Roma e dell'orbe dal principio della sua prigionia fino al presente.* 4 vols. Rome: G. Aurelj, 1872–1878.

Demarco, Domenico. *Pio IX e la rivoluzione del 1848: Saggio di storia economicosociale*. Modena: Società Tipografia Modenese, 1947.

Farini, Luigi Carlo. *Lo stato romano dall' anno 1815 al 1850*. 3rd ed. Florence: Le Monnier, 1853.

Fernessole, Pierre. *Pie IX, pape, 1792–1878*. 2 vols. Paris: P. Lethielleux, 1960–63.

Filipuzzi, Angelo. *Pio IX e la politica austriaca in Italia dal 1815 al 1848*. Florence: Le Monnier, 1958.

Gabriele, Mariano, ed. *Il Carteggio Antonelli-Sacconi (1858–1860)*. Rome: Istituto per la Storia del Risorgimento Italiano, 1962.

Ghisalberti, Carlo. "Il Consiglio di Stato di Pio IX: Nota storia giuridica." *Studi Romani* 2 (1954): 55–68.

Hales, E.E.Y. *Pio Nono: A Study in European Politics and Religion in the Nineteenth Century*. Garden City, N.Y.: Doubleday, 1962.

Hasler, August Bernhard. *How the Pope Became Infallible: Pius IX and the Politics of Persuasion*. Trans. Peter Heinegg. Garden City, N.Y.: Doubleday, 1981.

Hassard, John R.G. *The Life of Pope Pius IX*. New York: Catholic Publication Society, 1878.

Hayward, Fernand. *Pie IX et son temps*. Paris: Plon, 1948.

Kertzer, David I. *The Kidnapping of Edgardo Mortara*. New York: Knopf, 1997.

Leti, Giuseppe. *Roma e lo Stato Pontificio dal 1849 al 1870*. Ascoli Picenso: G. Cesari Editore, 1911.

Maioli, Giovanni, ed. *Pio IX da vescovo a pontefice: Lettere al Card. Luigi Amat. Agosto 1839–Luglio 1848*. Modena: Società Tipografia Modenese, 1949.

Martina, Giacomo. *Pio IX: Chiesa e mondo moderno*. Rome: Studium, 1976.

———. *Pio IX (1846–1850)*. Rome: Pontificia Università Gregoriana, 1974.

———. *Pio IX (1851–1866)*. Rome: Pontificia Università Gregoriana, 1986.

———. *Pio IX (1867–1878)*. Rome: Pontificia Università Gregoriana, 1990.

Martini, Angelo, ed. *Studi sulla questione romana e la conciliazione*. Rome: Cinque Lune, 1963.

Monti, Antonio. *Pio IX nel Risorgimento Italiano con documenti inediti illustrazioni*. Bari: Laterza, 1928.

Mourret, Fernand. *Le concile du Vatican d'après des documents inédits*. Paris: Bloud & Gay, 1919.

O'Reilly, Bernard. *A Life of Pius IX down to the Episcopal Jubilee of 1877*. New York: Collier, 1878.

Pasolini, Giuseppe. *Memorie, 1815–1876*. Ed. Pietro Desiderio Pasolini. Turin: Bocca, 1887.

Pii IX Pontificis Maxima acta. 9 vols. Rome: Atrium, 1854–1875.

Pirri, P. Pietro. *La laicizzazione dello Stato Sardo*. Rome: Pontificia Università Gregoriana, 1944.

———, ed. *La Questione Romana*. Rome: Pontificia Università Gregoriana, 1951.

Radice, Gianfranco. *Pio IX e Antonio Rosmini*. Vatican City: Libreria Editrice Vaticana, 1974.

Rava, Luigi, ed. *Epistolario di Luigi Carlo Farini*. Bologna: Zanichelli, 1911.

Rosmini, Antonio. *Della missione a Roma*. Turin: Paravia, 1881.

Rossi, Ernesto, ed. *Il Sillabo*. Florence: Parenti Editore, 1957.

Scott, Ivan. *The Roman Question and the Powers, 1848–1865*. The Hague: Martinus Nijhoff, 1969.

Serafini, Alberto. *Pio Nono: Giovanni Maria Mastai Ferretti dalla giovinezza alla morte nei suoi scritti e discorsi editi e inediti*. Vol. 1. Vatican City: Tipografia Poliglotta Vaticana, 1958.

Shea, John Gilmary. *The Life of Pope Pius IX and the Great Events in the History of the Church during His Pontificate*. New York: Thomas Kelly, 1878.

Thornton, Francis Beauschesne. *Cross upon Cross: The Life of Pope Pius IX*. New York: Benziger Brothers, 1955.

Vercesi, Ernesto. *Pio IX*. Milan: Corbaccio, 1930.

Wollemborg, Leo. "Lo statuto pontificio nel quadro constituzione del 1848." *Rassegna storica del Risorgimento* 22 (October 1935): 527–94.

LEO XIII (1878–1903): THE WORKING MAN'S POPE

Emiliana P. Noether

Pope Leo XIII (1878–1903) was born Vincenzo Gioacchino Pecci on 2 March 1810 at Carpineto Romano, province of Sabina (Papal States), into a noble family originally from Siena. His father Domenico Pecci had served in the Napoleonic army and had achieved the rank of colonel. His mother, Anna Prosperi, a deeply religious woman, belonged to the Third Order of St. Francis. With his elder brother Giuseppe (who also entered the church and became a cardinal), Vincenzo studied under the Jesuits at Viterbo from 1818 to 1823 and then continued his education at the Collegio Romano in Rome. In 1832, having completed his doctorate in theology, he was admitted to the Accademia dei Nobili Ecclesiastici, where members of the church from noble families prepared for a career in the church's diplomatic corps. He studied canon law at the University La Sapienza and filled several minor ecclesiastical offices to which Pope Gregory XVI appointed him by way of apprenticeship.

Ordained a priest on 31 December 1837, he was designated in February 1838 apostolic delegate to the small papal enclave of Benevento in southern Italy, then plagued by bandits, smugglers, and agitations by Mazzini's early disciples. There, despite his youth and relative inexperience, Pecci succeeded in restoring a modicum of order and curbing the most extreme manifestations of lawlessness. His next assignment came in 1841 with appointment as papal delegate to Perugia, a center of antipapal secret societies. Again the young priest succeeded in assuaging the potential revolutionary upheavals and earned a reputation as a social and municipal reformer.

Reflecting the growing esteem that he enjoyed at the papal court, his next appointment came in February 1843 when he was consecrated a bishop and named papal nuncio to Belgium. At that time the Jesuits and the Catholic University at Louvain were involved in a bitter conflict, a dispute Pecci, despite his many efforts at mediation, did not succeed in resolving completely. His three years in Brussels, however, expanded his political and diplomatic horizons beyond the somewhat limited perspectives offered by the Italy of the 1840s. King Leopold I, uncle of Queen Victoria, valued him highly and presented him to the English queen and her consort Albert on the young couple's visit to Belgium. At that time Bishop Pecci met many Englishmen, laying the basis for his later interest in bringing about a reconciliation between the Catholic and English churches, which, however, failed. He also met Archbishop Richard Whately of Dublin.

Remembering his moderate policies, the people and magistrates of Perugia petitioned at the beginning of 1846 that Pecci be appointed archbishop of their city and return to reside in it. But before going back to Italy, Pecci spent a month in London and two months in Paris, renewing old contacts and making new ones. Meanwhile, King Leopold requested that Pecci be given the cardinal's hat. Gregory XVI died before he could act on the recommendation, and Pecci's elevation to cardinal was delayed until 1853. Returning to Perugia, where he remained for some thirty years, Pecci devoted himself to his see. These years represented a turbulent period for Perugia and for Italy as a whole. A center of antipapal feeling, Perugia posed difficult challenges to Pecci. The situation became more complex after 1860. Then the formation of a unitary kingdom in Italy under Victor Emmanuel saw the end of papal rule in Perugia and the city's annexation to the new state. The changed political situation thus challenged the ingenuity of the papal representative, as new laws curtailed the authority of the church. Pecci opposed civil marriage and the confiscation of property belonging to religious orders. In 1870 he denounced the pope's loss of his temporal power and showed his opposition to the new political order by refusing to greet the king of Italy, Victor Emmanuel II, on the latter's visit to Perugia. Many of Pecci's policies and actions during his years in Perugia presaged the course he was to follow as pope. He devoted himself to elevating the intellectual and spiritual level of the clergy, and his pastoral letters during this period reveal an abiding concern for learning and social reform. In 1872 he established the Academy of St. Thomas Aquinas (later to be based in Rome), a clear indication of his abiding interest in Aquinan thought, and in 1875 he launched a program for diocesan missionaries.

As Pope Pius IX became increasingly opposed to the new forces shaping post-1848 Europe, Pecci walked a fine line, unwilling to join the reforming forces within the church, yet reluctant to support the reactionary tendencies in the papal court. A staunch supporter of the temporal power of the church, he was not ready to condemn all manifestations of the modern world. His restrained support of the Syllabus of Errors earned him for a time the displeasure of the pope. But in 1877, shortly after the death of Cardinal Antonelli, Pius IX appointed Cardinal Pecci to the important office of papal camerlengo, previously held by Cardinal Antonelli.

Theoretically, the camerlengo was disqualified from election to the papal throne. Practice proved otherwise at the conclave that followed the death of Pius IX on 7 February 1878. In a remarkably short time the cardinals elected Pecci on the third round of balloting on 20 February 1878, with forty-four out of sixty-one votes, or more than the mandatory two-thirds majority. What had inspired forty-four cardinals in their collective wisdom to choose the archbishop of Perugia, Pius IX's camerlengo, to lead them at such a crucial time in the history of the church? Relations were strained almost to the breaking point not only with Italy, but also with France's Third Republic and the new German Empire. The conclave itself, however, had been free from interference or pressure on the part of the European powers, whose attention was focused on the presence of a Russian army at the gates of Constantinople. Perhaps the fact that Pecci had only recently appeared at the papal court, after some three decades spent in Perugia, and thus had not intrigued in Rome made him a nonpartisan candidate.

Pope Leo XIII. (Courtesy of the Library of Congress)

It was rumored that he was chosen because of his age (he was then almost sixty-eight) and his frail health. The cardinals, it was said, wanted to prevent a hiatus in the leadership of the church at such a crucial time. Moreover, they did not want to elect another pope who would occupy the papal throne for an indeterminately long term. The various factions needed time to maneuver around a more powerful candidate. In short, they hoped for a short papal reign after the very long tenure of Pius IX. Cardinal Pecci appeared a good interim candidate. He enjoyed a good reputation. He was known to be a devout churchman and a circumspect administrator. His opposition to the new rulers of united

Italy and his support of the church's temporal power made him acceptable to conservative cardinals. His accomplishments in raising the religious and intellectual level of the clergy in his diocese and his social orientation won him the support of progressive cardinals in the conclave. His unswerving support of the church's temporal authority satisfied conservative cardinals. Thus Vincenzo Gioacchino Pecci was crowned in the Sistine Chapel on 3 March 1878, taking the name of revered predecessors to become Pope Leo. If the cardinals had hoped for a short reign, they were disabused. Leo XIII occupied the papal throne for twenty-five years.

Almost immediately the new pope asserted himself. His first papal allocution of 28 March 1878 defended the rights of the church. He also introduced frugal and austere reforms in the papal household. To serve in it, he called to Rome from Perugia members of the clergy who had been trained by him and were completely devoted to his wishes. Over the ensuing years a series of important encyclicals informed the faithful of the new pope's views. *Aeterni patris* (4 August 1879) focused on the teachings of St. Thomas Aquinas. This was followed by *Arcanum divinae sapientiae* (10 February 1880), which discussed the sacred nature of marriage and denied the validity of state authority over marriage. *Humanum genus* (20 April 1884) condemned Freemasonry. *Immortali Dei* (1 November 1885) considered the Christian constitution of states. *Libertas praestantissimum* (20 June 1888) examined human liberty. While these encyclicals reveal the breadth of Leo XIII's interests, it was *Rerum novarum* (15 May 1891) that earned him the sobriquet of the "working man's pope" and gave him a distinctive place among modern popes.

Rerum novarum reflected not only the pope's personal concerns, but also the thinking of a select group of Catholic thinkers and reformers, led by the economist Giuseppe Toniolo. They were increasingly troubled by the absence of attention in the church to the growing human misery engendered by the new economic forces at work in the Western world. The encyclical had a lasting impact on the social thinking of the church and was memorialized forty years later in another important encyclical, *Quadragesimo anno*. It made clear that the church was not insensible to the profound social and economic changes that were transforming Western society, creating deep fissures between the classes. But some Catholics interpreted the pope's words as license to work for a Christian democratic party. Leo XIII condemned their efforts in the strongly worded encyclical *Graves de communi* (18 January 1901). They were reminded that Catholics should defer to the church in all matters of "social charity and Christian justice." Efforts to create political parties linking Christian principles to secular doctrines like democracy or even socialism were contrary to church policies.

Leo XIII assigned great importance to education, particularly of the clergy, an activity that had occupied him as bishop of Perugia. He encouraged stricter theological education of all Roman Catholic clergy throughout the world. But he was also concerned that the laity be better informed on church doctrines. He furthered the study of the philosophy of St. Thomas Aquinas, with its reconciliation of faith and reason, which had informed his first encyclical *Aeterni patris*. He financed to a large extent the preparation and publication of the works of St. Thomas in a magnificent edition and encouraged centers for neo-Thomistic studies abroad at Paris, Fribourg, Salzburg, and Louvain, and also at the Catholic University of America. He promoted the study of church history and in 1883 opened the Vatican Archives and Library to scholars, for he believed that the disclosure of archival documents would not harm the church. He encouraged Christian archaeology and biblical studies. Not neglecting science, he equipped the astronomical observatory at the Vatican with the most modern instruments and brought scientists to the Vatican.

One of Leo XIII's most ambitious projects was to advance unity among all Christian denominations. He courted England, hoping to bring about its return to the Catholic world, addressing a specific encyclical, *Ad Anglos* (14 April 1895), to the English. This was followed by a general encyclical on the unity of the church, *Satis cognitum* (29 June 1896). At about the same time he extended his attention to Scottish Catholics and discussed Home Rule and "Americanism" with representatives of Irish and American Catholics. Expanding the authority of the church overseas, he established a diocesan hierarchy in India, with seven bishoprics and the archbishop of Goa designated patriarch.

From his predecessor, Pius IX, Leo XIII inherited troubled relations with Italy, France, and Germany. In all three countries the forces of nationalism militated against the supranational claims of the church. To Leo XIII fell the task of reestablishing better, if not completely amicable, relations with the rulers of these states, whereby the rights of the church in certain areas of human activities would be recognized. While not overtly successful in Italy, Leo XIII did restore a degree of civil discourse with France (Ralliement) and Germany (end of *Kulturkampf*). To be sure, this was not on the level the church would have desired, but it at least enabled the church to enjoy some freedom in carrying out its religious mission and rescuing Catholics in these countries from public hostility and even persecution. While the conflict between church and state was fought over control of what the church felt lay within its domain, such as education and marriage, it was in essence a political rather than a religious confrontation. The state in each of these countries would not countenance any outside power, to wit, the church, having a role in the public life of its citizens.

In Italy the crucial issue separating church and state was the temporal power of the church, which the occupation of Rome by the forces of Victor Emmanuel in 1870 had effectively abolished. Pius IX had sought refuge in the Vatican and had declared himself a prisoner in it. This remained the official papal position until the Lateran Accords of 1929 between the Italian state and the church ended their extant state of public enmity. During the pontificate of Leo XIII the situation did not appreciably improve, though talks did go on desultorily behind the scenes among shadowy representatives of church and state. Inevitably, however, such talks foundered on the issue of the church's temporal power. Both sides inclined to occasional conciliatory gestures, which, however, were often negated by some hostile manifestation or pronouncement. Until 1881 Leo XIII entreated the European powers to champion the church against the often-violent anticlerical tumults in Italy. But with the signing of the Triple Alliance in 1882 among Catholic Austria, Germany, and Italy, the pope turned his attention to strengthening the position of the church internationally by healing the breaches with France and Germany. In Italy a modus vivendi was reached with the secular authorities. Religious instruction was introduced in public schools. Civil marriage remained mandatory, but Catholics also married in church. Catholics developed a network of social and economic organizations gathered under the umbrella of the Opera dei Congressi.

A determined effort to unite Germany in more than name began after the inauguration of the German Empire in 1871 under the leadership of Prussia and its "Iron Chancellor" Bismarck. Politics, more than religion, motivated the struggle between German Catholics and the new state. The former organized themselves as the Center Party in the Reichstag. Bismarck refused to allow what he saw as a potential opposition to his policies, which aimed at making the authority of the state supreme. The struggle between the two sides, defined as the *Kulturkampf*, began with the "Falk laws" or "May laws" of 1872–73 that established considerable control in Prussia over the Catholic clergy. As resistance grew against the laws, the state retaliated with fines, imprisonment, and in some cases exile. Clerical exemption from compulsory military service was abolished. Papal criticism was answered by suppressing all religious orders save the nursing orders. When Leo XIII became pope in 1878, more than 2,000 priests had been fined, numerous dioceses and parishes were vacant, and some 500,000 church members lacked religious guidance in Germany. Leo XIII, faced with enmity in Italy, set about reaching a rapprochement with Germany. Motivated perhaps as much by the fear of a rising militant socialism, Bismarck slowly abated his antichurch stance. In 1885 he accepted Leo XIII's mediation in the conflict between Germany and Spain over the Caroline Islands in the Pacific. The pope recognized Spanish sovereignty over the islands, but gave Germany economic rights in them. This resolution pleased Germany, opening the way to better relations with Rome. While the "Falk laws" were not immediately abrogated, their enforcement lagged, and by 1887 they were largely repealed.

The Third Republic of France rose from the debacle of Napoleon III's empire and the bloodshed of the Paris Commune. From the start it was plagued by profound political and ideological divisions between conservative monarchists, republican liberals, and radicals. Conservatives, who had strong ties to the Catholic church, controlled the Republic during the 1870s. By 1879, however, both legislative bodies fell into the hands of the Republicans, and attacks on the church, considered an ally of the reactionaries, began. In 1880 the Jesuit Order was disbanded. In 1882 Jules Ferry succeeded in getting the legislature to pass his comprehensive law that laicized primary education and made it free and compulsory. The Dreyfus Affair in the 1890s further exacerbated anticlerical opinion in France and led to confrontations between clericals and their critics. Despite Leo XIII's conciliatory attitude toward the Third French Republic, his efforts were thwarted both by reactionary French Catholics, who remained impervious to the pope's appeal to rally to the support of the Republic, and by the deep-rooted anticlericalism of France's Republicans, which had its origins in the eighteenth-century revolution.

Elected to the papacy at a time when the fortunes of the church were at a low point, Leo XIII reoriented it. At his death it was no longer associated with the obscurantism of the Syllabus of Errors. Rather, it was a morally and intellectually revitalized church that came into the hands of his successor, Pius X, in 1903. The years of Leo XIII's pontificate, from 1878 to 1903, witnessed profound changes in the political, economic, and social character of Europe. The pope recognized these changes. More important, he understood that the church faced a potential danger of becoming a fossilized relic of the past in a rapidly changing world. Unlike Pius IX, he did not resort to blanket condemnations of the new secular ideologies and ways. Rather, he sought means by which the church could point the way to an amelioration of existing inequities, as *Rerum novarum* did in discussing the plight of labor. To the new materialist philosophies he opposed the neo-Scholasticism of St. Thomas Aquinas. He emphasized the importance of having a well-educated clergy and encouraged the study of church history and archaeology, and biblical studies among the laity. While he remained a man of the nineteenth century in his view of the church's temporal position, he opened the way for the church to enter the twentieth century.

SELECTED BIBLIOGRAPHY

Acta Sanctae Sedis. Rome: Ex Typographia Polyglotta, yearly from 1865 to 1908.
Burton, Katherine. *Leo the Thirteenth: The First Modern Pope*. New York: David McKay Co., 1962.
Carlen, Claudia, ed. *A Guide to the Encyclicals of the Roman Pontiffs from Leo XIII to the Present Day, 1878–1937*. New York: H.W. Wilson Co., 1939.

————, ed. *The Papal Encyclicals*. Vol. II: *1878–1903*. Wilmington, N.C.: McGrath Publishing, 1981.

————, ed. *Papal Pronouncements: A Guide, 1740–1978*. Vol. 1, *Benedict XIV to Paul VI*. Ann Arbor, Mich.: Pierian Press, 1990.

Coppa, Frank J. *The Modern Papacy since 1789*. Longman History of the Papacy. London and New York: Longman, 1998.

Crispolti, Filippo. *Pio IX, Leone XIII, Pio X, Benedetto XV: Ricordi personali*. Milan: Treves, 1932.

Fogarty, Gerald P. *The Vatican and the Americanist Crisis: Denis J. O'Connell, American Agent in Rome, 1885–1903*. Rome: Università Gregoriana Editrice, 1974.

Gargan, Edward T. *Leo XIII and the Modern World*. New York: Sheed & Ward, 1961.

Gilson, Etienne, ed. *The Church Speaks to the Modern World: The Social Teachings of Leo XIII*. New York: Image Books, 1954.

Holmes, J. Derek. *The Papacy in the Modern World, 1914–1978*. New York: Crossroad Publishers, 1981.

Houtin, Albert. *L'Americanisme*. Paris: Libraire Emile Nourry, 1904.

Hughes, John Jay. *Absolutely Null and Utterly Void: The Papal Condemnation of Anglican Orders, 1896*. Washington, D.C.: Corpus Books, 1968.

Kiefer, William J. *Leo XIII: A Light from Heaven*. Milwaukee: Bruce Publishing Co., 1961.

Koenig, Harry C., ed. *Principles for Peace: Selections from Papal Documents, Leo XIII to Pius XII*. Washington, D.C.: National Catholic Welfare Conference, 1943.

Leonis XIII Pontificis Maxima acta. 23 vol. Rome: Ex Typographia Vaticana, 1881–1905.

McCarthy, Justin. *Pope Leo XIII*. New York: F. Warne Co., 1890.

Miller, J. Bleeker. *Leo XIII and Modern Civilization*. New York: Eskdale Press, 1897.

O'Reilly, Bernard. *Life of Leo XIII, from an Authentic Memoir Furnished by His Order*. New York: John Winston Co., 1903.

The Pope and the People: Select Letters and Addresses on Social Questions by Pope Leo XIII, Pope Pius X, Pope Benedict XV, and Pope Pius XI. London: Catholic Truth Society, 1932.

Quardt, Robert. *The Master Diplomat: From the Life of Leo XIII*. Staten Island, NY: Alba House, 1964.

Sanctissimi Domini Nostri Leonis Papae XIII allocutiones, epistolae, constitutiones. 7 vols. Bruges and Lille: Desclée, 1887–1906.

Schmidt-Volkmar, Erich. *Der Kulturkampf in Deutschland, 1871–1890*. Göttingen: Musterschmidt, 1962.

Shahan, Thomas Joseph. *Leo XIII and the Hague Conference*. Washington, D.C.: New Century Press, 1902.

Soderini, Eduardo. *Leo XIII, Italy, and France*. Trans. Barbara Barclay Carter. London: Burns, Oates & Washbourne, 1935.

Staab, Giles. *The Dignity of Man in Modern Papal Doctrine: Leo XIII to Pius XII,*

1878–1955. Washington, D.C.: Catholic University of America Press, 1957.

Stehlin, Stuart. *Bismarck and the Guelph Problem, 1866–1890*. The Hague: Nijhoff, 1973.

Talbot, James F. *Pope Leo XIII: His Life and Letters*. Boston: Gately & Co., 1886.

Wallace, Lillian Parker. *Leo XIII and the Rise of Socialism*. Durham, N.C.: Duke University Press, 1966.

Watzlawik, Joseph. *Leo XIII and the New Scholasticism*. Cebu City, Philippines: University of San Carlos, 1966.

Wynne, John J., ed. *The Great Encyclical Letters of Pope Leo XIII*. New York: Benziger Brothers, 1903.

PIUS X (1903–14): THE POPE OF THE CURIA

WILLIAM ROBERTS

Born into a large family of modest means in the northeastern Italian village of Riese, province of Treviso, on 2 June 1835, Giuseppe Melchiore Sarto was elected pope on 4 August 1903. With the exception of Gregory XVI, who had a middle-class background, Pius was the only pope since Sergius IV in the eleventh century not to be an aristocrat. When he was canonized in 1954, Pius was also the only pope since 1712 to be declared a saint. During his pontificate Pius X established a number of essential doctrinal, institutional, and juridical principles in modern Catholicism that would characterize the church until the period of Vatican II and its aftermath. Among these were a strongly hierarchical ecclesiology that stressed papal and sacerdotal authority as opposed to episcopal collegiality or the participation of the laity, a standardized catechism, a uniform code of canon law, and a restructured central or curial government. Wavering always between reaction and renewal, Pius X and his policies have frequently been the subject of controversy and various conflicting interpretations.

Until his election at the conclave of 1903, Giuseppe Sarto had spent his entire career since his ordination in 1858, with the exception of nine years at Mantua, entirely in his native region of the Veneto, a stronghold of orthodox Catholicism in Italy. For all of that time as a priest and bishop he was almost entirely preoccupied with purely pastoral problems. After his studies at the seminary of Padua he was ordained, serving first as a curate in Tombolo (1858) and later as pastor of Salzano (1867). In 1875 he became chancellor of the diocese of Treviso and spiritual director of the diocesan seminary. Consecrated bishop of Mantua in 1884, he was named cardinal patriarch of Venice by Pope Leo XIII in 1893.

Cardinal Sarto was chosen pope at the conclave that followed the death of Leo XIII in July 1903. Sixty-three cardinals were present at its opening on 31 July, and on the following day at the first ballot or scrutiny, twenty-four voted for Cardinal Rampolla, the former pope's secretary of state. Rampolla's vote was increased at the next scrutiny, but then on 2 August the Polish cardinal, Archbishop Puzyna of Cracow, announced a veto in the name of the Austrian emperor. There was a painful scene while Rampolla protested this unwarranted intervention, and at the next scrutiny his vote was even further increased. However, the voting subsequently turned in favor of the patriarch of Venice, and on 4 August, at the seventh scrutiny, he was elected by an overwhelming majority of fifty-nine votes. Neither Sarto nor anyone else had expected this surprising result. The new pope-elect pleaded to be excused, but at the persuasion of the other cardinals he submitted with the words "Accepto in crucem." He then told them that he would take the name of Pius in memory of those pontiffs, especially Pius VII and IX, who had always defended the interests of the church. It was, as in all such cases, a symbolic choice, even a type of nom de guerre, and in the case of Pius X would in many ways prove to be apt. It clearly marked the beginning of the reign of one of the modern church's more unyielding and often-intransigent pontiffs.

Even during his early career Giuseppe Sarto had been known as a conservative, totally opposed to secular liberalism and to any compromise between rationalism and religion. In 1890, as bishop of Mantua, he had, in fact, defined himself as "intransigent to the core." Nonetheless, because of his innate sense of the practical, he always tried to establish a respectful modus vivendi with the local authorities. This pragmatism led him, as Cardinal Sarto, to personally construct a coalition between Catholics and moderate liberals in the Venetian municipal elections of 1895. That action was due in large part to his strong distrust of autonomous Catholic political parties. Later, during his pontificate, this would also be a factor in his support for alliances between moderates and the church, especially in the Italian national elections of 1904, 1909, and 1913. In fact, it seems that his real wish was that such parties never exist at all. He once said of the German Center Party or Zentrum, for instance, even with all of its history of resistance to Bismarck's *Kulturkampf*, "I do not like it because it is a Catholic party." There were several reasons for this opposition. First, he believed that a mixture of politics and religion was a dangerous hybrid for the church; he saw the two as incompatible. Second, because such parties fostered the participation of priests in politics, he believed that a conflict with the priestly vocation would likely occur. Last, he thought that such parties were useless, as Catholics could always seek support for their causes from those lay parties that proved favorable, or at least not hostile, to the church.

In terms of church structure, Pius X began his reign with a series of reforms that would, with his other policies, make him the most expansive reformer inside the church since the Council of Trent. These were concentrated mostly in the first five years of his pontificate and were aimed at renewing ecclesiastical and curial structures and reinvigorating Catholic spirituality and faith. In 1904, for instance, the right of veto, historically held by Catholic powers, in particular the Habsburg state, over choices in papal elections was abolished, and a rule of absolute secrecy was imposed on the deliberations of any future conclaves.

In his first encyclical, *Instaurare omnia in Christo*, Pius X announced what was to be the guiding principle of his pontificate, "to restore all things in Christ." In this regard, with his chief concern being the internal problems of the church and the religious life of the laity, he was able to find a capable and sympathetic supporter in Monsignor Rafael Merry del Val, the son of a former secretary to the Spanish Legation in London, whom he made a cardinal and secretary of state in November 1903. As such, Merry del Val was to play a prominent role in the first international crisis of the pontificate, the question of the church in France, where the policy of the radical Republicans was moving toward the inevitable separation of church and state. In fact, in the last years of Leo XIII the Holy See had already been engaged in a controversy with the French government over the interpretation of the clauses in the concordat of 1801 relating to the nomination of bishops and other matters of ecclesiastical rights and properties. Under Pius X a final crisis was provoked by the events of late 1903 and early 1904.

Painting of Pope Pius X by Pierl-Daronco. (Courtesy of the Vatican Library)

In 1903 the king of Italy, Victor Emmanuel III, paid a state visit to Paris. In response, the Holy See found it necessary to protest what it regarded as a public and formal recognition of the Italian king's sovereignty over Rome. In the following year the French president Émile Loubert returned the visit. Cardinal Merry del Val renewed the earlier protest in a letter that he unwisely allowed to be published in the French press. In response, the French government in July withdrew the staff of its embassy from Rome and severed diplomatic relations.

The French Republicans now pressed forward with plans for a law of separation, and as a preliminary measure it was deemed necessary to make provisions for the church's property and resources that were to be taken over by the state. To achieve this, the government proposed the formation of a number of *associations culturelles*, lay committees that were to be charged with the administration of the confiscated property on behalf of the state and were also to make provisions for the maintenance of the clergy and of public worship. One article in particular of the new law excluded the ecclesiastical authorities from any effective control over the associations. The French bishops were prepared to accept this situation, but not Pius. Nonetheless, the law of separation finally was passed in July 1905. In 1911 the Portuguese followed the French example and passed legislation providing for a separation of church and state.

In January of 1906, in his encyclical *Vehementer nos*, the pope protested against the unilateral denunciation of the concordat on the part of the French government as a violation of international law and an action incompatible with the divine constitution of the church and its essential rights. He argued that the law of separation in particular had disregarded the hierarchical nature of the church. Then, in defiance of the government, a few days later he consecrated fourteen new French bishops at the same time, while charging that the law encouraged schism. In fact, however, it seems that Rome actually was prepared to accept this legislation as a foregone conclusion, but was seeking to keep it confined to its stated limits and intentions. "We do not want any new Organic Articles," Pius protested in a private interview, referring to the limitations imposed on the church by Napoleon in his addendum to the concordat of 1801. In August, in a further action, Pius in his encyclical *Gravissimum* rejected the proposed regulations for the administration of church property.

But the separation of church and state in France did not prove to be the unmitigated evil that Rome feared at the time. Its most positive result was to free the church from the constant intervention of the state authority, as the church was to regain its freedom of action. It is to this pontiff's credit that he had refused to accept the compromise offered by the French government in the form of the associations. These would have given the secular authorities a jurisdictional control over the church that had been lost by the separation. Instead, the effect of the separation was to give the church full autonomy. As Pius supposedly said of the French bishops when reminded that they would now have to exist without the financial support of the state, "They will starve and go to heaven."

At the same time, between 1903 and 1904, Pius undertook his well-known liturgical reform of church music. In the encyclical *Tra le sollecitudini* he attacked what he saw as a scandalous secularization of the art form as practiced and performed in Catholic churches. Earlier composers of church music, inspired especially by opera and the theater, had decided that the best way to preserve the renown of various church choirs was to write music strongly influenced by these secular sources, in particular the opera. As a result, the congregations would often pay more attention to the music and the choir than to the liturgical services themselves. In many cases the liturgy had lost all of its sacred appeal and often became just an excuse for a concert. Pius's reform encouraged the restoration of Gregorian chant and polyphonic music. His purpose was to make the churches once again places of prayer and meditation centered on the liturgy itself. In fact, Pius already had behind him a record of similar reforms that he had successfully instituted when he had been archbishop in Venice.

Pius also initiated reforms in the sacramental life of the faithful. In a decree of 1905, *Sacra Tridentina Synodus*, he encouraged Catholics to practice frequent and even daily Communion, and in his statement of 1910, *Quam singulari*, he reduced substantially the age at which children were to be admitted to their first Communion. In all of these reforms can be seen Pius's concern that conformity and rote and the mere outward practice of religion were great evils to be overcome in the life of the church and its faithful. His actions in this regard were to enhance his image as a parish-priest pope, and a legend of sorts began to form that in spite of everything, he remained just that, a simple and humble pastor.

His reform of the curia, first undertaken in 1908, was itself based on other, more pragmatic concerns. Begun in the early years of his pontificate and promulgated in June 1908 in the apostolic constitution *Sapienti consilio*, Pius's efforts in that regard earned him the sometime title of "second founder of the Roman curia." In fact, the reform he initiated was not as radical or far-reaching as that phrase would denote. Instead, it was basically a technical reorganization of the various Vatican departments, with no other attempt to reform policies of recruitment, training, or personnel. However, the reforms he did undertake were truly essential, as the number of curial departments and subdepartments already had greatly multiplied under his immediate predecessors. They largely existed to provide posts for former officials of the civil pontifical administration who had been dismissed after the suppression of the Papal States. In redefining the curia's congregations and tribunals in this way, eliminating its obsolete offices, Pius definitely achieved a streamlining of the church's central administrative body. In the same spirit, he also undertook an important reform of canon law, thoroughly revising and recodifying it. The decision to begin this actually had been made in 1904, only a few months after his election, with the *motu proprio Arduum sane munus*, but the work was not completed until 1917, three years after his death. The final result of this effect was a new code of canon law comprising 2,414 articles.

The major crisis of Pius's reign concerned the modernist controversy. Presenting problems for the pontiff in theological, philosophical, and exegetic terms, modernism was actually a trend that had been developing within certain intellectual circles, especially in Western Europe and, to an extent, the United States. Essentially, it represented a growing dissatisfaction with what was seen as a static neo-Scholasticism and also a response to the development of evolutionary biological theory and new historical methodology, as well as the then not yet assimilated and changing relationship between the church and the social and political order.

Pius, intransigent as always in theological and philosophical matters, reacted with alarm to this liberalizing movement, which he perceived as an assault on dogma. After repeated warnings, he placed various suspect modernist writings on the Index. In the decree *Lamentabli* (3 July 1907) he branded modernism as a "synthesis of all heresies," and in the encyclical *Pascendi* (8 September 1907) he officially condemned sixty-five modernist propositions. This suppression finally was completed in a *motu proprio, Sacrorum antistitum*, issued in September 1910, in which an oath disavowing modernism was imposed on the clergy. A widespread and controversial investigation of scholars then ensued that further increased the chasm between the church and the intelligentsia. The expulsion of all suspect professors from seminaries and the appointment of diocesan censors and vigilance committees further exacerbated the issue. The antimodernist crusade so absorbed the pontiff's attentions that he was directly compromised in some of its more extreme aspects, such as his support of Monsignor Umberto Benigni's Sodalitium Pianum, a secret ecclesiastical espionage network that existed outside the hierarchy.

This controversy, which had initially been precipitated by the now-famous book *L'Évangile et l'Église*, written by the French biblical scholar Abbé Loisy, would be seen by many as an overreaction to what was much more an intellectual trend than an open assault on church authority or a heresy, as it was then viewed by Rome. In fact, modernism proved to be a short-lived issue, but the excessive response by the pope earned a reputation of reaction and paternalism for himself and his pontificate. However, this was balanced by the many constructive measures Pius had undertaken in terms of liturgical and curial reform and renovation.

In social and political terms, Pius's strict doctrinal orthodoxy and conservative views also led to a general distrust of any interconfessional labor or social organizations. In particular, this resulted in his condemnation of Romolo Murri's Christian Democratic movement in Italy and the Sillon of Marc Sangnier in France. Instead, Pius gave his support to the Catholic Action movement, which actually had its origins in his encyclical *Il fermo proposito* (1905). Moreover, his encouragement of electoral coalitions in Italy, based, as he had stated, on an alliance between clerical factions and "other honest defenders of order," was also to become the basis for his controversial protection of such groups as the Action Française. In all his political dealings Pius's concern was, of course, the religious interests of the church, thus explaining his various policies toward the secular sphere, as noted.

Known widely during his reign as a man of essential goodness and humanity, Pius X was often spoken of as a saint even before his death on 20 August 1914. Consequently, a process for his canonization was begun early, in 1923. Referred to as the "pope of the Eucharist" as well as the "pope of the curia," he was beatified on 3 June 1951 and canonized on 29 May 1954. His feast is celebrated on 21 August.

SELECTED BIBLIOGRAPHY

Aubert, Roger. "Documents sous le pontificat de Pie X relatifs au mouvement catholique italien." *Rivista di storia della Chiesa in Italia* 2, no. 3 (1948): 44–58.

Coppa, Frank J., ed. *Encyclopedia of the Vatican and Papacy*. Westport, Conn.: Greenwood Press, 1999.

Coppa, Frank J., and William Roberts, eds. *Modern Italian History: An Annotated Bibliography*. Westport, Conn.: Greenwood Press, 1990.

Dal-Gal, Girolamo. *Saint Pius X*. Trans. Thomas Murray. Dublin: M.H. Gill, 1954.

Falconi, Carlo. *The Popes in the Twentieth Century from Pius X to John XXIII*. Boston: Little, Brown, 1967.

John, Eric, ed. *The Popes: A Concise Biographical History*. New York: Macmillan, 1964.

Merry del Val, Cardinal Raphael. *Memories of Pope Pius X*. London: Burns, Oates, and Washbourne, 1939.

L'ordinamento dei seminari da s. Pio X a Pio XII. Vatican City: Tipografia Poliglotta Vaticana, 1958.

Roberts, William. "Napoleon, the Concordat of 1801, and Its Consequences." In *Controversial Concordats: The Vatican's Relations with Napoleon, Mussolini and Hitler*, ed. Frank J. Coppa. 34–80. Washington, D.C.: Catholic University of America Press, 1999.

Romana: Beatificationis et canonizationis Servi Dei Pii Papae X: Disquisitio circa quasdam obiectiones modum ugendi Servi dei respicientes in modernismi debellatione, una cum summario additionali ex officio compilato. Vatican City: Typis Polyglottis Vaticanis, 1950.

Romana: Beatificationis et Canonizationis Servi Dei Raphelis card. Merry del Val, secretarii status Sancti Pii Papae X. Vatican City: Typis Polyglottis Vaticanis, 1951.

Romanato, Gianpaolo. *Pio X: La vita di papa Sarto*. Milan: Rusconi, 1992.

BENEDICT XV (1914–22): POPE OF PEACE

Joseph A. Biesinger

Giacomo Della Chiesa (21 November 1854–22 January 1922), of an aristocratic Genoese family, was elected Pope Benedict XV on 3 September 1914. Even before Della Chiesa had entered the seminary in Genoa, he had completed a doctorate in civil law (1875). After his ordination on 21 December 1878 he earned doctorates in theology (1879) and canon law (1880). While attending the College for Noble Ecclesiastics in Rome, he was invited by Cardinal Rampolla del Tindaro, Leo XIII's secretary of state, to join the papal secretariat of state. In 1882 he became the personal secretary to Cardinal Rampolla who had been appointed papal nuncio to Spain. While there, Della Chiesa not only gained invaluable diplomatic experience, but also experience that would help him later to organize the Vatican relief agencies during World War I.

As undersecretary of state during 1901–2 he gained a reputation for shrewdness, was frequently consulted for his point of view, and exhibited a gracious sense of diplomacy. His fluency in French, German, and Spanish was an appropriate talent for a future pope. When Pius X was elected in 1903, Della Chiesa remained in the secretariat for four more years, but gently resisted the efforts of the new papal secretary, Rafael Merry del Val, to condemn some scholars. At the request of Merry del Val, Della Chiesa was encouraged by Pius X to accept the archbishopric of Bologna in 1907. Challenges of social unrest and socialist agitation confronted him there, and the Bolognese were disappointed over his physical appearance. Nonetheless, his pastoral solicitude and governance won him recognition. In 1914 he was elevated to cardinal just three months before being elected pope. Elected for his diplomatic skills to guide the church in time of war, he nonetheless manifested other characteristics befitting the vicar of Christ and apostle of peace to a war-torn world. A modest coronation took place in the Sistine Chapel.

Della Chiesa was diminutive and frail in appearance and was known as "il piccoletto" (the little gentleman). He walked with a limp due to an injury during childbirth that resulted in one eye, ear, and shoulder being noticeably higher. Nevertheless, it was said that as pope his bearing and presence were dignified and commanding, which made people lose awareness of his physical defects. His intellectual qualities included a remarkable memory that gave him a detailed recollection of people and events. Sometimes this was interpreted as minute attention to detail and reflective of a bureaucratic and uncreative mentality. He followed a rigorous routine, emphasizing punctuality. Certainly he was not a dynamic personality like his successor, Pius XI. Nonetheless, he manifested kindness, frankness, simplicity, and generosity even to his servants. He believed that everyone had a right to see the pope. It was said of him that he lacked the unction that was typical of ecclesiastics, although he was a man of sincere faith and piety. In conversation he could be witty, ironic, and usually friendly. Some observers thought that he was personally magnetic. Unlike Leo XIII, Benedict could make jokes about himself and was extremely generous with his money. As archbishop of Bologna and as pope, Benedict exhibited considerable pastoral solicitude.

The conflict between the modernists and the integralists had done great damage to the church in the seven years before Benedict's coronation. Among his notable achievements as pope was his peacemaking efforts among church factions, attempting to reconcile their opposing theological positions. He nonetheless continued to be a staunch antimodernist. In his first encyclical, *Ad Beatissimi*, Benedict renewed the condemnation of modernism as a "synthesis of all heresies." Benedict did condemn, however, the practices of the integral Catholics who questioned legitimate differences of opinion within the church over what had not been officially declared to be dogma. The integralists rigorously defended the past, opposed democracy, and supported absolute authority of the church against liberal tendencies and individual freedom. Earlier, as undersecretary of state, Monsignor Della Chiesa had opposed their methods in the Sodality (Sodalitium Pianum or Sapiniere) of Pius X, which has been thought to be the reason for his transfer to Bologna. While he was archbishop, Della Chiesa became very careful to avoid actions that the integralists could criticize. In his attempts to restrict the divisiveness of the integralists, Benedict fused the Congregation of the Index with that of the Holy Office. The integralist publication, *La Sapinière*, ceased publication, and in December 1921 the Sodality of Pius was disbanded.

Shortly after his coronation Benedict announced that he intended to intervene in the war in every possible way to bring it to an end. War horrified him, and he declared that it was the scourge of the wrath of God. In his first encyclical, *Ad Beatissimi*, issued on All Saints' Day 1914, Benedict repeated his hatred and condemnation of war. The encyclical also expressed the hopes and goals of his pontificate. Principal among them was the establishment of international peace, harmony between social classes and between factions within the church, charity, and apostolic zeal. Not until three years later, on 15 June 1917, did he issue *Humani generis*, in which he emphasized the importance of utilizing Holy Scripture in preaching, which he faithfully practiced in his own allocutions. A knowledge of Scripture, he believed, was a fundamental condition for an effective sermon, and he condemned as an abuse the reference to profane literature instead of the Bible. In fact, Benedict can be credited with the significant emphasis that the church placed on the Bible in the twentieth century. Discussion clubs to study the Bible were organized. In the United States the translation of the New Testament by the Confraternity of Christian Doctrine resulted. In *Spiritus Paraclitus*, published on 30 September 1920, Benedict praised St. Jerome's emphasis on the Bible and deplored the dangers of modern relativism in biblical studies. The pope pointed out the dangerous and unwarranted distinctions between relative and absolute truth, the denial of the historic truth in the Bible, and the misuse of principles suggested by Leo XIII. Considerable emphasis was placed on the Bible's place in the education of the clergy. Most of his other encyclicals were published between 1919 and 1921 and included appeals for the children of the dead and wounded for the peace conference in Versailles, and principles for peace to be applied between nations.

Pope Benedict XV. (Courtesy of the Library of Congress)

Although the reform of canon law had been initiated by Pius X, Benedict was responsible for the publication of a comprehensive codification of canon law on 28 June 1917. It was an unprecedented accomplishment, containing 2,414 canons that were both analyzed and synthesized. Benedict established rules for the teaching of the code and founded the commission for its interpretation. One example of a code for which Benedict himself was responsible was canon 245, which eliminated the permanent commission that decided which tribunal or sacred congregation was competent in doubtful cases. The canon ordained that the pope would appoint a new commission for each such case. Besides changes in some of the legislation, he substituted clearer language in others. Another case, especially pertinent to France, involved the number of vicars-general allowed in a diocese. Canon 366, paragraph 3, limited them to one, as had earlier been required by the Fourth Lateran Council (1215). Especially applicable to the United States was the decree reforming the procedure for the selection of new bishops (25 July 1916). The decree reduced the time required for the appointment of a new bishop to a vacant diocese.

During Benedict's pontificate, progress was made toward reconciliation with the Italian state. Benedict was the first pope since Italian unification who did not place obstacles in the way of good relations with Italy. Although he was a pope in the universalist tradition of Leo XIII and Rampolla, he nonetheless realized that the papacy's nineteenth-century policies toward the Italian state had become obsolete.

During World War I Benedict refused to embarrass the Italian government by trying to solve the "Roman Question" by international means. Nevertheless, he protested being a "prisoner in the Vatican" and deplored the restrictions that the war imposed on the church. When Italy entered the war, the Italian government promised to observe the rights of the pope according to the Law of Guarantees. Although the Italian government allowed the Prussian and Bavarian envoys to remain at the Vatican, they were required to communicate with their governments through the diplomatic service of the Holy See. This proved unacceptable, and they removed themselves to Lugano, Switzerland. Nevertheless, Benedict demonstrated his love for Italy and expressed fear for its future. He visited the injured from the earthquake that shook Rome in 1915. He wept after learning of the humiliating defeat of the Italian army at Caporetto in 1917. He recognized the king of Italy as "his majesty," whereas the Vatican had previously referred to him only as the "duke of Savoy." Departing from Vatican policy that the pope should not meet with world leaders who had visited with the king of Italy or with representatives of Protestant denominations, Benedict met with President Woodrow Wilson. In his encyclical *Pacem Dei munus* (23 May 1920) the pope also permitted Catholic rulers to henceforth visit with the Italian king. Finally, it was during the last year of Benedict's life that the pope urged his secretary of state, Cardinal Pietro Gasparri, to meet with Mussolini and discuss the conditions on which an accord might be concluded. Their meeting at the home of Count Santucci laid part of the foundation on which the 1929 Lateran Treaty would be based.

Reversing his predecessor's distrust of Catholic political parties that were independent of ecclesiastical control, Benedict permitted Don Luigi Sturzo to establish the Popular Party in December 1918. The dangers of a Communist or socialist government apparently encouraged this papal tolerance of the Popular Party. The party claimed to be politically independent of the Vatican, though it was led by a priest. Just prior to the 1919 Italian elections the pope removed the restrictions on Catholic political participation imposed by the *non expedit* (which specified that it was not expedient for Catholics in Italy to vote in national elections), allowing the Popular Party to win approximately 20 percent of the vote. Conservative Catholics opposed the party, and some Vatican officials preferred the organization Catholic Action. Relations between the Vatican and the Popular Party were initially harmonious, but became strained when the Popular Party did not share the Vatican's desire for a rapid solution to the Roman Question.

Benedict's apostolic zeal inspired him to radically reorganize the missionary activity of the church. In his encyclical *Maximum illud* (30 November 1919) he insisted on the establishment of native clergies and hierarchies. Breaking the church's connection with imperialism, Benedict condemned nationalism among missionaries and insisted that they respect native cultures. The defense of the church's missions at the Versailles Conference was placed in the hands of the pontifical representative, Monsignor Bonaventura Cerretti. He secured the rights of the church in the missions of the former German colonies. It was even more difficult to remove the church's missions in China from French protection. In 1918 the French reacted strongly to the appointment of a papal nuncio to Peking. The first pontifical representative arrived there only in 1922, during the pontificate of Pius XI. In order to establish native clergies and episcopates, Benedict reorganized the Society for the Propagation of the Faith and organized the Missionary Union of the Clergy. These efforts were continued by Pius XI, and by the beginning of World War II non-Europeans predominated in the hierarchy of the church.

World War I had calamitous consequences for Orthodox Christians in the East caused by the Bolshevik Revolution, the collapse of the Turkish empire, and the rise of Arab nationalism. While the hopes of Russian Catholics collapsed with the success of the Bolsheviks, Catholics in the Baltic states, Poland, and the Ukraine hoped for security for their religious freedom. As apostolic delegate to Poland, Lithuania, and Russia Benedict sent Monsignor Achille Ratti, the future Pius XI, who never entered Russia. On the other hand, the Bolshevik government sought to gain recognition from the Vatican, while the curia sought to safeguard the rights of the church and expand Catholic missionary efforts. The Vatican also desired to establish Catholic schools in Russia, which the regime refused to allow. As persecution escalated, negotiations ended in 1922.

The Vatican hoped for a rapprochement between Catholicism and the Eastern Orthodox church, and this was anticipated by the Apostolic Constitution that Benedict formulated for the Eastern rite and his apostolic letter favoring union of Eastern Christians with the Roman church. By removing the Eastern Uniate churches in 1917 from the competence of the Congregation of the Propagation of the Faith, Benedict reversed the Romanizing policies of Pius X, returning to the orientation of Leo XIII. He created the Sacred Congregation of the Eastern church (1917) as an independent department of the curia in order to protect the interests of Eastern Catholics. He also opened the newly formed Pontifical Institute for Oriental Studies to Orthodox students. Although Benedict expressed an interest in ecumenism, he forbade Catholic participation in organizations that promoted Christian unity. Nonetheless, Benedict continued the week of prayer for Christian unity.

Neutrality was the only realistic foreign policy for the pope during the war. Considering himself the spiritual father of all Christians, Benedict assumed a mediating role. His position was undoubtedly a difficult one, with Catholics on both sides. Although the nations of the Entente and the Central Powers sought to justify their positions and also gain the support of neutrals, Catholics would not have respected the pope's political intervention in this age of chauvinistic nationalism. If the pope had taken sides, he not only would have been required to morally, legally, and politically establish guilt or innocence, but he also would have jeopardized the interior unity of the church.

Benedict followed a policy of Christian pacifism and impartiality in the pursuit of peace. The new pope condemned the war on numerous occasions and repeatedly condemned the slaughter, cruelty, and injustices that the war perpetrated on its victims. His many pleas for peace began with his message of 8 September 1914. Appealing to the governments of the warring states not to pursue a military victory, he implored them to end the conflict with a just peace. Denying the applicability of the just-war theory, the pope believed that neither side fought from a position of justice. As the vicar of Christ and messenger of peace, he believed that war was an unnecessary evil and an immoral way for Christians to solve their conflicts. It was destructive not only of society but of the cause of Christ. He feared that a lengthy war, far from creating security, would inevitably lead to social revolution. He challenged the militaristic nationalism of Europe with his proposals for mutual disarmament and the abolition of general conscription. An international court of arbitration, freedom of communication and of the seas, and the establishment of an international organization of states were proposed to preserve peace.

Not unexpectedly, these proposals were rejected, and the pope was mistrusted and denounced by both sides for supporting the cause of the other. In his attempt to enlist the support of President Woodrow Wilson to end the war by returning to the prewar status quo, Benedict was unsuccessful. When the Vatican sought to keep Italy (1915) and the United States (1917) neutral, the Allies accused the papacy of favoring the Central Powers. Benedict did not take a stand on the moral guilt of Germany's violation of

Belgian neutrality, just as he did not on the Russian occupation of Galicia. Though the pope claimed that he had actually condemned the violation of Belgian neutrality with his categorical condemnation of violations of international law, the Allies considered this to be insufficient. The Germans received their share of papal criticism for sinking the *Lusitania* and the use of poison gas; impartially the pope chastised the perpetrators of both land and aerial bombardment of unfortified towns and the deportation of civilians. In 1915 Benedict's renowned prayer for world peace was recited throughout the world, yet it was not favorably received in France, where it was considered to be a threat to military morale.

The maintenance of Italian neutrality was of special importance to the Vatican, not only for the continuation of open lines of communication with the belligerents, but also for the administration of the universal church. Benedict secretly attempted to secure this by encouraging the Austrian government to cede the Trentino province to Italy as the price of continued neutrality. Negotiations were never successful, since both sides were too suspicious. The Italians had already signed the Treaty of London by which they were to join the Allies, and the Austrians were too mistrustful of Italian intentions.

Benedict's most important initiative was his famous peace note of 1 August 1917. It was not a detailed proposal, but rather a list of seven points that included the renunciation of the use of force, mutual disarmament, freedom of the seas, renunciation of reparations, the restoration of occupied territories, and international arbitration. The aim of Vatican diplomacy was to elicit a German promise of the restoration of Belgian independence, and the Austrian cessation of the Trentino to Italy. The new nuncio in Munich, Monsignor Eugenio Pacelli, was sent to Berlin to determine the German conditions for peace negotiations and was encouraged by the Kaiser's response. While the Allies were "cautious" and the German emperor was in favor of peace by Christmas, the appeal failed chiefly due to the continued refusal of the German government, especially Richard von Kühlmann of the Foreign Office, to restore the independence of Belgium. It is thought that this failed peace effort was the greatest disappointment of Benedict's pontificate.

On the day of his coronation the new pope already indicated what would be an area of notable accomplishment during his reign when a sizable amount of money was set aside for charitable purposes. His generous practice of Christian charity had already been evident when he was Cardinal Rampolla's secretary in Madrid and while he was archbishop of Bologna. It would be inaccurate to attribute his generosity to a progressive social conscience. Rather, his real motivation was the application of the teachings of the gospel combined with his belief that the upper classes should provide a Christian example to the lower and should be generous in their assistance to them. His personal donations usually exceeded what was asked of him.

The extensive needs that the killing and destruction of the war spawned demanded charity, to which Benedict impressively responded. The fifty pages that are devoted to these efforts by his biographer, Francesco Vistalli, serve as a testimonial to his extensive charitable work. Through every possible means the pope tried to help prisoners of war, the wounded, and refugees, acting as "a second Red Cross." Prisoners of war were hospitalized and exchanged, communications with families were established, and missing persons were sought. Numerous Catholic agencies were established, and hospital treatment was provided for the sick and wounded in Switzerland. Although he opposed the use of church property for military purposes, Benedict permitted the use of Catholic hospitals and schools by civil authorities. In 1915 French hostages were released due to papal pleas, and some Belgians in the hands of the Germans were spared execution. Large gifts of clothing, food, and medicine were distributed throughout Europe from France to Lithuania. Sometimes they were shipped in neutral vessels to at least ten countries affected by the war. Relief efforts even were made in Russia during the civil war and famine. The humanitarian measures of assistance to the Middle East, where more than a million people were massacred, deported, and starved, were without regard for religious, ethnic, or national membership. In recognition of this aid a monument for Benedict was erected in Constantinople during 1921 and an orphanage was named after him. All the various charitable enterprises, estimated to have required an expenditure of more than 82 million gold lire, left the Vatican treasury almost empty by 1922.

While Benedict had initially hoped for an invitation to the peace conference, the Vatican's participation at Versailles was prevented by the Italian government. Benedict had hoped for a postwar Europe in which no power would be dominant, and that the treaties would not arbitrarily impose a harsh peace on the defeated powers. The pope was disappointed in the dictated Treaty of Versailles, which was contrary to the moral and humanitarian ideals and goals of Benedict with its imposed territorial losses, reparations burdens, and lack of diplomatic balance in Europe. He favored the disarmament of both sides and a return of the German colonies. Although he favored the League of Nations, its restricted membership, which excluded the Vatican besides Germany and Russia, made him increasingly skeptical of its potential.

While the efforts of the Holy See had failed to bring about a negotiated peace, they had nonetheless given expression to the teachings of Christ in a wilderness of national hatreds and unprecedented technological destruction. Benedict's impartial Christian stand enhanced the stature of the papacy in the international community. Had the peace appeal of 1917 been accepted, millions of lives would have been spared. A Bolshevik dictatorship in Russia might have been avoided, as well as the rise of fascism and Nazism.

If diplomatic representation at the Vatican can be used as a guide, there was considerable improvement in the international stature of the papacy during Benedict's reign. His impartial Christian stand during the war enhanced the importance of the papacy in the international community. Between 1914 and the end of his pontificate in 1922 the number of states with representation at the Vatican rose from six to thirty-five. After the war ended, many new states desired diplomatic recognition that also secured their borders. Catholics were also preponderant in several newly independent nations, such as Ireland, Poland, Lithuania, and Czechoslovakia, and were numerous in Yugoslavia and Rumania. Although the church had earlier concluded concordats, a new age of concordats was initiated during Benedict's reign that was to be continued under Pius XI. Benedict also did a great deal to improve relations with such traditionally Catholic nations as France. In 1920, at the canonization of Joan of Arc, the French government reestablished diplomatic relations with the Vatican.

SELECTED BIBLIOGRAPHY

Acta Apostolicae Sedis. Vols. 6 (1914)–14 (1922).
Acta Sanctae Sedis. Vol. 16 (1883), "Saepenumero"; vol. 40 (1907), "Pascendi."
Althann, Robert. "Papal Mediation during the First World War." *Studies* (Ireland) 61, no. 243 (1972): 219–40.
Deuerlein, Ernst. "Zur Friedensaktion Papst Benedikts XV." *Stimmen der Zeit* 155 (January 1955): 241–56.
De Waal, Anton. *Der neue Papst unser heiligen Vater Benedikt XV.* Hamm: Breer & Thiemann, 1915.
Falconi, Carlo. *The Popes in the Twentieth Century.* London: Weidenfeld & Nicolson, 1967.
Herber, Charles. "Eugenio Pacelli's Mission to Germany and the Papal Peace Proposals of 1917." *Catholic Historical Review* 65, no. 1 (1979): 20–48.
Holmes, Derek J. *The Papacy in the Modern World, 1914–1978.* New York: Crossroad Publishing, 1981.
Lama, Friedrich Ritter von. *Die Friedensvermittlung Papst Benedikts XV und ihre Vereitlung durch den deutschen Reichskanzler Michaelis.* Munich: Kossel and Pustet, 1932.
Migliori, Giambattista. *Benedetto XV.* 2nd ed. Milan: 1955.
Peters, Walter H. *The Life of Benedict XV.* Milwaukee: Bruce Publishing, 1959.
Pollard, John F. *The Unknown Pope: Benedict XV (1914–1922) and the Pursuit of Peace.* London: Geoffrey Chapman, 1999.
Rope, Henry E.G. *Benedict XV, the Pope of Peace.* London: Catholic Book Club, 1940.
Rossini, Giuseppe. *Benedetto XV, cattolici, e la Prima Guerra Mondiale.* Rome: Edizoni 5 Lune, 1963.
Steglich, Wolfgang, ed. *Der Friedensappell Papst Benedikts XV vom 1 August 1917 und die Mittelmächte.* Wiesbaden: Franz Steiner Verlag, 1970.

Stehle, Hansjakob. *Eastern Politics of the Vatican, 1917–1979.* Trans. Sandra Smith. Athens: Ohio University Press, 1981.

Stehlin, Stewart H. "The Emergence of a New Vatican Diplomacy during the Great War and Its Aftermath, 1914–1929." In *Papal Diplomacy in the Modern Age.* Ed. Peter C. Kent and John F. Pollard. 75–85. Westport, Conn.: Praeger, 1994.

———. "Germany and the Proposed Vatican State, 1915–1917." *Catholic Historical Review* 60, no. 3 (1974): 402–26.

———. *Weimar and the Vatican, 1919–1933: German-Vatican Diplomatic Relations in the Interwar Years.* Princeton: Princeton University Press, 1983.

Vistalli, Francesco. *Benedetto XV.* Rome: Tipografia Poliglotta Vaticana, 1928.

Volk, Ludwig. "Kardinal Mercier, der Deutsche Episkopat, und die Neutralitätspolitik Benedikts XV, 1914–1916." *Stimmen der Zeit* 192 (1974): 611–30.

PIUS XI (1922–39): THE KINGSHIP OF CHRIST IN THE TWENTIETH CENTURY

PETER C. KENT

Pope Pius XI, between 1922 and 1939, effectively established the infrastructure and the direction for the Roman Catholic church for the balance of the twentieth century. Not only did Pius XI restore the temporal power of the papacy through the creation of Vatican City as a sovereign state, he also demonstrated a way for the church to contend with the secular materialism of the modern world that was becoming ever more pervasive in the twentieth century. The promotion by Pius XI of the Catholic Action movement as an apostolate of the laity to infuse the modern world with the spirit of the kingship of Christ was directly responsible for the emergence of Christian democracy as the dominant political movement in Europe after 1945. Within the church, participation in the life of the modern world was stimulated by Pius XI and culminated in the convocation of the Second Vatican Council by Pope John XXIII in 1962, ending the period of the Catholic "ghetto" and making the church more accessible to the laity of the late twentieth century.

The continuing influence of Pius XI in the latter years of the twentieth century was best symbolized by the election of Giovanni Battista Montini as Pope Paul VI in 1963. Montini was very much a product of the mission of Pius XI, having been active in the Italian Catholic Action movement under Pius XI, where he served as chaplain to the Association of Catholic University Students (FUCI) and was intimate with many of the future leaders of Italian Christian democracy. The effectiveness and presence of the Roman Catholic church in the world after 1945 was also due to its alliance with the capitalist West in the bipolar world of the Cold War.

When that bipolar world ended in 1989, the legacy of Pius XI faced its supreme test, under Pope John Paul II, of attempting to restrain the rampant secular materialism of contemporary capitalist society in the name of the kingship of Christ.

Ambrogio Damiano Achille Ratti was born at Desio, Lombardy, near Milan, on 31 May 1857, the fourth son of Francesco Ratti, a silk-factory manager, and Teresa Ratti. Educated at various schools and seminaries in Lombardy, Achille Ratti was trained for the priesthood in Milan and was ordained priest on 27 December 1879. His early life was noted for his love of, and skill at, mountain climbing, which led him, in the 1880s, to undertake the first Italian ascent of the Dufour peak of Monte Rosa in northern Italy. After teaching for six years at the seminary in Milan, Ratti was transferred to the staff of Milan's Ambrosian Library, where, proficient as both a scholar and an administrator, he became its prefect in 1907. In 1911 he was transferred to the Vatican Library as vice-prefect and in 1914 was named to the post of prefect.

In 1918 Achille Ratti's career as a scholar and librarian was interrupted when he received an important diplomatic appointment as apostolic visitor to Poland and, subsequently, as the first papal nuncio to the new Polish Republic. His task in Poland involved re-creating the organizational structure of the Roman Catholic church in a country that had been restored after being divided among the Prussian, Austrian, and Russian empires for over a century. The success of Ratti's mission to Poland ensured his 1921 appointment as archbishop of Milan, the second most important see in Italy. Pope Benedict XV died the next year, and Ratti was elected to succeed him as Pope Pius XI in February 1922.

From the beginning of his reign in 1922 Pius XI deliberately challenged the secularization of the age in which he lived, promoting a Christian reconquest of the world, through which Christian values would permeate modern society. He spoke of the "Peace of Christ in the reign of Christ." Pius XI believed that the problems confronting the world after 1918 could be traced to the attractions of materialism and secularism, which caused people to lose all sense of spiritual authority and belief in a higher power. After the horrors of the Great War, true peace would not return to the world, Pius claimed, until humanity turned once again to Jesus Christ. The papal message was adapted to the crises faced during that period—first, in relation to the unsettled legacy of the war and the Bolshevik Revolution, and second, in the context of the Great Depression and the increasing polarization of the 1930s that culminated in World War II.

This central objective of the pontificate formed the substance of Pius XI's first encyclical, *Ubi arcano Dei* of December 1922, and informed every action of this pope. To prepare the church for the task of restoring spiritual belief, Pius first concentrated on the training and preparation of the clergy, stressing the importance of sound scholarship and an awareness of modern developments in science and technology as a part of clerical education. Pius also believed that the laity must do their part in creating the "Kingship of Christ" and promoted the Catholic Action movement as the apostolate of the laity in order to permeate modern society with Christian values through separate Catholic lay organizations for men, women, and youth.

If the clergy and the laity were to enhance the spirituality of modern society, they had to do so in a world of secular states. The destruction of the Austro-Hungarian Empire in 1918 marked the end of the last great Catholic empire. It was clear to the pope that the security of the Roman Catholic church within the modern state system could only be ensured by negotiating concordats with individual states to protect the rights and independence of the clergy, the integrity of Catholic education, and the continued existence of Catholic Action. During his reign a large number of concordats were concluded with various European states. Yet the pope soon became aware that his message was being poorly received in major Catholic states, such as France and Italy. Issues of nationalism and anticlericalism clouded assessments of the papal mission in France, while in Italy opinion was dominated by the need for a settlement of the Roman Question that had been festering since 1870, when the army of the new Kingdom of Italy captured Rome

Pope Pius XI. (Courtesy of the Library of Congress)

from the pope and eliminated the temporal power of the Holy See.

In 1926 Pius XI addressed both the French and Italian issues in dramatic fashion, seeking to capture the attention of the people of both France and Italy for his central religious message. In that year he publicly condemned the reactionary nationalism of Charles Maurras's Action Française, thereby signaling that henceforth the Holy See and the Catholic church would recognize and deal only with the government of the French Third Republic. Also in 1926 Pius XI authorized the opening of secret negotiations with Benito Mussolini's Fascist regime that led to the Lateran Agreements of 1929 with Italy. This *Conciliazione* with Italy resolved the Roman Question by the conclusion of a concordat, a treaty, and a financial agreement between the Holy See and the Kingdom of Italy. These agreements regulated the relationship between church and state in Italy, including guarantees for the independence of Catholic Action, and returned secular independence and authority to the pope through the creation of Vatican City as a sovereign state. With the conclusion of the Lateran Agreements, the first phase of the pontificate came to a close, since Pius XI had laid his base well, and public opinion appeared now to have a clearer grasp of the papal mission. The encyclical *Casti conubii* of 1930 offered important papal teaching on marriage, the family, and Christian education at a time when the pope believed that European Catholics would prove more receptive to his message.

The second half of the pontificate of Pius XI was contingent upon the social and political upheaval associated with the Great Depression of the 1930s. Initially the Holy See had seen the Russian Revolution of 1917 as an opportunity to send missionaries to Russia in an attempt to persuade members of the discredited Russian Orthodox church toward union with Rome. Promising dealings with the Bolshevik government in the 1920s became futile once Stalin took power and began persecuting Russia's Roman Catholics. With the onset of the Great Depression Pius XI feared that the ideological challenge of the Communists might find a response among the unemployed masses of Europe. To meet this threat, the Holy See launched an active campaign against Communist atheism in 1930. In the following year, through his encyclical *Quadragesimo anno*, Pius XI challenged traditional Marxism by reiterating the conciliatory nature of Catholic social policy, which advocated class collaboration rather than class conflict in times of social distress.

In 1931 a conflict arose in Italy when the Fascist Party, feeling threatened by the growing popularity of Catholic Action, sought to limit and control the activities of the latter organization. Pius XI stood his ground and denounced the Fascist regime in the encyclical *Non abbiamo bisogno*, defending the significance of the Catholic Action movement. This conflict was resolved in September 1931 when both parties recognized that a compromise was in their mutual interest. Relations between church and state in Italy continued in a relatively amicable fashion throughout the balance of the 1930s. The success of the Italian concordat, the fear of communism, and the culmination of a long series of negotiations with the federal and state governments of Germany led to the conclusion of a controversial concordat with that country in July 1933, barely six months after Adolf Hitler's National Socialists had come to power. The pope had been willing to sacrifice the German Center Party and to give gratuitous international recognition to Hitler's Nazi revolution in return for promises of protection of the Catholic church in Germany. Like many other Europeans, the pope soon found that Hitler's promises were worthless, as 1933 was barely finished before the Nazis began an active persecution of the Catholic church in spite of the guarantee of the concordat. Pius XI realized that the polarization of European society between Communist and Fascist supporters in the mid-1930s would only serve to drive more people into the Nazi fold. The pope also feared that Mussolini, through a closer association with Hitler, would decide to emulate the Nazi persecution of the church within Italy. Yet the papal position was not clear to many anti-Fascists, many of whom believed that Pius XI had sacrificed his principles by signing the concordat with Hitler and by seemingly condoning Mussolini's invasion and conquest of Abyssinia in 1935–36. It was only, in fact, in the final phase of his papacy, between 1937 and 1939, that Pius XI resolved his ambiguous position with regard to totalitarianism and the denial of Christian principles.

Once Hitler and Mussolini had celebrated the creation of the Rome-Berlin Axis in late 1936, the pope sought to undermine the relationship. He refused to recognize the Spanish Civil War, teaming Hitler and Mussolini against the forces of the Left, as an ideological crusade. Then, through a series of unequivocal gestures, the pope firmly established the principles for which he stood and for which he expected Christians to stand. In March 1937 Pius XI released three important encyclicals within days of one another. Two of these encyclicals denounced the totalitarians of the Left and the Right—*Divini redemptoris* against atheistic communism and *Mit brennender Sorge* against Nazism—while the third; *No es muy*, denounced Mexican persecution of the church. In the eyes of the pope, it was impossible to use Christian principles as a guide for living in a society that was ideologically polarized.

To deter the Italian people and others from close dealings with the Nazis, Pius XI publicly denounced Hitler and his acts in 1938. The pope despaired of the *Anschluss*, demonstrably left Rome on the eve of Hitler's visit to that city, and attacked the racism of the Nazis. Once again Pius XI addressed public opinion clearly and unambiguously, warning Italians away from the German alliance and, more important, standing against racism on the basis of its infringement of Christian teaching on human rights. Just before he died, he commissioned the draft of a new encyclical, *Humani generis unitas*, against racism and anti-Semitism, which, because of his death, was never issued. The papal message reached its culmination in 1938 when its values of human rights and peace were forcefully conveyed to world opinion.

Before his death in February 1939 Pius XI had warned the world of the threat that Nazi Germany posed to Christian civilization. The historical legacy of Pius XI lay in the manner in which he had developed and encouraged Catholic Action as an institution for the promotion of Christian values in the increasingly intolerant, militarist, and authoritarian political cultures of the 1930s. With the defeat of the Axis powers in World War II, the Catholic Action movement effectively replaced Nazism and fascism because it produced much of the Christian democratic political leadership, organization, and value structure in postwar Europe. After 1945 European Christian democracy stood as the vindication of Pius XI's commitment to a new infusion of Christian values into the secular world of the twentieth century.

SELECTED BIBLIOGRAPHY

Agostino, Marc. *Le Pape Pie XI et l'opinion (1922–1939)*. Rome: École française de Rome, 1991.

Binchy, D.A. *Church and State in Fascist Italy*. London: Oxford University Press, 1941.

Cavalleri, Ottavio, ed. *L'Archivio di Mons: Achille Ratti visitatore apostolico e nunzio a Varsavia (1918–1921): Inventario*. Vatican City: Archivio Vaticano, 1990.

Clonmore, Lord William. *Pope Pius XI and World Peace: An Authentic Biography*. London: Robert Hale, 1937.

Coppa, Frank J. *Controversial Concordats: The Vatican's Relations with Napoleon, Mussolini, and Hitler*. Washington, D.C.: Catholic University of America Press, 1999.

———. "The Hidden Encyclical of Pius XI against Racism and Anti-Semitism Uncovered—Once Again!" *Catholic Historical Review* 84 no. 1 (January 1998): 63–72.

———. "Pope Pius XI's 'Encyclical' *Humani Generis Unitas* against Racism and Anti-Semitism and the 'Silence' of Pope Pius XII." *Journal of Church and State* 40, no. 4 (Autumn 1998): 775–95.

Falconi, Carlo. *The Popes in the Twentieth Century: From Pius X to John XXIII*. Trans. Muriel Grindrod. London: Weidenfeld and Nicolson, 1967.

Fogarty, Gerald P. *The Vatican and the American Hierarchy from 1870 to 1965*. Stuttgart: Anton Hiersemann, 1982.

Hughes, Philip. *Pope Pius the Eleventh*. New York: Sheed & Ward, 1937.

Kent, Peter C. "Between Rome and London: Pius XI, the Catholic Church, and the Abyssinian Crisis of 1935–36." *International History Review* vol. 11, no. 2 (May 1989): 252–71.

———. "The Catholic Church in the Italian Empire, 1936–38." *Historical Papers of the Canadian Historical Association*, 1984, 138–50.

———. *The Pope and the Duce: The International Impact of the Lateran Agreements*. London: Macmillan, 1981.

———. "A Tale of Two Popes: Pius XI, Pius XII, and the Rome-Berlin Axis." *Journal of Contemporary History* 23, no. 4 (October 1988): 589–608.

———. "The Vatican and the Spanish Civil War." *European History Quarterly* 16, no. 4 (October 1986): 441–64.

Kent, Peter C., and John F. Pollard, eds. *Papal Diplomacy in the Modern Age*. Westport, Conn.: Praeger, 1994.

Keogh, Dermot. *Ireland and the Vatican: The Politics and Diplomacy of Church-State Relations, 1922–1960*. Cork: Cork University Press, 1995.

Lewy, Guenter. *The Catholic Church and Nazi Germany*. New York: McGraw-Hill, 1964.

Novelli, A. *The Life of Pius XI*. Trans. P.T. Lombard. Yonkers, N.Y.: Mount Carmel Press, 1925.

Passelecq, Georges, and Bernard Suchecky. *The Hidden Encyclical of Pius XI*. Trans. Steven Rendall. New York: Harcourt Brace, 1997.

Pollard, John F. *The Vatican and Italian Fascism, 1929–32: A Study in Conflict*. Cambridge: Cambridge University Press, 1985.

Rhodes, Anthony. *The Vatican in the Age of the Dictators, 1922–1945*. London: Hodder & Stoughton, 1973.

Stehle, Hansjakob. *Eastern Politics of the Vatican, 1917–1979*. Athens: Ohio University Press, 1981.

Stehlin, Stewart A. *Weimar and the Vatican, 1919–1933: German-Vatican Diplomatic Relations in the Interwar Years*. Princeton: Princeton University Press, 1983.

PIUS XII (1939–58): CONTROVERSIAL "POPE OF PEACE"

CHARLES F. DELZELL

Eugenio Maria Giuseppe Giovanni Pacelli, a conservative and very controversial Roman pontiff, reigned as Pius XII (1939–58) during World War II and postwar reconstruction. Born in Rome on 2 March 1876, he was the second of four children of Filippo Pacelli, a lawyer, and Virginia Graziosi, minor but respected members of the papal or "black" aristocracy. Young Pacelli studied philosophy at the Gregorian University and theology at Sant'Apollinare (the Lateran University). In April 1899 he was ordained a priest. Next he studied canon law and earned a doctorate in 1902. After entering the Vatican Secretariat of State (1901) he collaborated with Pietro Gasparri on the huge task of preparing the code of canon law. He also taught canon law at the Rome Seminary and published numerous legal studies. From 1909 to 1914 he was a professor of ecclesiastical diplomacy at the Ponteficia Accademia dei Nobili Ecclesiastici. In 1914 he was named secretary of the Congregation for Extraordinary Ecclesiastical Affairs.

To further Pope Benedict XV's efforts to halt the Great War, Pacelli was appointed (May 1917) apostolic nuncio to Bavaria, with the honorary title of archbishop of Sardes. His dealings with the wartime leaders of the German Empire foundered over the question of Belgium's future status. During the Spartacist rising in turbulent Munich in 1919 armed Communists burst into his nunciature. Pacelli stood his ground and ordered them to leave, which they did. The harrowing confrontation left an indelible impression upon him. In June 1920 Pacelli became the first apostolic nuncio to the new German Republic and remained in Berlin until

1929. He developed great affection for the German people and spoke their language fluently. Pacelli believed strongly in the importance of concordats that preserved the church's privileges and freedom of action, even with regimes hostile to Christian principles. He helped to negotiate concordats with the states of Bavaria (29 March 1924), Prussia (14 June 1929), Austria (5 June 1931), Baden (12 October 1932), and finally with Adolf Hitler's Third Reich (20 July 1933). He regarded this last one as a "calculated risk," at best.

Recalled to Rome, Pacelli was created cardinal by Pius XI in December 1929. The following year he succeeded Pietro Cardinal Gasparri as Vatican secretary. In 1935 he was appointed camerlengo, holding both important posts simultaneously. The new secretary of state traveled extensively on papal missions in North and South America, France, and elsewhere. He was principal advisor to Pius XI on how best to deal with Hitler's regime and helped draft the encyclical *Mit brennender Sorge* (With deep anxiety) of 14 March 1937, in which the pontiff rejected the myths of race and blood (though avoiding explicit mention of anti-Semitism). Four days later the pontiff, with the help of Pacelli, balanced this with *Divini redemptoris* (On atheistic communism), a strong encyclical focusing on religious persecution in the Soviet Union, Spain, and Mexico. When Hitler's foreign minister Joachim von Ribbentrop came to Rome in 1938, the austere secretary of state received him coldly, and he was also sharply critical of Hitler's annexation of Catholic Austria that year. In the wake of Pius XI's death Cardinal Pacelli was elected his successor on 2 March 1939 in the shortest conclave since 1623. He took the name Pius XII. His reign was to be marked by much controversy.

Aspiring to be a new "pope of peace" in the style of Benedict XV, Pius XII tried desperately to stave off World War II by proposing a new international conference to deal with Hitler's demands against Poland. But Britain, which had recently been disillusioned by Hitler's cynical repudiation of the four-power agreement on Czechoslovakia that had been drawn up at Munich on 29 September 1938, declined to participate in another such conference, and Hitler, who did not want to be deprived of a Nazi blitzkrieg against Poland, also expressed no interest. Pius had to give up this plan on 10 May 1939. Next, he offered his good offices for bilateral talks between Germany and Poland and between France and Italy, but to no avail. Instead, Hitler and Mussolini forged their Pact of Steel military alliance (22 May). On 23 August Germany and the Soviet Union startled the world by agreeing to a ten-year neutrality and nonaggression treaty, which also contained a secret protocol for partitioning Poland between them. Nevertheless, Pius made an anguished appeal to the world (24 August): "Nothing is lost by peace, but everything may be lost by war" (Konig, 585).

On 1 September 1939 Hitler invaded Poland, and three days later Britain and France responded by declaring war against Germany. In less than one month Germany conquered the western half of Poland and allowed Stalin to take the eastern half. On 20 October 1939 Pius issued his first encyclical, *Summi pontificatus* (On the Limitations of the Authority of the State), in which he outlined a possible path to peace. Between November 1939 and February 1940 he relayed messages between the German resistance movement and the Western Allies. On Christmas Eve he broadcast to the world the first of his notable Christmas messages during the war.

In it he expressed his hope to bring an end to the selfish nationalism that had led to war. But Pius focused most of his attention that first winter of the war on keeping Italy out of it. (Knowing that Fascist Italy was exhausted by his recent wars in Ethiopia, Spain, and Albania, Mussolini had announced on 2 September 1939 that Hitler had agreed that Italy would remain "nonbelligerent" for the present.) The pope's most important action was to arrange an unprecedented exchange of visits between himself and Italy's royal family, a move that was clearly designed to put pressure on King Victor Emmanuel III to restrain the Duce.

Pope Pius XII. (Courtesy of the Library of Congress)

In April 1940, when Hitler's forces invaded Denmark and Norway, the Vatican organ, *L'Osservatore Romano*, condemned this extension of the war, whereupon Mussolini tried to prevent its circulation. The pope appealed again to the Duce to stay neutral, but on 30 April Mussolini replied that he could no longer guarantee this. (By then he had secretly promised Hitler that Italy would soon enter the war.) Early in May Pius learned from German army officers in the anti-Nazi underground that Hitler was about to invade not only France but the neutral Low Countries as well. The pope quickly forwarded this news to the three Benelux sovereigns and, in the wake of the actual invasion on 10 May, dispatched telegrams expressing his sorrow that their countries had been invaded "against [their] will and right" and assuring them of his paternal affection and of prayers that full freedom and independence would soon be restored. These telegrams, which some observers likened to extreme unction, were published in the Vatican newspaper on 12 May. They were the pope's most courageous public protest against German aggression. They were also his last. For the duration of the war he maintained public silence on the question of who was to blame for the war, much to the bewilderment of millions of Catholics and non-Catholics. He believed that if he singled out any one belligerent, he might ruin whatever slim chance remained for him to mediate the conflict. Moreover, he did not wish to do anything to alienate those Catholics who were fighting under the banner of nationalism, or to jeopardize the concordats that had been negotiated with Mussolini's Italy and Hitler's Germany.

Angered by the pope's messages to the Benelux rulers, Mussolini once again blocked distribution of *L'Osservatore Romano*. In a tense meeting with Italy's ambassador, Pius raised his voice: "Whatever may happen, We have absolutely nothing to be ashamed of, and We do not even fear deportation to a concentration camp. . . . We were not afraid of the revolvers pointed at Us once before; We are even less so this second time" (Alfieri, 17). But the Vatican gave in, and thereafter its newspaper expressed only the most anodyne comments on the war. The Vatican felt that it had no choice because, in a showdown, Mussolini could have silenced the paper completely and cut off the Holy See from easy communication with the outside world. Thus on 10 June 1940, when Mussolini attacked France and Britain, *L'Osservatore Romano* published without comment the news of Italy's declaration of war. In the wake of France's surrender to Germany and Italy a few days later, the Vatican urged Britain also to make peace, but Prime Minister Winston Churchill adamantly rejected such advice.

In December 1940 and in February 1941 the pontiff issued protests against Nazi euthanasia and sterilization policies. In general, however, he sought to be evenhanded in dealing with both the Axis powers and the Western democracies. When Nazi Germany invaded the Soviet Union in June 1941, the pope's dilemma became acute. He certainly had no liking for communism, but since the Soviet Union had now become the wartime ally of Britain, he felt that he could not say anything critical of Stalin unless he also did so about Hitler, so he maintained public silence insofar as possible. On 25 December 1939 President Franklin D. Roosevelt named Myron C. Taylor, an Episcopalian layman, to be his "personal envoy" to Pius XII. The United States' formal entry into the war in December 1941 added a new dimension to Vatican diplomacy. Pius was dismayed when the president announced the Allies' "unconditional surrender" policy in January 1943; he feared that this would needlessly prolong the war. The pontiff thought that Roosevelt was naïve to imagine that Stalin's conciliatory religious policies during the war would continue afterward, or that the Kremlin would refrain from territorial and ideological expansionism.

The influence of the Vatican in seeking peace reached its low point during 1941–42. So, too, did efforts of the Vatican Information Service to find out about hundreds of thousands of refugees, though Catholic charities continued to deliver humanitarian assistance as best they could. The published *Actes et documents du Saint Siège relatifs à la seconde guerre mondiale* shed much light on this spreading atmosphere of pessimism in the Vatican. For Pius XII, the most horrendous problem was the genocidal "Final Solution," which Hitler launched in Eastern Europe after his invasion of Russia in June 1941 and soon extended throughout Nazi-occupied Europe. During the next four years at least 9,000,000 people were systematically murdered in death camps in Poland and elsewhere. Of these victims, about 6,000,000 were Jews. Other categories destined for extermination included Gypsies and homosexuals. There can be little doubt that the Vatican received much reliable information about these crimes.

Toward the end of his lengthy Christmas message of 1942 Pius XII inserted a short paragraph that mentioned "hundreds of thousands who, without fault on their part, sometimes only because of race or nationality, have been consigned to death or to a slow decline" (Konig, 804). This was, of course, a guarded reference to the Jews, but the pope did not specifically identify Hitler's Nazis as the perpetrators, apparently deciding that this would be counterproductive. Thereafter, and to the puzzlement of millions, he left it to local church leaders to interpret his thoughts in whatever way they deemed best. A brave minority did speak out against Nazi atrocities in France, the Low Countries, Germany, and elsewhere, always at grave danger. Sometimes their protests achieved limited success, but on other occasions quite the opposite. It should be noted that during 1942–43 the Vatican did manage to persuade the Axis satellite states of Slovakia, Hungary, and Rumania to prevent deportations, but by 1944 the Nazis had brutally taken full control and countermanded such interventions.

Upon Mussolini's entry into the war on 10 June 1940, Pius tried unsuccessfully to get all the belligerents to recognize Rome as a demilitarized "open city" and spare it from aerial bombardment. Italian Fascists seem to have been responsible for a bomb that fell on the Vatican on 1 March 1943. On 19 July the Allies, hoping to knock Mussolini's Italy out of the war after their successful invasion of Sicily, ordered a massive aerial bombardment of the railway yards in the San Lorenzo quarter of Rome. Shortly thereafter the pope toured this sector, which had suffered many casualties. The Allied raid unquestionably hastened the royal and military coup d'état that deposed Mussolini on 25 July. On the night of 8 September 1943 the new non-Fascist government of King Victor Emmanuel III and Marshal Pietro Badoglio announced Italy's surrender to the Allies. Hitler, anticipating this, had greatly reinforced his troops in Italy. They quickly overpowered the confused Italian armies in the north and began to move into Rome. He also ordered the rescue of Mussolini, who was soon installed as Germany's puppet head of a northern Italian Social Republic, with its capital at Salò on Lake Garda. Meanwhile, before dawn on 9 September the King and Marshal Badoglio fled from Rome to join the Allies in the south. They left no instructions for the city's defense. As soon as German units seized Rome, Hitler toyed briefly with a scheme to deport the pope, but fortunately his aides talked him out of this. Rome's terrified inhabitants, which included a well-assimilated Jewish community of 8,000, looked to the pope for protection. He remained at the Vatican throughout the German occupation.

Late in September SS Major Herbert Kappler threatened the leader of Rome's Jewish community that 200 Jews would be deported unless a ransom of fifty kilograms of gold was paid at once. Rome's Jews, helped by many Catholics and with a generous offer from the pope to make up the balance if necessary, raised the fifty kilograms and delivered the ransom to the German Embassy. But their sense of relief was brief. Heinrich Himmler ordered Kappler (who had obtained a list of all Jewish families in Rome) to round up all of the city's Jews for deportation and liquidation. The pope was alerted to this by Ernst von Weizsacker, the German ambassador. Pius quickly instructed all monasteries and convents owned by the Vatican and claiming "extraterritorial" status to open their doors to Jews and also to well-known Italian anti-Fascists. About 4,700 of Rome's Jews took shelter in this way, but many others unwisely stayed in their homes. Suddenly, on the night of the Sabbath, 16 October 1943, the SS invaded the old Jewish ghetto, located across the Tiber from St. Peter's. There they rounded up 1,259 residents. The pope at once instructed Bishop Alois Hudal, rector of the German Catholic church in Rome, to seek the release of those who could be shown to be either Aryans or of mixed marriage. Hudal succeeded in gaining the release of 252 such people, but the remaining 1,007 Jewish prisoners were hauled off in freight cars to Auschwitz, where more than 800 met immediate death in the gas chambers. Altogether, about 7,600 of Italy's Jews perished at the hands of Nazis during the twenty months of German occupation of northern Italy.

On 23 March 1944 young Italian partisans detonated a bomb that killed thirty-two members of an SS police detachment marching down Via Rasella in central Rome. Hitler, in a fury, wanted to destroy a whole sector of the city, but aides persuaded him to order, instead, reprisals at a ratio of ten to one SS officials, aided by the collaborationist Italian chief of police, exceeded this target, seizing 335 Italians (77 of them Jews) from Rome's Regina Coeli prison. They hauled them to the Ardeatine Caves on the city's outskirts. There they forced the men, hands tied behind their backs, to kneel and be shot in the back of the head. Pius strongly criticized the ambush on Via Rasella but could not prevent the ensuing massacre ordered by Hitler, the worst atrocity to occur in Italy in World War II.

On 4 June 1944, as Allied units neared Rome, Germany's field marshal Albert Kesselring, mindful of the pope's wishes that the Eternal City be

spared but also worried about his own Tenth and Fourteenth armies, secured Hitler's approval for withdrawal of German forces and avoidance of destruction that could enrage the whole Catholic world. The next day thousands of Romans crowded St. Peter's Square to acclaim Pius XII as their *defensor civitatis*. The Allies permitted Italy's royal government to return quickly to Rome. It had gained "co-belligerent" status on 13 October 1943, when it declared war on Germany. The Vatican continued to recognize this government and not the puppet one of Mussolini. During the remaining year of fighting in northern Italy the Vatican worried much about the growing strength of communism. Quite a few local priests (but none of the higher clergy) took part in the Catholic wing of the Armed Resistance.

Three weeks after the final defeat of Nazi Germany Pius XII delivered an allocution (2 June 1945) to the sacred college of cardinals. Referring to the German people, he said, "We nourish faith that they can restore themselves to new dignity and to new life, now that they have rejected the satanic specter of National Socialism, and after the guilty parties . . . have expiated the crimes they have committed" (Rossi, 460–61). Despite the pope's words about the need for expiation of crimes, a number of Germans accused of such crimes managed to find temporary shelter in Vatican buildings in Rome and help in escaping abroad.

When Italy moved into the post-Fascist era, Pius XII had not initially favored formation of a Christian democratic party that would function independently of the church. He preferred to make use of Azione Cattolica Italiana (Italian Catholic Action), the militantly conservative organization of Catholic laymen headed by Professor Luigi Gedda of Milan and supervised by the bishops. But when an autonomous, centrist Christian democratic party was formed by Alcide De Gasperi, Pius accepted it. The precarious balance between Christian Democrats and Communists in Italy's postwar republic, however, led Pius to encourage Gedda's "civic committees" to intervene in parliamentary politics in a more right-wing direction. When De Gasperi, who was Italy's strong Christian Democratic premier from 1945 to 1953, protested such meddling, he incurred considerable disfavor at the Vatican. Clerical intrusion in public life in Italy, as well as in France, reached a high pitch by the mid-1950s when Pius XII's failing health left power increasingly in the hands of ultraconservative cardinals. The pontiff stirred up much resentment among left-wing Catholics when he denounced the new ministry of French "worker-priests" and called upon them to return to traditional religious tasks.

The Vatican was not involved in the organization of the United Nations in 1945. Pius XII generally looked with favor on it, though he had misgivings about the composition of the Security Council and its voting system. He preferred the more inclusive General Assembly, and he regretted the East-West stalemate that long delayed admission into it of such Catholic countries as Italy, Spain, Portugal, Ireland, and Austria. Pius looked favorably on the role of many specialized agencies of the United Nations, and he was generally pleased with the U.N. Declaration of Human Rights (1948). As soon as UNESCO established headquarters in Paris, a special "Vatican Mission" to it was created and placed under the Paris archdiocese. With regard to the status of the Holy Places in Palestine, he favored an international statute for Jerusalem. The Vatican played no role in drafting the Paris peace treaties in 1947 with the former Axis satellite states, but Pius warmly welcomed the American Marshall Plan to rebuild Europe's economies. The same was true for the Congress of Europe promoted by Winston Churchill at The Hague in May 1948. He also applauded efforts of such statesmen as Jean Monnet and Robert Schuman to promote the economic integration of Western Europe, a process that culminated in the European Economic Community (1957).

The pope condemned Stalin's imposition of Communist regimes in Eastern Europe after 1944, and as the Cold War intensified, he was shocked by the long imprisonment of such prelates as Cardinal Joszef Mindszenty of Hungary and Cardinal Stefan Wyszinski of Poland. In 1949 and 1950 the Holy Office excommunicated Catholics who freely and knowingly joined the Communist parties in France, Italy, and Czechoslovakia. Pius gave his approval to the West's formation of the NATO defensive military alliance in 1949, but he always stopped short of advocating a crusade against the Soviet Union, and in the apostolic letter *Carissimis Russiae populis* (7 July 1952) he carefully distinguished between the Communist system and the Russian people. The ascetic pontiff was unquestionably a gifted scholar, an astute diplomat, and deeply spiritual, but he could hardly be called an innovative leader. He reaffirmed the encyclicals of Leo XIII (*Rerum novarum*, 1891) and of Pius XI (*Quadragesimo anno*, 1931). He was especially conservative in his attitude toward marital relations, making a number of pronouncements about the "safe period" but without carrying discussion much beyond the position of his predecessor. Nor did he do much to further Christian ecumenism. On the subject of religious tolerance, however, Pius stated (6 December 1953) that the church, mindful of the good faith of those who live in "invincible ignorance," should practice toleration toward other religious-ethical confessions. On 7 September 1955 he rejected the medieval notion that all temporal authority comes from God through the pope as Christ's representative.

Both during and after the war Pius promoted excavations under St. Peter's Basilica. These resulted in important archaeological discoveries and fixed with certainty the location of the original grave of the Apostle St. Peter. The pontiff's scores of scholarly addresses to specialized audiences touched on urgent moral and social problems, on the dictates of conscience, and on the need for Catholic schools. Motion pictures and the media of radio and television were the focus of his encyclical *Miranda prorsus* (8 September 1957). One of Pius XII's greatest encyclicals was *Divino afflante Spiritu* With the help of the Divine Spirit, 30 September 1943 which gave fresh impetus to the study of the Scriptures in their historical setting. Such studies had been hampered by the inquisitorial atmosphere engendered in 1907 by Pius X's denunciation of the errors of modernism. The new encyclical welcomed most of the techniques of modern biblical scholarship. In 1950, however, a conservative encyclical, *Humani generis* (Of the human race), seemed to restrain the kind of theological speculation that *Divino afflante Spiritu* had encouraged. *Mistici corporis Christi* (1943) was a profound study of the church as the Mystical Body of Christ. *Mediator Dei* (Mediator of God, 1947) forwarded the liturgical movement, aiming at restoring a community character to public worship, but cautioning against extravagant experimentation. In *Munificentissimus Deus* (1 November 1950) Pius proclaimed the dogma of the Bodily Assumption of Mary, while in *Ad caeli Reginam* (11 October 1954) he elucidated the sublime dignity of Mary. Pius summoned two consistories (18 February 1946; 12 January 1953) to create fifty-six cardinals. The college numbered fifty-seven at his death. For the first time there were fewer Italians than non-Italians in it. He canonized thirty-three saints. The number of dioceses increased from 1,696 in 1939 to 2,048 in 1958. Hierarchies were established in China (1946), Burma (1955), and several parts of Africa. In 1953 a concordat with Franco's Spain was concluded. In February 1955 Pius resolved the long dispute concerning the Knights of Malta by reconciling their claim to sovereignty with their status as a religious order.

In failing health, Pius XII died in his summer palace at Castel Gandolfo on 11 October 1958 at the age of eighty-two. His death marked the end of a conservative era for the Roman Catholic church, which was soon to embark on monumental renovations under the charismatic leadership of Pope John XXIII (1958–63).

SELECTED BIBLIOGRAPHY

Alfieri, Dino. *Dictators Face to Face*. Trans. David Moore. Westport, CT: Greenwood Press, 1978.

Alvarez, David, and Robert A. Graham: *Nothing Sacred: Nazi Espionage against the Vatican, 1939–1945*. London: Frank Cass, 1997.

Bentley, Eric, ed. *The Storm over "The Deputy."* New York: Grove, 1964.

Blet, Pierre. *Pius XII and the Second World War: According to the Archives of the Vatican*. Trans. Lawrence J. Johnson. New York: Paulist Press, 1999.

Blet, Pierre, Robert A. Graham, Angelo Martini, and Burkhart Schneider, eds. *Actes et documents du Saint Siège relatifs à la seconde guerre mondiale*. 11 vols. Vatican City: Libreria Editrice Vaticana, 1965–81.

Buonaiuti, Ernesto. *Pio XII*. Florence: Parenti Editore, 1958.

Carlen, Claudia, ed. *The Papal Encyclicals*. Vol. 4, *1939–1958*. Wilmington, N.C.: McGrath, 1981.

Catti De Gasperi, Maria Romana. *De Gasperi, uomo solo*. Milan: Mondadori, 1964.

Chadwick, Owen. *Britain and the Vatican during the Second World War*. Cambridge: Cambridge University Press, 1986.

Charles-Roux, François. *Huit ans au Vatican, 1932–1940*. Paris: Flammarion, 1947.

Cornwell, John. *Hitler's Pope: The Secret History of Pius XII*. New York: Viking, 1999.

De Felice, Renzo. *Storia degli ebrei italiani sotto il fascismo*. 4th ed. Turin: Einaudi, 1988.

Delzell, Charles F. *Mussolini's Enemies: The Italian Anti-Fascist Resistance*. Princeton: Princeton University Press, 1961; rev. ed., New York: Howard Fertig, 1974.

———, ed. *The Papacy and Totalitarianism between the Two World Wars*. New York: Wiley, 1974.

———. "Pius XII, Italy, and the Outbreak of War." *Journal of Contemporary History* 2, no. 4 (October 1967): 137–61.

Dinneen, Joseph F. *Pius XII: Pope of Peace*. New York: Robert M. McBride, 1939.

Di Nolfo, Ennio, ed. *Vaticano e Stati Uniti, 1939–1952: Dalle carte di Myron C. Taylor*. Milan: F. Angeli, 1978.

Falconi, Carlo. *Gedda e l'Azione cattolica*. Florence: Parenti, 1958.

———. *The Popes in the Twentieth Century*. London: Weidenfeld & Nicolson, 1967.

———. *The Silence of Pius XII*. Trans. Bernard Wall. Boston: Little, Brown, 1970.

Friedlander, Saul. *Pius XII and the Third Reich: A Documentation*. Trans. Charles Fullman. New York: Alfred A. Knopf, 1966.

Giovannetti, Alberto. *El Vaticano y la guerra 1939–1940*. Trans. Felice Ximenez de Sanoval. Madrid: Sposa-Calpe, S.A., 1961.

Einaudi, Mario, and François Goguel. *Christian Democracy in Italy and France*. Notre Dame, Ind.: University of Notre Dame Press, 1952.

Graham, Robert A. "Pius XII und seine Zeit: Der politische und kulturelle Rahmen eines historischen Pontifikats." In *Pius XII zum Gedächtnis*. Ed. Herbert Schambeck. Berlin: Duncker & Humblot, 1977.

Halecki, Oscar, and James F. Murray, Jr. *Pius XII: Eugenio Pacelli, Pope of Peace*. New York: Farrar, Straus & Young, 1954.

Herzer, Ivo, ed. *The Italian Refuge: Rescue of Jews during the Holocaust*. Washington, D.C.: Catholic University of America Press, 1989.

Hilberg, Raul. *The Destruction of the European Jews*. 3 vols. New York: Holmes & Meier, 1985.

Hochhuth, Rolf. *The Deputy*. Trans. Richard Winston and Clara Winston. New York: Grove Press, 1965.

Holmes, J. Derek. *The Papacy in the Modern World 1914–1978*. London and New York: Crossroad, 1981.

Jemolo, Arturo C. *Chiesa e stato in Italia dalla unificazione a Giovanni XXIII*. Turin: Giulio Einaudi, 1965.

Katz, Robert. *Black Sabbath: A Journey through a Crime against Humanity*. New York: Macmillan, 1969.

———. *Death in Rome*. New York: Macmillan, 1967.

Konig, Harry C., ed. *Principles for Peace: Selections from Papal Documents from Leo XIII to Pius XII*. Washington, DC: National Catholic Welfare Conference, 1943.

Lamb, Richard. *War in Italy, 1943–1945: A Brutal Story*. New York: St. Martin's Press, 1993.

Lapide, Pinchas E. *Three Popes and the Jews*. New York: Hawthorn, 1967.

Leiber, Robert. "Pius XII." *New Catholic Encyclopedia* 11 (1967): 414–18.

———. "Pius XII." *Stimmen der Zeit: Monatschrift für das Geistesleben der Gegenwart* 163, no. 2 (November 1958): 81–100.

Levai, Jeno. *Geheime Reichssache: Papst Pius XII hat nicht geschwiegen*. Cologne: Wort & Werk, 1966.

Lewy, Guenter. *The Catholic Church and Nazi Germany*. New York: McGraw-Hill, 1964.

Lichten, Joseph L., ed. *Pius XII and the Holocaust: A Reader*. 1963. Repub., Milwaukee: Catholic League for Religious & Civil Rights, 1988.

Maccarone, Michele. "Pius XII." *Enciclopedia cattolica* 9 (1952): 1544–52.

Marchione, Margherita. *Pope Pius XII: Architect for Peace*. Mahwah, N.J.: Paulist Press, 2000.

———. *Yours Is a Precious Witness: Memoirs of Jews and Catholics in Wartime Italy*. Mahwah, N.J.: Paulist Press, 1997.

Miccoli, Giovanni. *I dilemmi e i silenzi di Pio XII: Vaticano, Seconda guerra mondiale, e Shoah*. Milan: Rizzoli, 2000.

———. "Santa Sede e Chiesa Italiana di Fronte alle Leggi Antiebraiche del 1938." *Studi Storici* 29, no. 4 (October–December 1988): 821–902.

Michaelis, Meir. *Mussolini and the Jews: German-Italian Relations and the Jewish Question in Italy, 1922–1945*. Oxford: Clarendon Press, 1978.

Morley, John F. *Vatican Diplomacy and the Jews during the Holocaust, 1939–1943*. New York: KTAV, 1980.

Murphy, Francis X. *The Papacy Today*. New York: Macmillan, 1981.

Nichols, Peter. *The Politics of the Vatican*. New York: F.A. Praeger, 1968.

———. *The Pope's Divisions: The Roman Catholic Church Today*. New York: Holt, Rinehart & Winston, 1981.

Nobecourt, Jacques. *"Le Vicaire" et l'histoire*. Paris: Editions du Seuil, 1964.

Palazzini, Pietro. *Il clero e l'occupazione tedesca di Roma: Il ruolo del Seminaro Romano Maggiore*. Rome: APES, 1995.

Picciotto Fargion, Liliana. *Il Libro della Memoria: Gli ebrei deportati dall'Italia (1943–1945)*. Milan: Mursia, 1991.

———, ed. *L'occupazione tedesca e gli ebrei di Roma: Documenti e fatti*. Rome: Carucci, 1979.

Podellaro, Nazareno. *Portrait of Pius XII*. London: J.M. Dent, 1956.

Purdy, William A. *The Church on the Move: The Characters and Policies of Pius XII and John XXIII*. London: Hollis & Carter, 1966.

———. "Pius XII." *The New Encyclopedia Britannica: Micropaedia* 9 (1992): 1487–88.

Raddatz, Fritz J., ed. *Summa iniuria; oder, Dürfte der Papst schweigen? Hochhuths "Stellvertreter" in der öffentlichen Kritik*. Reinbek bei Hamburg: Rowohlt Taschenbuch Verlag, 1964.

Reese, Thomas J. *Inside the Vatican: The Politics and Organization of the Catholic Church*. Cambridge, Mass.: Harvard University Press, 1996.

Rhodes, Anthony. *The Vatican in the Age of the Dictators, 1922–1945*. New York: Holt, Rinehart & Winston, 1973.

Riccardi, Andrea. *Il potere del papa da Pio XII a Paolo VI*. Rome: Laterza, 1988.

Rossi, Ernesto. *Il Managnello e l'aspersorio*. Florence: Parenti, 1948.

Sarfatti, Michele. *Gli ebrei nell'Italia fascista: Vicende, identità, presecuzione*. Turin: Einaudi, 2000.

Schambeck, Herbert, ed. *Pius XII zum Gedächtnis*. Berlin: Duncker & Humblot, 1977. Smit, Jan Olav. *Pope Pius XII*. London: Catholic Book Club, 1951.

Stehle, Hansjakob. *Eastern Politics of the Vatican, 1917–1979*. Trans. Sandra Smith. Athens: Ohio University Press, 1981.

Tardini, Domenico. *Pio XII*. Vatican City: Tipografia Poliglotta Vaticana, 1960.

Taylor, Myron C., ed. *Wartime Correspondence between President Roosevelt and Pope Pius XII*. New York: Macmillan, 1947. Reprint, New York: Da Capo, 1975.

Valiani, Leo, Gianfranco Bianchi, and Ernesto Ragionieri. *Azionisti, cattolici, e comunisti nella Resistenza*. Milan: Franco Angeli, 1971.

Webb, Leicester C. *Church and State in Italy, 1947–1957*. Carlton, Australia: Melbourne University Press, 1958.

Webster, Richard A. *The Cross and the Fasces: Christian Democracy and Fascism in Italy*. Stanford: Stanford University Press, 1960.

Weisbord, Robert G., and Wallace P. Sillanpoa. *The Chief Rabbi, the Pope, and the Holocaust: An Era in Vatican-Jewish Relations*. New Brunswick, N.J.: Transaction, 1992.

Zolli, Israele (later Eugenio). *Before the Dawn: Autobiographical Reflections*. New York: Sheed & Ward, 1954.

Zuccotti, Susan. *The Holocaust, the French, and the Jews*. New York: BasicBooks, 1993.

———. *The Italians and the Holocaust: Persecution, Rescue, and Survival*. New York: Basic Books, 1987.

———. *Under His Very Windows: The Vatican and the Holocaust in Italy*. New Haven: Yale University Press, 2000.

JOHN XXIII (1958–63): THE FATHER OF THE SECOND VATICAN COUNCIL

PATRICK GRANFIELD

Angelo Giuseppe Roncalli, better known as John XXIII or "Good Pope John," can rightly be called a notable pope. His long path to the chair of Peter was unusual in many respects, and his pontificate lasted only four and a half years, but in that time he made a major contribution to the church and the world by convoking the Second Vatican Council. His life, character, and accomplishments merit serious reflection.

Sotto il Monte, a village in northern Italy six miles from Bergamo, was the place of his birth on 25 November 1881. The third of thirteen children, he was born of poor but pious parents who were sharecroppers. Always grateful for his humble beginnings, he said on his deathbed, "I had the great grace to be born into a Christian family, modest and poor but with the fear of the Lord." After attending the seminary in Bergamo, he studied theology at the Roman Seminary, St. Apollinare. For a year he served in the Italian army, which he found to be a purgatory, and Babylonian captivity. On his return he earned a doctorate in theology and was ordained a priest in Rome on 10 August 1904. His family did not attend the ordination because they could not afford the trip to Rome.

His first major assignment as a priest, one that lasted nine years, from 1905–1914, was to be secretary to the new bishop of Bergamo, Giacomo Radini Tedeschi. During that period he also taught church history and apologetics at the seminary and published several short monographs on the historian Cesare Baronio and on St. Carlo Borromeo. In 1915 he was called back to the army and eventually became a lieutenant in the chaplains' corps. After the war he served as spiritual director in the seminary, and he established a hostel in Bergamo for students. In 1921 he was made a monsignor. That same year Benedict XV appointed him director of the Society for the Propagation of the Faith in Italy. He lived in Rome for five years, until 1925, but he traveled widely.

The next period of his life, nearly thirty years, was spent in the diplomatic service of the Holy See, although he was never formally trained in diplomacy. Yet he served in three foreign posts, each for roughly ten years. The first assignment was to Bulgaria (1925–34). At the age of forty-three he was consecrated the titular archbishop of Areopolis and appointed apostolic visitor to Bulgaria with a residence in Sofia. His episcopal motto was *Obedientia et Pax* (Obedience and Peace). He felt these words reflected in his life and history. In Bulgaria he found relatively few Eastern-rite or Latin-rite Catholics, since the majority of the people were Orthodox, which was the state church.

His second assignment was as apostolic administrator to Turkey and Greece with a residence in Istanbul (1935–44). It was a difficult assignment, since there were few Catholics and Turkey was a secular state with some antireligious and anti-Catholic laws. Catholic schools were closed, and no clerical clothing was allowed in public. He called his efforts in Turkey "bee's work." However, he encouraged the use of Turkish in some liturgical prayers and maintained positive relations with the government. He helped many Jews who were fleeing European persecution. His work in Greece was also trying, since there was a strong anti-Catholic and anti-Italian feeling there too.

His third diplomatic position was as nuncio to France (1944–53). He lived in Paris and had to face many delicate political and ecclesiastical problems that emerged during the last year of World War II and the postwar period. His gracious nature enabled him to resolve many of them, and he developed a good relationship with French politicians and French bishops. His position on the worker-priest experiment is unclear. In an effort to evangelize the dechristianized workers, some French priests—not more than one hundred—wore secular dress, worked in factories, celebrated Mass in their apartments, and were often involved in partisan politics. The movement was eventually suppressed by a decree of the Holy Office on 3 July 1959. Likewise, it seems that as nuncio he was not directly involved in the debate over the theological movement known as '*nouvelle théologie*' or "the new theology" that Pius XII condemned in the encyclical *Humani generis* in 1950.

At the age of seventy-one his life took a different turn when Pius XII named him a cardinal in November 1952 and appointed him patriarch of Venice in January 1953. He prayed about it, and answered *Obedientia et Pax*. It seemed that this assignment would be his last, and shortly after arriving in Venice he observed that he found himself on the threshold of eternity. In 1958 he published the fifth and last volume of documentation on the apostolic visitation in 1575 to Bergamo by Carlo Borromeo that he had been working on for fifty years. In his five years in Venice (1953–58) he was an active and caring pastor warmly received by his people.

After the death of Pius XII (9 October 1958) a conclave elected Roncalli pope on the eleventh ballot on 28 October 1958. When asked by Cardinal Eugene Tisserant, dean of the college of cardinals, if he accepted the election, he replied that he accepted, bowing his head before the cup of bitterness and his shoulders before the yoke of the cross. He took the name John XXIII. John was his father's name, the name of the parish in which he was baptized, and the name of twenty-two legitimate popes before him. Since he was only a month short of his seventy-seventh birthday, many considered him to be a *papa di passaggio*, a caretaker or transitional pope who would have a brief and uneventful reign. Little did his electors or the church at large realize what was in store for them.

Pope John XXIII. (Courtesy of the Vatican Library)

On 25 January 1959, at an extraordinary consistory of cardinals at the Benedictine Basilica of St. Paul's outside the Walls in Rome, the pope announced three major plans: a synod for the diocese of Rome; an ecumenical council for the universal church; and the revision of the code of canon law. The cardinals greeted these announcements with silence. The next day *L'Osservatore Romano* mentioned them only briefly, not on the front page but on page 3. John was disappointed with the lack of interest, but he was not deterred. After a year of preparation the synod, the first in the history of Rome, took place in January 1960. The result was 755 articles that were accepted by the participants. Some dealt with disciplinary matters: clerics were to wear cassocks in public, to have tonsures, and to avoid such events as operas, movies, or plays. Yet article 35, written by the pope himself, showed his remarkable kindness. He was distressed that priests who had left the active ministry were often shunned. Thus article 35 noted, "No one is to be deprived of the friendliness of his fellow priests or consolation in his difficulties or even material help should it be needed." The updating of the code of canon law was a more ambitious project. John XXIII established a pontifical commission for the revision of the code on 28 March 1963. John Paul II finally promulgated the revised code of canon law on 25 January 1983, twenty-four years to the day after it was first announced by Pope John.

The Second Vatican Council (1962–65) was the crowning achievement of the pontificate of Pope John. According to his secretary, Loris Capovilla, the idea of calling a council came to the pope shortly after his election. John said that the idea was an inspiration from God. Three years (1959–62) were devoted to preparing the council. In the midst of these preparations John mused on the idea that he was thought by some to be a provisional pope. On 10 August 1961, he wrote in his diary, "Yet here I am, already on the eve of the fourth year of my pontificate, with an immense program of work ahead of me to be carried out before the whole world, which is watching and waiting" (John XXIII, *Journal of a Soul*, 303). The first session of the council began on 11 October 1962. Pope John was almost eighty-one years old.

In his opening address he exhorted the council fathers to zeal and dissociated himself from those "prophets of doom" who constantly predict disaster. Rather, he said, "at this historical moment Divine Providence is leading us towards a new order in human relationships." The purpose of the council, he explained, was to help the church, in conformity with tradition, bring its teaching and discipline up to date, to renew the religious life of Catholics, and to seek the unity of all Christians. The council was to be a pastoral event, a celebration of faith. Exhortation rather than condemnation should characterize it. He perceived the council not as a speculative assembly, but as a living, vibrant organism. The first session debated the schemas on the liturgy, revelation, and the church. At times the debate was heated, fueled by the tension between members of the curia who had prepared the schemas and some of the council fathers. Bishop Émile-Joseph de Smedt of Bruges, Belgium, for example, in a memorable address, criticized the schema on the church by condemning its triumphalism, clericalism, and juridicism.

John was aware of the ideological conflicts within the council, and he frequently encouraged the fathers to work together collegially. Although he did not attend the daily meetings of the council, the pope followed the proceedings on closed-circuit television in his quarters. He intervened in the proceedings only occasionally. During the debate on the schema on revelation, however, the pope suspended the two-thirds voting rule and ordered that the schema be revised by a special mixed commission. The first session, the only one presided over by John, ended on 8 December 1962. He appointed a commission to continue conciliar business during the recess.

Besides his work with the council, John had an active pontificate. Conscious of his role as bishop of Rome, he often visited churches, hospitals, and prisons in Rome. Although he never left Italy as a pope, in 1960 he went by automobile to Roccantica to the villa of the Roman Seminary, and in 1962 he traveled by train to Loreto and Assisi. He canonized ten saints, beatified five, including Mother Elizabeth Seaton, and declared St. Lawrence of Brindisi to be a doctor of the church. He enlarged and internationalized the college of cardinals, creating fifty-four cardinals in four years. At the end of his pontificate there were eighty-seven cardinals (plus three *in pectore* who remain unknown), which was at that time the highest number ever in history.

The most noteworthy of his seven encyclicals were *Mater et magistra* (15 May 1961) and *Pacem in terris* (11 April 1963). *Mater et magistra* endorsed the concept of the modern welfare state as a manifestation of the common good but insisted on certain safeguards. It supported cooperatives and unions. *Pacem in terris* was an international encyclical addressed to all people of good will. It insisted on the freedom of conscience, especially freedom of worship, and appealed for peace and the protection of fundamental human dignity. Concern was shown for the people of the third world and their cultural and political rights.

On 23 September 1962 doctors told John that he had stomach cancer. He suffered much in the spring of 1963, and by the end of May his death seemed imminent. During his final anointing he pleaded for unity in the church and for mankind. John XXIII died on the evening of 3 June 1963, just as the words "Ite, missa est" were said at the public mass being celebrated in St. Peter's Square just below his bedroom.

Having seen the main features of the life of Pope John XXIII, how should we evaluate it? Here are some observations to help us understand better both the man and his pontificate. First, John was a paradoxical figure. On the one hand, he appeared to be a product of the Tridentine church: traditional, conservative, pious, and cautious. He seemed to embody the classical virtue of *Romanitas* with its emphasis on moderation, reason, and stability. For example, he was unenthusiastic about liturgical experiments and about priests in politics. He also insisted on Latin as the language of the church and of the council. Thus his apostolic constitution *Veterum sapientia* (22 February 1962) promoted the study of Latin and required professors in seminaries throughout the world to lecture in Latin. On the other hand, his desire for the reform of the church, his support of ecumenism, and his progressive economic and political ideas surprised many.

John is correctly portrayed as a simple, warmhearted person, an extrovert with a ready wit and an unaffected manner. He was a deeply spiritual person who put his trust in Divine Providence. Yet his piety and simplicity should not be taken as lack of intelligence. In fact, he was a cultured man who had a great love and knowledge of history, archaeology, art, and music. He spoke seven languages and took delight in reading and rereading Latin and Italian literary classics. Never fearing reality, John XXIII was aware of his own limitations, his advanced age, and his talents. Knowing that his papacy would be relatively short, he established his own priorities. He did not reform the Roman curia nor significantly transform the episcopate or the cardinalate. But he did have a vision of a reformed and united church, and he worked tirelessly, under the guidance of the Holy Spirit, to give life to that vision.

Second, John demythologized the papal office by personalizing it. His outgoing nature and his jovial manner contrasted sharply with the style of his predecessor, Pius XII. John XXIII rarely used the tiara, did not wear the traditional satin slippers, and did not require Vatican officials to bow three times when they entered his office or to address him on their knees. His meals were usually with members of the curia or visiting guests. He did not like the bureaucracy of the Vatican or its political intrigues. His managerial style was not to micromanage, but to give people as much freedom as possible. Although he preferred to intervene only when necessary, he was always aware of what was going on. His approach is reflected in one of his favorite maxims, attributed to St. Bernard: "Omnia videre, multa dissimulare, et pauca corrigere" ("See everything, overlook much, and correct a few things").

Third, John championed the cause of Christian unity and interreligious dialogue. The experience he had dealing with the Orthodox Jews and Muslims in his years in Bulgaria and Turkey instilled in him respect for the religious beliefs of others. One of his first important decisions was to establish in 1960 the Secretariat for Promoting Christian Unity under the direction of Cardinal Augustin Bea. The secretariat later played a major role in the council; John also invited Orthodox and Protestant observers to attend the council; eventually their number reached one hundred. His relations with Jews were also positive, as is evidenced by his deleting the expression "perfidious" Jews from the Good Friday liturgy. It was said that he once welcomed Jewish visitors with the words "I am Joseph, your brother." The attitude of John XXIII conveyed a positive image of the papacy. He was seen as a genuine, caring person and not as aloof, imperialistic, or authoritarian. As a result, many non-Catholics were able to lay aside many stereotypes of the pope and the Catholic church.

Fourth, John ushered in a new epoch for the church. His pontificate was a watershed in the history of Christianity. The pope wanted the Second Vatican Council to promote reform in the church, encourage unity with other Christians, and act as a catalyst for good in the world. After John the council eventually treated such major issues as the church, liturgy, revelation, the church and the world, ecumenism, Eastern Catholics, religious freedom, education, non-Christian religions, priesthood, episcopacy, laity, religious life, missions, and communication. John's universal vision convinced him that the church should not be isolated but should energize modern society. John XXIII, and later Paul VI, enabled the church to confront the needs of the twentieth century. Vatican II, a pastoral council, has left us with a rich heritage that we are still, more than thirty-five years later, trying to understand and to implement. We are all indebted to the pope from Bergamo. John XXIII was hardly a caretaker pope. He initiated an exciting new phase in the life of the church. As one commentator put it, "It is rare to achieve greatness in old age, but that is exactly what pope John XXIII achieved." For this we can all be grateful. John Paul II beatified John XXIII on 3 September 2000.

SELECTED BIBLIOGRAPHY

Alberigo, Angelina, and Giuseppe Alberigo. *Giovanni XXIII: Profezia nella fedeltà*. Brescia: Editrice Queriniana, 1979.

Aradi, Zsolt, James I. Tucek, and James C. O'Neill. *Pope John XXIII: An Authoritative Biography*. New York: Farrar, Straus & Cudahy, 1954.

Bonnot, Bernard R. *Pope John XXIII: An Astute Pastoral Leader*. New York: Alba House, 1979.

Capovilla, Loris. *Giovanni XXIII*. Vatican City: Libreria Vaticana, 1963. English translation by Patrick Riley, *The Heart and Mind of John XXIII, His Secretary's Intimate Reflection*. New York: Hawthorn, 1964.

———. *Giovanni XXIII: Quindici letture*. 3rd ed. Rome: Edizioni di Storia e Letteratura, 1970.

———. *Papa Giovanni XXIII, gran sacerdote come lo ricordo*. Rome: Edizioni di Storia e Letteratura, 1977.

———. *Ite Missa Est*. Padua: Messagero, Bergamo: Grafica e Arte, 1983.

Caprile, Giovanni. *Il concilio Vaticano II*. 5 vols. Rome: Civiltà cattolica, 1964–69.

Conzemius, Victor. "Mythes et contre-mythes autour de Jean XXIII." *Cristianesimo nella storia* 10 (1989): 553–77.

Feldman, Christian. *Pope John XXIII: A Spiritual Biography*. New York: Crossroad, 2000.

Giovanni XXIII. *Discorsi, messaggi, colloqui del Santo Padre Giovanni XXIII*. 5 vols. Vatican City: Tipografia Poliglotta, 1961–67.

———. *Il giornale dell'anima*. Ed. Loris Capovilla. 5th ed. Rome: Edizioni di Storia e Letteratura, 1967.

———. *Lettere ai familiari, 1901–1960*. Edited by Loris Capovilla. 2 vols. Rome: Edizioni di Storia e Letteratura, 1968. English translation by Dorothy White, *Pope John XXIII: Letters to His Family*. New York: McGraw-Hill, 1970.

———. *Lettere, 1958–1963*. Ed. Loris Capovilla. Rome: Edizioni di Storia e Letteratura, 1978.

Hales, E.E.Y. *Pope John and His Revolution*. London: Eyre & Spottiswoode, 1965.

Hebblethwaite, Peter. *Pope John XXIII, Shepherd of the Modern World*. Garden City, N.Y.: Doubleday, 1985.

Hughes, John Jay. "John XXIII (1958–1963)." In *Pontiffs: Popes Who Shaped History*. Huntington, Ind.: Our Sunday Visitor, 1994, 225–95.

Johannes XXIII. *Acta summi pontificis Johannis XXIII*. In *Acta et documenta concilio oecumenico Vatican II apparendo*, ser. 1, volume 1; ser. 2, vol. 1. Vatican City: Typis Polyglottis Vaticanis, 1960, 1964.

———. *Prima romana synodus A.D. MDCCCCLX*. Vatican City: Typis Polyglottis Vaticanis, 1960.

John XXIII. *The Encyclicals and Other Messages of John XXIII*. Washington: The Pope Speaks, 1964.

———. *Journal of a Soul*. Trans. Dorothy White. New York: McGraw Hill, 1965.

Johnson, Paul. *Pope John XXIII*. Boston: Little, Brown, 1974.

Roncalli, Angelo Giuseppe. *Gli atti della visita apostolica di S. Carlo Borromeo a Bergamo (1575)*. Edited in collaboration with Pietro Forno. 5 vols. Florence: L. Olschki, 1936, 1937, 1938, 1946, 1957.

———. *In memoria di monsignor Giacomo Radini Tedeschi, vescovo di Bergamo*. 3rd ed. Rome: Edizioni di Storia e Letteratura, 1963. English translation by Dorothy White, *My Bishop: A Portrait of Mgr. Giacomo Radini Tedeschi*. London: Geoffrey Chapman, 1969.

———. *Scritti e discorsi, 1953–1958*. 3 vols. Rome: Paoline, 1959.

———. *Souvenirs d'un nonce: Cahiers de France, 1944–1953)*. Rome: Edizioni di Storia e Letteratura, 1963. English translation by Dorothy White, *Mission to France, 1944–1953*. London: Geoffrey Chapman, 1966.

Trevor, Meriol. *Pope John*. London: Macmillan, 1967.

Trisco, Robert. "John XXIII, Pope." *New Catholic Encyclopedia* 7: 1015–20.

Zizola, Giancarlo. *L'utopia di papa Giovanni*. 2nd ed. Assisi: Cittadella Editrice, 1973.

PAUL VI (1963–78): CATHOLICISM'S BRIDGE TO THE MODERN WORLD

RICHARD J. WOLFF

The life of Pope Paul VI (Giovanni Battista Montini) may be divided into three segments: his work with university students from 1926 to 1933, his position in the Vatican Secretariat of State from 1934 to 1953, and his pastoral assignments that began with his consecration as archbishop of Milan in 1954 and culminated in his elevation to the throne of St. Peter in 1963. Vatican II unleashed powerful forces provoking strong traditionalist reactions. From the close of the council in 1965 to the end of his reign in 1978, Pope Paul presided over a divided church, attempting to ensure that the council reforms took root while avoiding the permanent alienation of conservative Catholics.

This future pope was born on 26 September 1897 to a family steeped in Catholic political activity. His father, Giorgio Montini, was asked by Pope Benedict XV to serve as president of the Unione Elettorale Cattolica Italiana, which prepared the way for the launching of the Partito Popolare Italiano (PPI). Immediately after the war Montini was elected to the Chamber of Deputies on the Popolare list from Brescia and held his seat until 1926, when Mussolini eliminated all opposition parties. Battista's mother offered a unique model for an Italian woman at the turn of the century. Active in Catholic causes, she enrolled in the Red Cross during World War I and was a leader of the Unione di Donne Cattoliche from 1923 to 1931. At the age of six Battista was enrolled in the Jesuit Collegio Cesare Arici, where he remained until 1916. Until the age of thirteen Battista was an active, if not robust, child. An enthusiastic bicyclist, he was compelled to abandon this sport in 1910 when a heart seizure left him unable to engage in strenuous exercise.

After completing his studies at the Jesuit college in 1916, young Montini entered the diocesan seminary in Brescia. Giacinto Gaggia, the bishop of Brescia, gave the physically frail young man permission to study at home. Consequently, Montini was able to remain in close contact with his friends. From 1918 to 1925 Montini collaborated in the publishing of a journal called *La Fionda* (The Sling) for Catholic students in Brescia. In the first year alone the seminarian contributed nine articles, and in doing so he began to articulate his views on personal liberty, faith, and social reform. Montini's strong religious sentiments, combined with his interest in politics, did not make him either conservative or intransigent. Much like his father, as well as Don Sturzo and the Catholics of the left wing of the PPI, the young Montini demonstrated political tolerance, going so far as to advocate cooperation with elements of the Socialist Party if they would renounce class struggle, materialism, and Communist tendencies.

The Fascist political violence against the Popolari during the immediate postwar years did not stop Montini from expressing his views in *La Fionda*. In fact, his support for the Christian democratic movement endured the hardships of twenty-one years of Fascist rule and continued in the post–World War II period. On 20 May 1920 Bishop Gaggia ordained Montini. The next day Montini celebrated his first mass. Montini's abilities and family contacts resulted in his immediate enrollment in the Gregorianum and the faculty of literature at the University of Rome. However, one of Giorgio Montini's acquaintances intervened with Cardinal Pietro Gasparri, the Vatican secretary of state, to secure Battista a place at the prestigious Accademia dei Nobili Ecclesiastici, the training school for Vatican diplomats. Montini viewed this intervention with mixed emotions. Eventually he resigned himself to the situation noting that if Christ could be a carpenter, he could serve as an office boy.

When in 1921 his friend Gian Andrea Trebeschi received his university degree, Montini congratulated him, revealing that his first love was the work that the two of them had undertaken with students in Brescia. In January 1922, Pope Benedict XV died. Early in 1922 the college of cardinals met to select a successor, electing the cardinal of Milan, who took the name Pius XI. At the beginning of his papacy Pius XI expressed the wish to be remembered as the "pope of Catholic Action," and his vigorous support of the Catholic lay movement and its youth groups often brought him into conflict with the Fascist leader, Benito Mussolini. From 1922 to his death in 1939 the Roman church was led by a pontiff who, like young Montini, believed in the importance of the apostolate among university students. Pius XI had strong personal ties to the Montini family. In May 1923 Montini became the youngest Vatican diplomat in the field when at the age of twenty-six he was posted to the nunciature in Warsaw under Monsignor Lorenzo Lauri. Montini remained in Poland only until October of the same year.

Upon his return to Rome in 1923 Montini sought a position with university students. In December he was appointed *assistente ecclesiastico* of the *circolo romano*, a local chapter of the Federazione Universitaria Cattolica Italiana (FUCI). Founded in 1896 as an autonomous branch of Catholic Action, the FUCI in ensuing years developed strong links to the young Christian democratic movement. Unlike conservative Catholics, the members of the organization (known as *fucini*) warmly greeted the formation of the PPI. The FUCI's attachment to the liberal wing of postwar Catholicism pleased the new *assistente*. Living in Rome, where his father spent much of his time and where his family's friend, papa Ratti, sat on the papal throne, young Montini was happy.

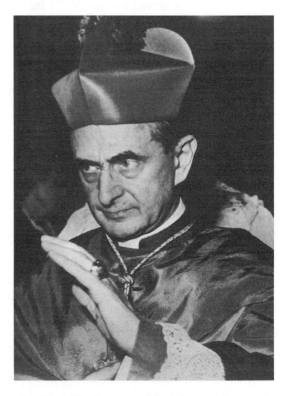

Pope Paul VI. (Courtesy of the Library of Congress)

As Mussolini consolidated his regime and ended the multiparty parliamentary system, the position of the PPI became increasingly precarious. The Duce, despite his anticlerical past, held out an olive branch to the Vatican in the guise of educational reforms, and in the hopes of weaning papal support from the Popolari. The growing popularity of fascism among the Italian people alarmed Montini. Viewing Mussolini's movement as "anticlerical" and "beneath bestiality," young Montini was well suited in outlook and politics for his role among the Catholic students. In 1925 the *fucini* assembled in Bologna for their annual national meeting. To avoid clashes with Fascist students, the FUCI president, Pietro Linzier, and the *assistente ecclesiastico generale*, Don Luigi Piastrelli, placed the convention under the official protection of the king. Since the Vatican did not recognize the legitimacy of the Italian state, this was an imprudent act.

The reaction of Pius XI was swift and stunning. Piastrelli was dismissed and the reelection of Linzier was annulled. In their places, the Vatican chose Montini and Igino Righetti, a law student from the University of Rome. Thus Montini, at the age of twenty-eight, came to head the national Catholic organization of university students. Fearing that their independence would be severely restricted by the Vatican, the *fucini* greeted Montini coldly. Nonetheless, in a short time Montini and Righetti endeared themselves to the Catholic students for their willingness to oppose the totalitarian aspects of the regime and to distance the FUCI from the growing "clerical conservatism" of the church. Montini promptly turned his attention to the publications of the FUCI, *Azione Fucina* (a weekly) and *Studium* (a monthly founded by Montini and Righetti in 1928).

The year after Montini was appointed to the FUCI national post, the Fascist effort to suppress the remnants of the parliamentary system culminated in the Aventine secession and the subsequent disbanding of all political parties except the Fascists. In August the FUCI national congress in Macerata was disrupted by the Fascists, and many Catholic students were injured in a day of violence. Three months later, in November, Montini wrote to his father, who was a part of the Aventine secession, condemning the burning of the offices of *Il Cittadino*. In the same month Giorgio Montini was barred from taking his seat in the Chamber of Deputies.

The FUCI of Montini and Righetti, characterized by strong antifascism, called for a Catholic presence in every aspect of Italian life. The majority of *fucini* believed that fascism was a new form of anticlericalism. Fearing that a settlement between the church and the state would mean an end to Vatican protection, they privately expressed dissatisfaction with the *conciliazione* of 1929. Montini himself disapproved of the Lateran Accords as "useless." The settlement between church and state notwithstanding, the Catholic student leadership refused to permit its members to enroll in the Fascist university organization, the Gioventù Universitaria Fascista (GUF). From 1925 to 1931 Montini's quiet yet persistent intransigence toward fascism served the Vatican. During these years Pius XI attempted to establish the rights of the church vis-à-vis the government and utilized first the Popolari and then the *fucini* to do so. In 1931 the smoldering feud between Mussolini and the pope concerning the education of Italian youth flared up in six months of polemics, violence, and suppression. The FUCI, accused of attempting to infringe on the prerogatives of the GUF and of training a political elite to replace the Fascist leadership, was singled out for Fascist reprisals. Incidents of violence against FUCI offices and Catholic students steadily increased until the organization was suppressed and its records confiscated in May. Montini was confined to his Vatican apartments, and Righetti joined him to avoid arrest.

After a summer of tension that witnessed the condemnation of the regime in the encyclical *Non abbiamo bisogno*, the pope and Mussolini settled their differences in the September compromise. For Montini's students, this meant an official change of name from the FUCI to the Associazione Universitaria di Azione Cattolica and the placement of local groups under diocesan control, but little else. Montini and Righetti remained unrepentant. The *assistente* praised the *fucini* for their "ability to fight back, to resist, and to persevere" during the worst of the violence against Catholic Action. In recognition of his contributions to the Vatican's cause, Montini was made a domestic prelate on 8 July 1931. By 1933, however, Monsignor Montini's view of an activist organization of Catholic university students with a mandate to bring Christian values to every aspect of Italian life had become an embarrassment to the Vatican. In a climate of compromise and cooperation with the state, the intransigence of the FUCI was politically undesirable. The Brescian priest, with his attachment to the Popolari and his evident dislike of fascism, had many enemies in a curia predominantly constituted of clerical conservatives. Thus in March 1933, only a few weeks after he had been reconfirmed in his post by the pontiff, Montini was suddenly asked by Cardinal Giuseppe Pizzardo to resign from the FUCI. An obedient priest, Montini announced his "resignation" for the reasons given him by Pizzardo and continued to work at the Secretariat of State.

From 1933 to 1937 Montini served in the Secretariat of State, reporting directly to Monsignor Domenico Tardini, the undersecretary of state. He found these years in the diplomatic service "boring," but he enjoyed teaching papal diplomatic history at the Pontifical Academy. When Tardini was made the head of the section of extraordinary ecclesiastical affairs, Montini took his place as undersecretary of state to Cardinal Eugenio Pacelli, thus beginning a long and close working relationship between Montini and Pacelli. As Pius XI grew increasingly hostile toward fascism and Nazism, Montini's close connections with the left wing of the Popolari no longer worked against him within the Vatican, where he now lived full-time. Although Montini had occasional access to the pope, he had regular contacts with Pacelli and Tardini. Within a year of Montini's appointment as undersecretary Pius XI was dead; and in March 1939, on the eve of World War II, Eugenio Pacelli was elected pope, taking the name Pius XII.

Montini surrounded himself with anti-Fascists. Roberto Farinacci, the leading Italian Fascist propagandist, accused Montini of being anti-Italian and pro-Allied, while inside the Vatican, cardinals sympathetic toward Mussolini worked against him. But Pacelli never wavered in his support of Montini during the war years. At the same time, there can be no question that Montini was a strong supporter of Pius XII, recognizing the need for wartime neutrality on the part of the Vatican. He preferred to work "behind the scenes." He discussed with Princess Maria José, wife of the heir to the throne, plans to overthrow Mussolini and transmitted this information to the Americans. He met in his Vatican apartments with the exiled *democristiani* to discuss Italy after fascism. All the while, however, he played the part of the consummate diplomat, protesting neutrality and attending Axis diplomatic functions. Montini's connections with the democrats within the Italian Catholic movement played a role in enabling the church to establish itself firmly within the postwar Italian state. Montini, in the face of opposition by Tardini and Cardinal Ottaviani of the Holy Office, supported Alcide De Gasperi as the future leader of the Christian Democrats.

Pius XII retained serious reservations about political Catholicism, but he realized that Christian democracy represented a necessary bulwark against a powerful Italian Communist movement. Within the curia, however, debate raged over the direction of the Catholic political movement. Montini was seen as firmly in the camp of De Gasperi and Giuseppe Dossetti, the latter the leader of the left wing of the party with strong connections to the Communists. More conservative Catholics, such as Luigi Gedda, found Montini's liberalism troubling, but as the 1948 elections drew near, Catholics united to oppose the Communists. Setting aside his differences with conservative Catholics, Montini funneled money into Gedda's conservative civic committees, local lay parish organizations designed to turn out the Catholic vote as a bloc. At Montini's direction, the Vatican bank provided one hundred million lire to bring out the Catholic vote. The results of the 1948 election were favorable for the Christian Democrats, who captured 48.5 percent of the vote, compared to 31 percent for the Communist-Socialist front.

Montini's strong support of De Gasperi and his left-leaning wing of the Christian Democrats created problems for him in the early 1950s. The Roman municipal elections of 1952 brought the issue to a head. With the Communists threatening to capture city hall, Pius pressured De Gasperi to form a common list with the right-wing parties. De Gasperi refused. Pius never forgave De Gasperi for his refusal. This growing rift between the conservative Catholics in the curia and De Gasperi undermined Montini within the Vatican. In addition, Montini had been identified as sympathetic to the French "worker-priest" movement. In fact, he had long-standing close relationships with liberal French theologians and with Jacques Maritain and at first welcomed the new initiative to involve priests in the workplace. However, when the movement was condemned by Pius XII in 1953, Montini supported the pontiff. Nonetheless, within months of the papal condemnation of the worker-priest movement, Montini's enemies made their move against him. First, the conservatives ousted Montini's close allies. Next, critics began to openly attack Montini, calling him a creature of Amintore Fanfani and other Christian Democrats who were attempting to bring about a Catholic alliance with the left-wing parties. Finally, Cardinal Pizzardo, a longtime Montini nemesis, criticized Montini for a preface to a book he had written that seemed to imply that he supported the worker-priests.

When Milan's Cardinal Ildefonso Schuster died in 1954, Montini was quickly named his successor. The appointment, although officially couched in favorable terms, was a blow to Montini. Montini served the see of Milan from 1955 to 1963. Upon his arrival he quickly established himself as the "workers' archbishop." With Milan's increasingly secularized society less inclined to come to the church, the new archbishop determined to take the church to the workers, an interesting echo of the French worker-priest movement. Soon Montini was a familiar figure in factories and mines and on the docks, often wearing a hard hat. He made an extra effort to reach out to the many in his diocese who voted Communist, and he sponsored a new movement among the *fucini* and ex-*fucini* to encourage Catholic social activism among the poor and working classes.

In 1957 Archbishop Montini inaugurated a diocesan-wide movement called "Mission to Milan," a two-week period of intense pastoral activity, accompanied by the staging of numerous publicized events. All over the diocese, in the streets of working-class neighborhoods, in cinemas, in public squares, in factories and offices, thousands of orchestrated sermons on living a Christian life in the modern world were delivered. The "monster mission," as it was dubbed by the press, was a resounding success. Montini's episcopate was also marked by an unusual level of ecumenical activity, particularly with the Anglican church. At the same time, his longtime friendship with Angelo Roncalli, now primate of Venice, was strengthened during these years as both men, trained as diplomats, struggled to administer large and influential dioceses. Roncalli was convinced that Montini would be the next pope, but Pius had not granted the Milanese archbishop a cardinal's hat. Thus when Pacelli died in 1958, Montini was not a member of the college of cardinals; Roncalli left for the conclave without his friend and confidant.

On 28 October 1958 the primate of Venice, Cardinal Roncalli, was elected pope. He took the name John XXIII. Three weeks later the new pope announced that he would make Montini the first cardinal of his papacy. When Pope John announced his intention of calling an ecumenical council, Montini quickly endorsed the idea. The cardinal of Milan played an important role in the preparations for the council, and the pope appointed him to the central preparatory commission, charged with establishing the agenda for the council. Although the pope envisioned only one session, Montini proposed three. In his view the council should concentrate on the "mystery of the church" in the first session. The second should focus on the "mission of the church," and the third should deal with the church's relationship with the world. This, in fact, was more or less how the Second Vatican Council developed. John XXIII lived to guide the church through the first session of Vatican II, which ended on 8 December 1962. The old pope, unfamiliar with the ways of the curia, relied upon Montini to steer him through the labyrinthine passages of the Roman secretariats. Aware that he was dying of cancer, John confided in his Jesuit friend, Robert Tucci, that he feared that the next conclave would attempt to "destroy all that I set out to achieve." Tucci thought that John was hoping that Montini would succeed him to ensure that his work continued.

In June 1963, when John XXIII died, Cardinal Montini entered the conclave as a clear favorite to be the next pope. He had worked closely with John and was committed to continuing the council. Montini was also a favorite of the French and the curial cardinals who sought change. In the end, Montini was chosen pope, a compromise between the progressive and conservative forces. Montini recognized the difficulties of assuming the papacy. He had worked closely with both Pius XII and John for years, and he understood the problems confronting the uncompleted council. The new pope realized that he would have to contend with a powerful conservative bloc within the church that was generally hostile to the direction that John had taken. No wonder he is said to have answered, when asked if he would accept election to the chair of Peter, that he found himself crucified with Christ.

The new pope took the name Paul VI, emphasizing his desire to reach out to the modern world in the manner of St. Paul the Apostle. For Pope Paul, this began with the unfinished work of the council. The pope was concerned with two critical issues: the organization of the council, which was still an impediment to its effectiveness, and the alienation of the conservative minority from the work of the first session. He set about addressing both problems. He appointed personal moderators: the liberal cardinals Leo Suenens and Giacomo Lecaro and the conservatives Pietro Agagianian and Julius Dopfher. The moderators would serve as the pope's "representatives" to the working sessions, setting the agenda and ensuring papal input into deliberations and conclusions.

The second council session opened on 29 September 1963. Paul's opening remarks focused on the subjects that he wished considered: collegiality, the relationship between the bishops and the pope, and ecumenicism. At the same time, the new pope strongly emphasized the primacy of the papal role, to the surprise of some of his liberal supporters. In this second session there were struggles between the ten presidents appointed by John to manage the day-to-day agenda of the council and the new moderators designated by Paul to undertake essentially the same task. In the end, the moderators, who were decidedly more liberal than the majority of presidents, carried the day. The session ended with progressive views on episcopal collegiality and liturgical reform voted in overwhelming numbers, demonstrating that the conservatives were in a decided minority. In a characteristic stroke of diplomacy, Paul shocked the liberals and gratified the conservatives at the session's end by unilaterally declaring Mary as the "mother of the church."

The third session was marked by a counterattack by the conservative bishops, led by Cardinal Arcadio Larraona's and Archbishop Marcel Lefebvre's sharp criticisms of the notion of "collegiality." The conservatives warned of impending chaos should the primacy of the pope be weakened.

Paul was genuinely shaken by the conservative challenge. He believed that the enhancement of the role of bishops would strengthen the primacy of the bishop of Rome. Still, he was acutely aware of the need to walk a tightrope between the procollegiality and anticollegiality camps. Paul consistently supported the views of the progressive majority of the council, but he repeatedly took steps to ensure that the minority felt that their views were respected. To accomplish the latter, Paul often had to act unilaterally, after a vote had been taken. This angered the progressives, who felt that the pope was flying in the face of the collegiality that he supported.

The promulgation of *Mater Ecclesiae* in November 1964 provides an example of how Paul's attempts to bridge the ideological chasms within the church went largely unappreciated by both sides. The conservatives rejoiced, for not only had the pope acted on his own, upholding the principle of primacy, but he had also settled the nettlesome question about the role of Mary in favor of the traditionalists. But Paul never retained the support of conservatives. They quickly forgot his favors and loudly protested the "drift toward disintegration" within the church. The progressive majority, on the other hand, objected strenuously to *Mater Ecclesiae*'s content and its unilateral promulgation.

The concluding session occurred between September and December 1965. In his opening remarks Paul announced the establishment of the synod of bishops that would be convened periodically by the pontiff "for consultation and collaboration." Although the synod was clearly under the authority of the pope, the progressive majority warmly welcomed Paul's initiative. The last session was also characterized by the promulgation of the decree on religious liberty, which worried the traditionalists. Cardinal Giuseppe Siri adhered to the maxim that error has no rights and that other religions could at best be "tolerated" by God. The majority, represented by the Jesuit Cardinal Augustin Bea, proposed that there exists a natural right to religious liberty, while firmly maintaining revealed doctrine on the one true religion for all. The council was paralyzed over the decree. Late in September Paul summoned both sides to his study. There he listened patiently and then declared that a vote would go forward on the basis of Bea's formulation. The decree was promulgated: 1,997 for, 200 against. Paul had shown decisive leadership.

The final session of the council was notable as much for matters that were not addressed as for those that were. The pope decided that the issues of both celibacy of the priesthood and birth control would be the preserve of the pope. The pope also intervened in the drafting of the chapter on marriage in *Gaudium et spes*, warning about the separating of love from procreation and citing Pius XII's encyclical that recommended the natural method of birth control. Paul genuinely believed that both celibacy and contraception were issues that would be vigorously debated by the bishops and that this public debate would be the cause of confusion among the faithful. For these reasons—and not because he caved in to the minority, as some commentators noted—Paul again acted quickly and decisively.

In December 1965 Vatican II drew to a close. The liturgy had been modernized; the role of the bishops had been defined and strengthened; ecumenism had been endorsed; and the seeds of a renewal of the church had been sown. The next thirteen years of Paul's papacy would be marked by the reverberations of the council. The push and pull of both conservative and liberal extremists that Paul had deftly managed at the council would continue. Paul's primary task was to foster the renewal wrought by the council without permitting the church to splinter in two.

In the course of his fifteen-year reign Paul VI authored five encyclical letters: *Ecclesiam suam* (1964), *Mysterium fidei* (1965), *Sacerdotalis caelibatus* (1967), *Populorum progressio* (1967), and *Humanae vitae* (1968). Quite unfairly, the pope is most remembered for *Humanae vitae*, which, although a rich and thoughtful letter on the human condition, was reduced by the press upon its publication to nothing more than the papal banning of artificial birth control. In fact, Paul's encyclicals were not, by and large, treated well by the popular press, which tended to focus on the most sensationalist sections and rarely bothered to fully analyze the text.

Ecclesiam suam described the way in which the church should function in the modern world. It called for "awareness," "renewal," and "dialogue," but it was the call for dialogue that drew attention to the encyclical. Conservatives in the council were not pleased with the emphasis on dialogue with the modern world. They wanted no concessions to the world, particularly to godless communism or to other religions. Perhaps to assuage their concerns, Paul explicitly condemned communism in the letter and restated the primacy of the papacy. Conservatives could find nothing to carp about; progressives emphasized the passages on the need for dialogue with the modern world. Paul's first encyclical mirrored his council strategy: support the progressive majority; respect the conservative minority.

Paul's second encyclical letter, *Mysterium fidei*, was issued at the beginning of the final session of the council in 1965. In the letter Paul clarified the mystery of the Eucharist and transubstantiation on traditional grounds and the teachings of Trent. Paul viewed the question of the Eucharist as urgent and within the jurisdiction of the papacy, even though the council fathers were about to open the fourth session. He deliberately chose not to deflect the issue to a commission, but addressed what he viewed as erroneous theological writings on transubstantiation before they could take root within the church. In doing so, he again caused grumbling among the liberals. Despite being pleased with the encyclical, conservatives did not offer effusive praise for the pope. Rather, they thought that Paul simply did what he should have done, believing that his coddling of the progressives was the cause of the outrageous views the encyclical condemned.

In 1967 Paul issued two encyclicals: *Sacerdotalis caelibatus*, which rein-forced traditional church teaching on priestly celibacy, and *Populorum pro-gressio*, which addressed the social and economic problems of the world. In *Sacerdotalis caelibatus* the pope cited the long tradition of celibacy in the Roman church, its practical value that freed men to serve God alone, and the lack of empirical evidence that celibacy negatively impacted vocations. After scolding priests who abandoned their vocations, Paul allowed that, under some circumstances, they could be granted dispensations. For the liberals of North America and Europe, *Sacerdotalis caelibatus* seemed a slap in the face. Defections from the priesthood continued, and the popular press in developed countries depicted Paul as an obscurantist. At the same time, conservatives worried that the pope had gone too far in his letter by admitting that some priests who rejected celibacy in favor of marriage might receive dispensations and "live as good Christians."

Populorum progressio was Paul VI's first attempt in an encyclical to speak not just to Catholics, but to people of the world. Broadly defined, his concern was "human development," and he insisted that the real crisis in the world was caused by the "North-South" divide, not by the conflict between the East and the West. Addressing the problems of the poor "third world," Paul said that the problems of poverty, hunger, and disease would only be solved by cultivating global solidarity. He attacked unbri-dled capitalism and directed a pointed message to the wealthy "first world" of Europe and North America, repeating that the superfluous wealth of rich countries should be placed at the benefit of poor nations. He rejected the "free market" and argued that "trickle-down economics" did not help the underclasses. The reaction to *Populorum progressio* was predictable. Lib-eral theologians, poor nations, and leftist intellectuals in the West ap-plauded its sentiments. Outside the first world the secular press, by and large, welcomed Paul's challenge to the world's wealthiest nations, but in the United States papal criticisms of capitalism and the free market were largely ignored. Some conservatives even believed that the ideas expressed in the encyclical were subversive, pointing to it as the breeding ground for liberation theology, if not encouraging Communist agitation.

By far, Paul's most controversial and misunderstood encyclical was *Hu-manae vitae*, promulgated in 1968. The encyclical appeared during the so-cietal turbulence of that year: student rebellions in Europe and North America that challenged authority and protested U.S. involvement in Vi-etnam, and the beginnings of the so-called sexual revolution, resulting in incipient recognition of gay rights and increasing acceptance of divorce and remarriage. Cardinal Suenens had urged Paul to call a synod of bishops to discuss family life and, by extension, birth control, but Paul believed that artificial birth control was an attack upon the sanctity of human life and, therefore, did not call for extended discussion. The encyclical insisted that the "defense of human life must begin at the very origin of human existence" and went on to condemn forced birth control in the third world as a violation of basic human rights and unacceptable government interference in family life. At the same time, Paul was sensitive to the plight of married couples who struggled with the birth-control issue, refusing to characterize the use of birth control as a mortal sin. The thoughtfulness and care of the language and meaning of the encyclical were lost on the mass media. They portrayed the encyclical as merely the "banning of the pill," and public opinion polls in Europe and the United States stressed how out of touch the pope and the Vatican were with the daily life of Catholics.

Paul was careful never to claim infallibility for *Humanae vitae*, nor did he regret the inclusion of the pastoral section, which seemed, by admitting a role for individual conscience, to soften the blow to Catholics practicing artificial birth control. This was characteristic of Paul VI: every authoritative action that he took seemed to include salve for the wound, reflecting a keen sense of pastoral care. What did sting the pope was the astounding antipapal reaction from the press and vocal Catholic groups in Europe and the United States, many of which dismissed the encyclical as nothing more than the private opinions of the bishop of Rome. The shaken pontiff never issued another encyclical, although his pontificate continued for ten more years.

Paul's acknowledgment of the eightieth anniversary of Leo XIII's *Rerum novarum* did not result in an encyclical. Instead, in 1971 the pope issued a letter to Cardinal Maurice Roy, the head of the Justice and Peace Commission, entitling it *Octogesima adveniens*. By this document Paul breathed new life into Catholic social teaching, calling upon Catholics to find in the gospel solutions for their particular circumstances. Although the letter condemned the excesses of both socialism and capitalism, it recognized that socialism had several faces, not all of which were objectionable to Catholics. Further, the pontiff criticized developing nations' tendencies to provide lip service to human rights while allowing "flagrant discrimination, continued exploitation and actual contempt" of the poor to exist. Liberation theologians and the church in Latin America, Africa, and Asia praised Paul's letter, and *Octogesima adveniens* solidified Paul's reputation there. In Europe and the United States the words of the pontiff were treated as inconsequential.

Paul VI took the seeds of the ecumenism planted by John XXIII and nurtured them during the entire fifteen years of his papacy. Before Vatican II and Paul, Rome viewed other religions as simply "in error" and their adherents as objects of the missionary work of the Propagation of the Faith. The pope's strong support of ecumenism was evident in 1965 when he presided at the first ecumenical service ever attended by a Roman pontiff. Joined by representatives of the Orthodox and Protestant churches, Paul spoke of the importance of Christian unity. Paul took a particular interest in the final council decree on ecumenism, intervening at the last moment to turn back a conservative effort to water down the notion of religious liberty, defining it as freedom from coercion of belief. Early in his pontificate he established two new and important Vatican offices to promote the ecumenical movement, the Secretariat for Christian Unity and the Secretariat for Non-Christian Religions. Although papal ecumenical initiatives were fairly broad under Paul, his greatest efforts were reserved for the Orthodox and Anglican churches.

In 1964, during the pope's historic visit to the Holy Land, Paul met three times with the patriarch of Constantinople, Athenagoras. The pope and patriarch developed strong personal ties, and their churches grew closer together during Paul's pontificate. In 1965, in Rome, Paul and Athenagoras mutually lifted the thousand-year-old "anathemas of 1054" that marked the formal schism between Rome and Constantinople. Since the two churches' differences were essentially rooted in acceptance of papal primacy and not in doctrinal or sacramental issues, the road of ecumenism was the least difficult of all to hoe. There is little doubt that Pope Paul knew more about the Church of England than any previous pope. He had hosted Anglican visitors as archbishop of Milan even before Vatican II stirred the winds of ecumenism, and he forged a good relationship with Michael Ramsey, the archbishop of Canterbury. The Anglican Roman Catholic International Commission, with members from both denominations, was established as a standing commission charged with the ongoing examination of theological and doctrinal issues with an eye toward greater unity. In 1977 the new archbishop of Canterbury, Donald Coggan, visited Rome.

Ecumenical services, intercommunion, talk of married priests or women priests, the exodus from religious life, the new liturgy, the Dutch catechism, collegiality, liberation theology, focus on the third-world poor—to ultraconservative Catholics, these "abominations" spelled the ruin of Catholicism under Pope Paul VI. The case of Archbishop Marcel Lefebvre was characteristic both of the conservative opposition to Paul's papacy and of the pope's reaction to dissension. Lefebvre, a French Holy Ghost priest and a missionary bishop, was an outspoken leader of the conservative opposition during the council. On several occasions he joined forces with others to try to prevent the council and the church from being infiltrated by the "errors of modern ideas": collegiality, liturgical reform, and ecumenism. After the council Lefebvre continued to speak out against the implementation of the council's reforms. In particular, he objected to the new Mass, which made minor revisions in the Tridentine one and was to be celebrated in the vernacular.

In 1971 Lefebvre founded a seminary to perpetuate his views in Econe, Switzerland. There he railed against the errors of the council, continued to say Mass in the precouncil form, and ordained priests against the wishes of the pope. The pope used intermediaries to appeal to Lefebvre, but was rebuffed. In 1976 the conflict finally came to a head when Lefebvre published his inflammatory book *J'accuse le Concile*, in which he rejected the Second Vatican Council as a betrayal of Roman Catholicism. In July the congregation of bishops formally suspended Lefebvre, forbidding him to say Mass or administer any of the sacraments.

Paul still sought diplomatic solutions. He had been one of the closest aides of Pius XII and had helped maneuver the church through the difficult years of World War II. As pope, Paul had a coherent, focused foreign policy that sought to place the Vatican in the role of advocate for the developing nations of the world while steering clear of the pitfalls of the Cold War. Perhaps the highlight of Paul's diplomatic efforts came early in his reign when, in October 1965, he became the first Roman pontiff to address the United Nations General Assembly. In some ways the pope's speech set the tone for the diplomatic direction of his pontificate. He came to the United Nations, Paul said, to speak on behalf of the poor, disinherited, and suffering, for all those who hunger for justice, for dignity and progress. He recognized the United Nations as an instrument for peace, although he understood that it had yet to achieve this lofty goal. Chiding the superpowers, the pope suggested that nations had to cease their struggles for prestige, domination, colonialism and egoism. In calling for an all-out assault on poverty in the third world, Paul told nations to provide for the poor, not to solve the problem by limiting the birth of the poor.

On 1 January 1968 Paul inaugurated his first "World Peace Day." He urged nations to set aside ideological, economic, and racial differences in favor of peaceful coexistence. His Justice and Peace Commission was established to promote these values worldwide and to challenge first-world nations to respond to the needs of the developing ones. The pope personally worked to bring about peace, meeting with President Lyndon Johnson twice, in 1965 in New York and in 1967 in Rome, to attempt to mediate peace in Vietnam. It was through Vatican intervention that the Paris peace talks were opened in the spring of 1968.

In the developing world Paul placed tremendous emphasis upon Latin America with its strong Roman Catholic traditions. In 1968 the pope decided to visit Colombia, his trip coinciding with the Eucharistic Congress and the second Latin American Bishops Conference (CELAM), an organization established by Paul. In his speech to the bishops Paul emphasized the themes of his encyclical *Populorum progressio*, and he was well received by liberal prelates more focused on papal social teaching than on the first-world concerns of married and women priests. Paul responded over the years by appointing like-minded bishops throughout Latin America who shared the Vatican's views on justice and peace. In short, Paul attempted to steer a course between the old Latin American church, which was closely

aligned with ultrarightist politicians and the military, and the forces unleashed by liberation theology, which sometimes used means that were too
radical for the pope.

In Europe the Vatican pursued *Ostpolitik*, a policy that sought to achieve
better relations with the countries under Communist control. Paul believed that Communist domination of Eastern Europe was a temporary
phenomenon and that *Ostpolitik* would not only improve the lot of Catholics in these nations, but also contribute to the weakening of communism.
The basic assumptions of Vatican policy in Eastern Europe were not uni-
versally accepted; many saw the pope's initiatives as "sellouts" to Marxist
tyrants. Nonetheless, in the name of *Ostpolitik*, Joszef Cardinal Mindszenty,
the symbol of Catholic anticommunism in Hungary, was persuaded in
1971, after fifteen years of self-imposed exile, to leave the U.S. Embassy
in Budapest and relinquish de facto control of the Hungarian church. The
Hungarian government kept its half of the bargain by allowing vacant sees
to be filled by papal appointments.

In Poland Paul made Karol Wojtyla, archbishop of Krakow, a cardinal
and relied upon him more than upon the old hard-liner and primate, Cardinal Stefan Wyszynski. Although both Wojtyla and Wyszynski were implacable anti-Communists, Krakow's archbishop saw the merits in Paul's
Ostpolitik that escaped the old primate. In 1977 the pope received Edward
Gierek, the Polish leader, whom he admonished to implement in Poland
the human rights provisions of the Helsinki accords. The pope lectured
Gierek on the Polish government's promotion of abortion and birth control and demanded the church's right to develop without hindrance. By
this time the Communist regimes of Eastern Europe were beginning to
suffer a major erosion in popular support, resulting in the collapse of the
Berlin Wall in 1989.

On 6 August 1978 Pope Paul VI died at Castel Gandolfo. Almost immediately there was an evaluation of his pontificate. In the era of Vatican
II the church and the papacy needed a leader with the energy, vision, and
organizational ability to bring the council to a successful conclusion. With
Catholic life transformed as a result of the council, the church required
leadership that could ensure that Vatican II's reforms took hold without
causing a conservative backlash that might result in schism. In Paul VI,
Giovanni Battista Montini, the church had such a leader. Paul rejected
authoritarianism, appealed to his followers with reasoned argument, and
demanded the social justice of the Gospels. He was not swayed by pressure
from either the left or right. His legacy was a Roman Catholic church
transformed into a modern force by Vatican II and able to interact more
meaningfully in human affairs than perhaps at any other time in history.
His pontificate was Catholicism's bridge to the modern world.

SELECTED BIBLIOGRAPHY *BY FRANK J. COPPA*

Abbott, Walter. *The Documents of Vatican II*. New York: America Press, 1966. London: Chapman, 1966.

Acta synodalia Sacrosancti Concilii Oecumenici Vaticani II. 26 vols. Vatican City: Typis Polyglottis Vaticanis, 1970–86.

Adornato, Giselda, ed. *Giovanni Battista Montini, archvescovo di Milano, Al mondo del lavaro. Discorsi e scritti (1954–1963)*. Rome: Edizioni Studium, 1988.

Anni e opere di Paolo VI. Ed. Nello Vian, introd. Arturo C. Jemolo. Rome: Instituto della Enciclopedia Italiana, 1978.

Antonetti, Nicola. *La FUCI di Montini e di Righetti: Lettere di Igino Righetti ad Angela Gotelli (1928–1933)*. Rome: AVE, 1979.

Caprile, Giovanni, ed. *Il Concilio Vaticano II*. 5 vols. Rome: Civiltà Cattolica, 1965.
———, ed. *Il sinodo dei vescovi. Paolo VI: Interventi e documentazione*. Rome: Edizione Studium, 1992.

Carlen, Claudia, ed. *The Papal Encyclicals*. Vol. 5, *1958–1981*. Raleigh: Pierian Press, 1981.

Clancy, John G. *Apostle for Our Time: Pope Paul VI*. London: Collins, 1964. *De Ecclesia: The Constitution on the Church of Vatican Council II Proclaimed by Pope Paul VI, November 21, 1964*. Glen Rock, N.J.: Paulist Press, 1965.

Enchiridion delle encicliche. Vol. 7, *Giovanni XXIII e Paolo VI (1958–1978)*. Bologna: EDB, 1994.

Fappani, Antonio, and Franco Molinari. *Giovanni Battista Montini giovane, 1897–1944: Documenti inediti e testimonianze*. Turin: Marietti, 1979.

Felici, Pericle. *Il lungo cammino del Concilio*. Milan: Ancora, 1967.

Flannery, Austin, ed. *Vatican Council II: The Conciliar and Post Conciliar Documents*. Grand Rapids, Mich.: Eerdmans Publishing Co., 1992.

Giovanni e Paolo, due papi: Saggio di corrispondenza (1925–1962). Ed. Loris Capovilla. Brescia: Instituto Paolo VI, 1983.

Guitton, Jean. *Dialogues avec Paul VI*. Paris: Fayard, 1967.
———. *Paul VI secret*. Paris: Desclée, 1979.

Hebblethwaite, Peter. *Paul VI: The First Modern Pope*. New York: Paulist Press, 1993.
———. *The Runaway Church*. London: Collins, 1978.
———. *Understanding the Synod*. Dublin: Gill, 1968.
———. *The Year of Three Popes*. New York: Collins, 1979.

Hitchcock, James. *Catholicism and Modernity: Confrontation or Capitulation?* New York: Seabury Press, 1979.

Insegnamenti di Paolo VI. 16 vols. Vatican City: Libreria Editrice Vaticana, 1965–79.

Jaeger, Lorenz. *The Ecumenical Council, the Church and Christendom*. London: Chapman, 1961.

Magister, Sandro. *La politica Vaticana e l'Italia, 1943–1978*. Rome: Riuniti, 1979.

Montini, Giovanni Battista. *Discorsi e scritti sul Concilio (1959–1963)*. Brescia: Istituto Paolo VI; Rome: Studium; Quaderni dell' Istituto, 1983.
———. *Lettere ai Familiari, 1919–1943*. Ed. Nello Vian. Brescia; Instituto Paolo VI, 1986.

————. *Lettere a un giovane amico*. Ed. Cesare Trebeschi. Brescia: Querinaina, 1979.

Our Name Is Peter: An Anthology of Key Teachings of Pope Paul VI. Ed. Sean O'Reilly. Chicago: Franciscan Herald Press, 1977.

Paolo VI. *Discorsi e documenti sul Concilio (1963–1965)*. Brescia: Istituto Paolo VI, 1986.

Paul VI. *Address of His Holiness Paul VI to the General Assembly of the United Nations, October 4, 1965*. Vatican City: Typografia Poliglotta Vaticana, 1966.

Paulus PP. VI (1963–1978): Elenchus Bibliographicus. Ed. Paolo Vian. Brescia: Paul V Institute, 1981.

The Teachings of Pope Paul VI. Vatican City: Libreria Editrice Vaticana, 1968.

Wolff, Richard J. "Giovanni Battista Montini and Italian Politics, 1897–1933: The Early Life of Pope Paul VI." *Catholic Historical Review* 71, no. 2 (April 1985): 228–47.

JOHN PAUL II
(1978–)

Roy P. Domenico

When Karol Wojtyla assumed the throne of Saint Peter as Pope John Paul II in 1978, he inaugurated perhaps the most volatile epoch in the history of the modern papacy. His pontificate witnessed and contributed to the end of one age and helped to launch a new one. John Paul clearly recognized the watershed nature of the era in his first encyclical, *Redemptor hominis* (1979), issued on 4 March 1979, in which he asked "in what manner should we continue? What should we do, in order that this new advent of the church connected with the approaching end of the second millennium may bring us closer to (the) . . . 'Everlasting Father?' " Historical currents merged with John Paul's own actions to create an office very different from the one he assumed in the late 1970s. Upon reflection two decades later, commentaries from the first years of his pontificate that debated how he would adapt to the heritage of the second Vatican council appeared misdirected. Whereas the forces affecting the church from both within and without had led many to judge the second Vatican council as the defining moment of modern Catholicism, comparable to the council of Trent, it now seems just as likely that history may consider John Paul's pontificate to be of even greater consequence.

The second Vatican council deliberated in a world limited by the Cold War, and then only on the verge of the technological revolution which overcame the globe in the 1980s and 1990s. Cold War issues have now become historically framed; but innovations in information science, the flood of industry and technology to the less developed world, the explosion of consumerism with its concomitant materialism and skepticism, and the decline of the nation-state generated greater challenges for Rome than those faced by Popes John XXIII and Paul VI. Furthermore, John Paul II was an activist who confronted these problems and whose controversial approaches redefined the papacy and its relation to other aspects of the Catholic church. While detractors criticized him as a reactionary, guilty of fostering a papal cult, and indifferent to legitimate voices of change, supporters believed that his pontificate would be remembered as a pastoral success, one that successfully revived the church without serious doctrinal compromises.

Karol Wojtyla was born on 18 May 1920 to a petit bourgeois family in Wadowice, Poland. Despite a childhood of modest comfort, tragedy struck twice the boy's family: the deaths of his mother, Emilia, in 1929, and of his older brother, Edmund, in 1932. His father, also named Karol, died in 1941. The young Wojtyla displayed an active interest in the theater and poetry and frequently participated in circles dedicated to them. His formal education in philology and literature at Krakow's Jagiellonian University was interrupted by Germany's invasion of Poland in 1939, but he nevertheless continued untutored readings while working in a chemical plant.

Wojtyla's life as a Catholic until the world war had been typical of that of many young Poles. The youth in Wadowice and Krakow participated in the Marian Sodality, and devotion to the Madonna subsequently enjoyed a special place in his life. He also gained an appreciation of Poland's nineteenth-century Catholic and nationalist poets such as Adam Mickiewicz and Zygmunt Krasinski. As a Pole informed by their tradition, Wojtyla was often suspected of identifying a messianic role for his homeland in its subsequent struggle against Russian Soviet domination. George Huntston Williams, however, has noted that Wojtyla's favorite poet, Cyprian Norwid, was critical of the messianic school.

Central to Wojtyla's spiritual formation was the influence of a Catholic activist and mystic from Krakow, Jan Tyranowski (1900–1947). Immediately upon their first meeting, at a February 1940 theological discussion group that he chaired, Tyranowski exerted a profound influence on the young man. He intensified Wojtyla's devotion to Mary and introduced him to the work of St. John of the Cross, St. Teresa of Avila, and the Carmelites. Barely two years after his first encounter with Tyranowski, from 1942 until the end of the war, Wojtyla and four other students undertook training for the priesthood, clandestinely sheltered and educated within the walls of the archiepiscopal palace, where he enjoyed the protection of Krakow's Cardinal Adam Sapieha. Sapieha took an early interest in Wojtyla and nurtured his career until his own death in 1951.

After his ordination in 1946 Wojtyla continued his studies and earned two doctorates, one at the Angelicum College in Rome in 1948 and the other at the Jagiellonian University in Krakow in 1952. At the Jagiellonian

Wojtyla worked under the direction of the Dominican Thomist scholar Reginald Garrigou-Lagrange. His dissertation on the question (later sometimes published as the "doctrine") of faith in the work of St. John of the Cross was successfully defended in June 1948. Work toward a second doctorate, in philosophy, was undertaken back in Poland on the insistence of Cardinal Sapieha. Wojtyla's study on the compatibility of Christian ethics with the work of the German phenomenologist Max Scheler earned him a doctorate from Jagiellonian's faculty.

Much of Wojtyla's analysis contained in this work, informed by a familiarity with Thomism acquired during his Roman studies, later found elaboration in his major philosophical treatise, *The Acting Person*. His interest in poetry continued, and he continued to publish works in the Catholic weekly, *Znak*, under the nom de plume Andrzej Jawien. Many of "Jawein's" works were translated into English and released as *Easter Vigil and Other Poems*.

Karol Wojtyla's academic work earned him a position with the faculty of Christian philosophy at Poland's Catholic University at Lublin in 1954. Wojtyla devoted himself exclusively to the Catholic University until 1958, when he was named auxiliary bishop of Krakow. He nevertheless maintained a part-time role at Lublin for many years thereafter and never completely cut his ties with the institution. His new responsibilities in the diocese of Krakow coincided, in 1960, with the publication of one of his most pastoral works, *Love and Responsibility*.

Pope John Paul II visits England and conducts a service at Westminster Cathedral in London. (Hulton/ Archive by Getty Images)

On 30 December 1963 Wojtyla learned of his appointment as archbishop of Krakow by Pope Paul VI, and on 28 June 1967 he received the cardinal's hat. In his new capacities Wojtyla traveled more frequently to Rome. He spoke on religious freedom to the Second Vatican Council in 1964, attended meetings of the Consilium de laicis and its Iustitia et pax commission, participated in the drafting of Pope Paul's encyclical *Humanae vitae*, and frequented the bishops' synods that began in 1967. His relationship with Pope Paul matured, and Wojtyla was asked to lead the 1976 Lenten retreat for the pontiff and the curia. Meditations he composed for this retreat were later printed in English as *Sign of Contradiction*. Wojtyla's expanding responsibilities and presence at the Vatican mixed with his extraordinary position as cardinal from a Communist nation to give him a certain distinction in Roman politics. Upon the death of Paul VI on 6 August 1978, and during John Paul I's short pontificate, which ended on 28 September 1978, Wojtyla's reputation had been firmly established in the curia.

On 16 October 1978 Karol Wojtyla was elected pope after (probably) eight ballots. A deadlock between rival camps of Italian candidates had created the opportunity for the first "foreign" pontiff since the sixteenth-century Dutch pope Hadrian VI. After the conundrum of electoral deadlock became apparent, a German-Spanish–Latin American bloc formed, led by Vienna's cardinal Franz König and Munich's Joseph Ratzinger, that ultimately triumphed behind Wojtyla, who took the name John Paul II.

John Paul's first years on the throne revealed a pastoral pontiff with an ambiguous fealty to the reforms of the Second Vatican Council and a political leader drawn from an embattled East European church who faced squarely the rapidly changing situations of communism, of the underdeveloped nations, and of the West. His responses were to apply pressure to the Communist regimes, to evangelize as never before beyond European cultures, and to reject the materialism of the West while embracing its technology. At the same time, John Paul turned his attention to changing the look of the administration of the Holy See and ecclesiastical leadership around the world.

At the highest church levels, and with a determination that unsettled many, John Paul restructured power into the hands of conservatives such as Cardinal Franjo Seper, prefect of the Congregation for the Doctrine of the Faith, and Alfonso Lopez Trujillo, head of the Latin American Episcopal Conference. His decisions to promote to the college of cardinals Joseph Hamer (Seper's assistant and then head of the Congregation on Religious and Secular Institutes), Miguel Obando y Bravo, John O'Connor, Bernard Law, and he appointed Cardinal Joseph Ratzinger prefect of the Congregation for the Doctrine of the Faith in 1981. These actions as well as his disciplinary measures or replacement of bishops in Brazil, the Netherlands, Austria, and the United States were interpreted as indications of a more conservative pontificate and a step away from the spirit of Vatican II. One observer referred to the new pontificate as the "Restoration" after Paul VI's revolutionary tenure.

John Paul's treatment of certain orders, furthermore, elicited criticism from those who discerned an authoritarian streak in his methods. He clearly favored the growth of the controversial Opus Dei, for example, approving both its status as a prelature in 1982 and, in 1992, the beatification of its founder, José Maria Escrivà de Balaguer. The pontiff's harsher side, however, showed in his approach toward the Jesuits and Carmelites.

The Holy See and the Jesuits had been at odds, particularly over Latin American issues, since the beginning of the pontificate. When the order's superior-general, Pedro Arrupe, expressed his wish to resign for health reasons and to call a congregation, the pope pressured for a delay. But in August 1981 Arrupe suffered a debilitating stroke and appointed as a temporary successor the American Vincent O'Keefe. In October, however, John Paul intervened and, in an unprecedented move, appointed Paolo Dezza as his personal representative to manage the society. The pontiff finally permitted a Jesuit congregation in September 1983 at which the Dutch Peter-Hans Kolvenbach was elected superior-general of the partly demoralized and weakened order.

John Paul also intervened in Carmelite affairs, an act prompted by protests to him from sisters dissatisfied with their experimental 1977 charter. That document looked back to the original intent of St. Teresa of Avila while incorporating many of the principles of *aggiornamento* associated with the Second Vatican Council. The objections came from about 20 percent of the order who were led primarily from two Spanish convents associated with the Opus Dei. In October 1984 Secretary of State Agostino Casaroli announced that the Holy See would administer the order and rewrite the Carmelite constitution. On 8 October 1990 John Paul nullified the 1977 document and pressed on the Carmelites the revised, more conservative one.

Pope John Paul's plans were not limited to the hierarchy or the orders. The new pontiff bluntly addressed dissent from all factions: clergy and lay Catholics. As early as *Redemptor hominis* he lamented that the church suffered from "... an excessive self-criticism" and launched measures to tame it. A bishops' synod in 1980, for example, was called on questions of the family at which voices critical of *Humanae vitae* were stifled. Taking special aim at academics, furthermore, the apostolic constitutions *Sapientia Christiana* (1979) and *Ex corde ecclesiae* (1990) sought to enhance the Catholic essence of pontifical and Catholic universities and the work of their faculties. *Sapientia Christiana* was among the earliest of John Paul's declarations in this direction, although much of the planning behind the document had been the effort of Pope Paul VI. Nevertheless, John Paul's approval of the constitution coincided with a Roman offensive against rebellious clerics and academics. The most celebrated case concerned Hans Küng, the Swiss-born theologian at the University of Tübingen, who had long sounded a controversial voice in Catholic debates.

In 1979 leading newspapers around the world published an open letter by Küng that doubted John Paul's abilities, as a representative of an embattled East European church, to administer fairly the global Catholic population. Küng, furthermore, cast reservations about John Paul's familiarity with modern theological currents. Eight weeks after this publication Rome declared Küng unfit to teach from the pontifical chair of theology that he occupied. Many supporters felt that John Paul was correct to discipline Küng considering the public manner of the attacks and because the theologian's writings had been so abrasively critical, equating, for example, the West German bishops' conference with the Nazis. The Italian Catholic political leader and professor of religion Rocco Buttiglione argued against Küng's position by claiming that John Paul's years in Communist Poland, where he had witnessed the near annihilation of a traditional culture, facilitated his task as the first pope of the postmodern age. John Paul's assaults on communism and capitalism, he continued, were not born of a fear of things to come, but were undertaken because of the failures of these systems.

More disturbing disciplinary measures, however, were Roman actions to censure the more moderate Belgian Edward Schillebeeckx, the French Jacques Pohier, and the American Charles Curran, moves that appeared as attempts to force the submission of Catholic scholars to a Vatican line. John Paul's Marian encyclical *Redemptoris Mater* (1987) and his document *Mulieris dignitatem* (1988), furthermore, emphasized his reluctance to address feminist concerns. His response to feminism in these texts was to promote the Marian devotional and maternal ideals for all Christian women and condemn discrimination and violence against them while underscoring the differences between the masculine and feminine worlds.

Not all contraventions concerned figures who favored modernizing trends. The rebellious traditionalist, French cardinal Marcel Lefebvre, anxious to preserve the Tridentine church in the face of Vatican II reforms, also felt the sting of John Paul's hand. A determined reactionary who rejected most Vatican II reforms and who had been suspended from priestly functions by Paul VI, Lefebvre launched what became a schismatic integralist church. John Paul clearly wished a dialogue, but after Lefebvre consecrated bishops in 1988, he had no choice but to excommunicate the cardinal. Lefebvre died in 1991, outlived by his dissenting movement.

John Paul's discipline held great consequences for the church, but it was for his travels that the pontiff will probably be best remembered around the world. Many of the controversies and ambitions associated with him, such as the papal cult, the embrace of modern technology, a fresh if problematic approach toward the church in developing nations, and criticisms of the Communist East and the capitalist-consumerist West, were accentuated in the daunting travel burden that he assumed upon becoming pope. Before his coronation Karol Wojtyla had visited Oceania in 1973 and the United States in 1976. His work on the fourth bishops' synod, devoted to "evangelization and the modern world," and at the pontifical council (commission) on justice and peace also spurred an awareness of extra-European Catholicism. On becoming pope, John Paul undertook a policy of frequent travel, pastoral encounters, and pilgrimages that enjoyed spectacular success. In his 1982 trip to Spain, for example, approximately one-half of the entire nation saw him in person. Attendance by hundreds of thousands, or even a million, at special masses in all corners of the globe became commonplace.

These showcase trips grew out of the pope's ready embrace of twentieth-century technology, in particular the jet, the television, and elements of mass communication. In 1982, for instance, he granted approval to the American publishing concern the Marvel Group for the release of a comic-book biography, *The Life of Pope John Paul II*. He also allowed, in 1983, an accord with Daniel Serra, an Italo-Brazilian bossa nova singer, to synchronize on record a musical selection with one of his homilies. The significance of John Paul's "showmanship" as well as his pilgrimages must be considered along with his encyclicals and statements as parts of a whole plan to revitalize the church.

The first nation with which John Paul made extended and meaningful contact was Italy. That he was the first "foreign" pope in over four centuries, as well as his clear concern for his native land, created some apprehension among Italians. Upon assuming the throne, John Paul ordered the introduction of Polish broadcasts on Vatican Radio and directed that the Vatican newspaper, *L'Osservatore Romano*, downplay its customary devotion to Italian news. Some considered, however, that his reliance on Secretary of State Cardinal Agostino Casaroli was undertaken to placate the Italians. In the end, most embraced John Paul as one of their own, often noting that he was more Italian than the Italians. He built upon his knowledge of their language and developed an impressive fluency, using it as a matter of course in public appearances in Italy. As bishop of Rome, the pontiff made frequent pastoral visits to local churches and to other Italian cities. His concern with Italy's society and politics, furthermore, assumed a paternal dimension that was often translated into action. During trips to Sicily and the south and from the Vatican itself, for example, he delivered harsh criticisms of Italian organized crime. He also unsuccessfully urged voters to overturn Italy's abortion law in a 1981 referendum.

That vote came only days after a Turkish gunman, Mehmet Ali Agca, attempted to kill the pontiff as he rode in an open-air vehicle greeting well-wishers in St. Peter's Square. Subsequent investigations by Italian magistrates and by the American journalist Claire Sterling indicated that Agca, a Muslim fundamentalist, was part of a Bulgarian-engineered conspiracy, with probable Soviet involvement. Papal support of Polish liberation from the Moscow orbit may have been the motive for the attempted murder. The assassin's bullet, however, had little effect on John Paul's determination to travel. Despite serious health complications from the attack and other medical problems, including the removal of a tumor in 1992, the pope undertook unprecedented and extensive visits to nations on all inhabited continents. Reception varied from place to place. Among his European trips the pope was greeted in 1979 by joyous throngs in

Ireland and by scenes of insult and ridicule during his 1985 Netherlands visit.

John Paul's native Poland, however, assumed the center stage of his travels and politics, notably during the first half of his pontificate. His determination to use his status to call attention to Poland's plight under the Communists was evident even before his election, in veiled statements on a "deep hunger for freedom and justice," for example, to the Philadelphia Eucharistic Congress in 1976, or later in clear pronouncements such as his June 1980 address at UNESCO headquarters in Paris, when he used Poland to illustrate the importance of national cultures in resisting oppression. The day after his coronation John Paul addressed his "beloved countrymen" to emphasize the particular role, or "special witness," of the Polish church.

Undertaken amid labor turmoil generated by Lech Walesa and the Solidarity movement, John Paul's controversial first trip to Poland in 1979 occasioned statements on the rights of workers to organize and strike, pronouncements that clearly situated the Holy See on the side of working-class rebellion, at least in Eastern Europe. John Paul's Polish declarations on behalf of workers and struggle combined with impressions received from visits to the United States and Mexico that same year and presaged his first major encyclical on labor, *Laborem exercens* (1981). Through subsequent visits to his homeland and maneuvers from Rome, John Paul took up the task of referee in Poland's transition toward democracy wherein he cultivated close relationships with Walesa and the head of the martial-law government, Wojciech Jaruzelski. As such, the pope was a political negotiator as well as a source of practical help, directing, for instance, the distribution from Western episcopates of two billion U.S. dollars in aid for Polish farmers.

Visits to underdeveloped nations put the pope in contact with desperate and widespread poverty, problems of Marxism, and competition from both Protestant evangelism and creeping consumerism. Despite ambiguous pronouncements in Rome and contradictory actions taken against liberation theology, these trips nevertheless echoed many of the principles of Paul VI. On the one hand, Cardinal Joseph Ratzinger disciplined Brazilian theologian Leonardo Boff, and the pope ordered Nicaraguan clerics to cease participation in the Sandinista government. On the other hand, John Paul's 1979 trip to the third Latin American Episcopal Conference in Puebla, Mexico, was hailed as a step forward in keeping with Vatican II. With papal consent, the lay presence at Puebla was expanded, and Brazil's progressive Aloisio Lorscheider was chosen as its chair. Although many feared that conference organizer Archbishop Lopez Trujillo would assure a conservative outcome, John Paul surprised the conference participants when, after the Puebla meeting, he recast his speech to the Oaxaca Indians into an impassioned attack on the injustice of concentrated wealth and the anguish of poverty in the third world.

John Paul frequently reemphasized these sentiments, as on his 1980 trip to Brazil, where he confronted President J.B. Figueiredo and embraced Dom Helder Camara; his 1981 trip to the Philippines, where he criticized the Marcos regime; his 1985 visit to Latin America; his 1990 address in commemoration of the World Day of Peace; and his encyclical *Sollicitudo rei socialis* (1987) on the twentieth anniversary of Paul's *Populorum progressio*. In a 1991 visit to Brazil, and at the fourth general conference of Latin American bishops at Santo Domingo in 1992, while John Paul sounded a conservative clarion regarding priestly celibacy and the threat of Protestant fundamentalism, observers noted that liberation theology did not suffer an attack. The movement had been granted a respite in this new and fruitful, if quiet, phase.

The impact of John Paul's trips was also felt in sub-Saharan Africa, where he sought to cultivate the church while preventing the retention of pre-Christian "Africanisms," such as a polygamous priesthood, which conflicted with Catholic teachings. African Catholicism on the whole made enormous strides during his pontificate. Ranks of the faithful there expanded 56 percent in the 1980s to 78,300,000. Between 1978 and 1990 forty-nine new seminaries opened in Africa. John Paul also directed a sustained Vatican diplomatic offensive in the Middle East. His controversial meetings in the Vatican with Yasir Arafat and members of the Palestine Liberation Organization were balanced by the extraordinary recognition of the State of Israel in December 1993.

The fall of Eastern Europe's Communist regimes permitted the pope to turn his scrutiny to the West, where criticisms were directed toward injustice in the capitalist marketplace as well as toward consumerist culture. John Paul's judgments on the West's economic system had been long evident from *Redemptor hominis*, which affirmed the worth and dignity of the person, through *Laborem excercens, Sollicitudo rei socialis*, and *Centesimus annus* (1991). In commemoration of Pope Leo XIII's 1891 encyclical *Rerum novarum, Centesimus annus* applauded the end of atheistic and inefficient communism that had violated the essential human dignity of the workers, but it also reproached Western capitalism, urging a reformation of its market system within a juridical framework that placed it at the service of human freedom. Such assaults triggered responses from capitalist skeptics, including one from London's *Financial Times*, which labeled John Paul a leading socialist.

In other declarations, particularly his 1993 encyclical *Veritatis splendor*, the pontiff disparaged what he considered to be the consumerist offspring of an individualistic and socially irresponsible capitalism. He cautioned against the moral bankruptcy of the wealthy nations, proportionalism, relativism, and rampant greed that cheapened the human being, ruined social cohesion, and poisoned the global environment. During his first papal visit to America John Paul had ordered U.S. bishops at a Chicago conference to draw strict lines against such Western "ills" as divorce, homosexuality, and contraception. Later, even in Poland, John Paul began to attack the maladies of a consumerist society. His disappointing 1991 visit there was distinguished by a scolding of his countrymen who, after their heroic victory over atheistic communism, had turned away from church teachings and had succumbed to atheistic materialism. He lamented their lack of devotion and their embrace of "ills" associated with the West such as drugs, selfishness, divorce, and abortion. He criticized the Polish parliament, for example, as he did the American president Bill Clinton in 1993, for its decision to legalize abortion. Abortion became a focus of U.S.-Vatican disputes, particularly during the 1994 United Nations Conference on Population and Development in Cairo.

When this entry was written, John Paul still occupied the throne of St. Peter, and discussions of his demise and successor were only speculative. Final historical judgments on his pontificate remains open.

SELECTED BIBLIOGRAPHY

Bernstein, Carl, and Marco Politi. *His Holiness: John Paul and the Hidden History of Our Time*. New York: Doubleday, the Penguin, edition, 1996.

Buttiglione, Rocco. *The Thought of the Man Who Became Pope John Paul II*. Grand Rapids, Mich.: William B. Erdmans, 1997.

John Paul II (Karol Wojtyla). *The Acting Person*. Boston: D. Reidel, 1979.

———. *The Encyclicals of John Paul II*. Ed. by J. Michael Miller. Huntington, Ind.: Our Sunday Visitor, 2001.

———. *Gift and Mystery: On the Fiftieth Anniversary of My Priestly Ordination*. New York: Doubleday, 1996.

———. *Insegnamenti di Giovanni Paolo II*. Vatican City: Libreria Editrice Vaticana, 1978– .

John Paul II (Karol Wojtyla), and Vittorio Messori. *Crossing the Threshold of Hope*. Ed. Vittorio Messori. New York: Knopf, 1994.

Hastings, Adrian, ed. *Modern Catholicism: Vatican II and After*. New York: Oxford University Press, 1991.

Hebblethwaite, Peter. *In the Vatican*. Bethesda, Md.: Adler & Adler, 1986.

———. *Introducing John Paul II: The Populist Pope*. London: Collins, 1982.

———. *Pope John Paul II and the Church*. Kansas City: Sheed & Ward, 1995.

McDermott, John M., ed. *The Thought of Pope John Paul II: A Collection of Essays and Studies*. Rome: Editrice Pontificia Università Gregoriana, 1993.

Sterling, Claire. *The Time of the Assassins*. New York: Holt, Rinehart & Winston, 1984.

Szulc, Tad. *Pope John Paul II: The Biography*. New York: Scribner's, 1995.

JOHN PAUL II (1978–)

Weigel, George. *Witness to Hope: The Biography of Pope John Paul II*. London HarperCollins, 1999.
Williams, George Huntston. *The Mind of John Paul II: Origins of His Thought and Action*. New York: Seabury Press, 1981.

BIBLIOGRAPHIC NOTE

The most important repository for the modern papacy is the Archivio Segreto Vaticano (ASV), where the papers of the popes from Pius VI (1775–99) to Benedict XV (1914–22) are accessible. In February 2002, the Vatican announced that within the next decade it will open part of the papers of Pope Pius XI (1922–39) and Pius XII (1939–58). The ASV also contains the archives of the various nunciatures. Some documents on the administration of the Papal States will be found in the Archivio di Stato di Roma (ASR), while the Central Museum of the Risorgimento, also in Rome, contains rich sources on the policies of the popes who confronted the Risorgimento.

These repositories can be supplemented by a series of printed sources, including the *Acta Apostolicae Sedis* (*AAS*) or Acts of the Apostolic See (Rome: Typis Vaticanis, 1909–   ), which contains the laws, pronouncements, and addresses of the pope as well as the major documents issued by the various departments of the Vatican. The *AAS* has replaced the older *Acta Sanctae Sedis* (*ASS*), which was published in Rome from 1865 to 1908 by Typographia Polyglotta. These can be supplemented by the *Annuario pontificio* (*AP*) or Annual Papal Directory, which some have seen as a descendant of the compendium *Notizie*, and which remains essential for an understanding of yearly developments in the church. The *Bullarii romani continuatio*, edited by Andrea Barberi, contains the papal bulls and other important letters and documents from 1835 to 1857 (Rome: Camera Apostolica).

Claudia M. Carlen has edited five volumes of *The Papal Encyclicals* (Wilmington, N.C.: McGrath Publishing Co., 1981), which include the formal circular letters produced by the popes from 1740 to 1981. Carlen also has edited *A Guide to the Encyclicals of the Roman Pontiffs from Leo XIII to the Present Day, 1878–1937* (New York: H.W. Wilson Co., 1939). Other papal encyclicals and pronouncements are found in Carlen's two-volume *Papal Pronouncements: A Guide, 1740–1978* (Ann Arbor, Mich.: Pierian Press, 1990). These volumes also contain many sermons, *motu proprios* or papal decrees, and homilies, providing more than five thousand documents shedding light on the modern papacy. Henry C. Koenig has edited *Principles for Peace: Selections from Papal Documents Leo XIII to Pius XII* (Washington, D.C.: National Catholic Welfare Conference, 1943). In some seven hundred pages Koenig has included papal documents on many of the major contemporary religious, political, and social issues from the 1870s through the pontificate of Pius XI (1922–39). The papal encyclicals can also be found in Eucardio Momigliano, ed., *Tutte le encicliche dei sommi pontefici* (Milan: dall'Oglio, editore, 1959).

A series of volumes on papal teachings has been selected and arranged by the Benedictine Monks of Solesmes. One is on *Education*, trans. Aldo Rebeschini (Boston: St. Paul Editions, 1960), and contains most of the pertinent texts on education from the pontificate of Pius VII (1800–1823) to that of Pius XII (1939–58), as well as some of the early documents of Pope John XXIII (1958–63). There is a volume of Papal Teachings on *Matrimony*, trans. Michale J. Byrnes (Boston: St. Paul Editions, 1963), contains the papal teachings on matrimony from Benedict XIV (1740–58) through John XXIII (1958–63).

L'Osservatore Romano is the newspaper of the Holy See and has existed as a daily since 1861. Among other things, it publishes the texts of papal speeches, pronouncements, and announcements. There is an Italian Sunday edition published separately known as *L'Osservatore della Domenica*. The fortnightly review *La Civiltà Cattolica*, under the direction of the Society of Jesus, provides insights into papal thought and policy on social, religious, and political issues.

Regarding the specific pontificates in this part, John McManners provides a good overview of the Church and the French Revolution in *The French Revolution and the Church* (New York: Harper and Row, 1969). Pius VII's correspondence with the Austrian emperor is published in Friedrich Engel-Janosi, ed., *Die politische Korrespondenz der Päpste mit den österreichischen Kaisern (1801–1918)* (Vienna: Herold, 1964), while that with the Russian tsar is found in Sophie Olszamowska-Skowronska, ed., *La correspondance des papes et des empereurs de Russie (1814–1878)* (Rome: Pontificia Università Gregoriana, 1970). Among the early important secondary works on Pius VII is Alexis François Artaud de Montor's *Histoire du Pape Pie VII* (Paris: Lecler, 1836), as well as the later one by Margaret M. O'Dwyer, *The Papacy in the Age of Napoleon and the Restoration: Pius VII, 1800–1823*

(Lanham, Md.: University Press of America, 1985). There are several good studies of the relationship between Pius VII and Napoleon; the best in English is E.E.Y. Hales, *The Emperor and the Pope* (Garden City, N.Y.: Doubleday, 1961), while the most thorough is Ilario Rinieri's five-volume *La diplomazia pontificia nel XIX secolo* (Turin: Unione Tipografico, 1901–6). Henry H. Walsh provides a detailed English account of the condordat with Napoleon in *The Concordat of 1801* (New York: Columbia University Press, 1933). Relations with England are explored by John Tracy Ellis, *Cardinal Consalvi and Anglo-Papal Relations, 1814–1824* (Washington, D.C.: Catholic University of America Press, 1942), while relations with Austria are covered in Alan J. Reinerman, *Austria and the Papacy in the Age of Metternich*, volume 1, *1809–1830* (Washington, D.C.: Catholic University of America Press, 1979).

For Pius IX, important printed primary sources are the *Atti del Sommo Pontefice Pio Nono, felicemente regnante. Parte Seconda che comprende i motu-propri chigografi editti, notificazioni, ec. per lo stato pontificio* (Rome: Tipografia delle Belle Arti, 1857), useful for a study of the political actions of the first two years of his pontificate and the institutions this pope provided the Papal States following the 1849 restoration. *Pii IX Pontificis Maxima acta* (Rome: Atrium, 1854–1875) contains papal allocutions and encyclicals and other documents of an ecclesiastical nature. Pasquale de Franciscis has collected in four volumes the discourses of Pius following the loss of Rome, 1870–1878, *Discorsi del sommo pontefice Pio IX pronuziati in Vaticano ai fedeli di Roma e dell'orbe dal principio della sua Prigionia fino al presente* (Rome: Tipografia di G. Aurelj, 1872–78).

Mastai-Ferretti's early correspondence can be found in Giovanni Maioli, ed., *Pio IX da vescovo a pontefice: Lettere al Card. Luigi Amat* (Modena: Società Tipografica Modenese, 1949), while his later correspondence with Leopold II of Tuscany and Vittorio Emanuele of Piedmont-Sardinia can be found, respectively, in *Pio IX e Leopoldo II*, edited by Giacomo Martina (Rome: Pontificia Università Gregoriana, 1967), and the two volumes edited by P. Pietro Pirri entitled *Pio IX e Vittorio Emanuele II dal loro carteggio privato* (Rome: Università Gregoriana, 1944, 1951). Paolo Dalla Torre has published their later correspondence in *Pio IX e Vittorio Emanuele II dal loro carteggio privato negli anni del dilaceramanento (1865–1878)* (Rome: Istituto di Studi Romani, 1972). Part of the correspondence with the nuncios has been published, including *Il Carteggio Antonelli-Sacconi (1858–1860)* with Paris (Rome: Istituto per la Storia del Risorgimento, 1962), *Il Carteggio Antonelli-Barili (1859–1861)* with Madrid (Rome: Istituto per la Storia del Risorgimento, 1973), *The Vatican and Hungary, 1846–1878* (Budapest: Akadémiai Kiadó, 1981), and *Il Carteggio Antonelli–De Luca, 1859–1861* with Vienna (Rome: Istituto per la Storia del Risorgimento, 1983). The reports of Odo Russell, the unofficial English representative at the court of Rome, have been edited by Noel Balkiston in *The Roman*

Question: Extracts from the Despatches of Odo Russell from Rome, 1858–1870 (London: Chapman & Hall, 1962). Another English account of the papal court during the pontificate of Pius IX is found in the reports of the U.S. ministers to Rome. These have been collected by Leo Francis Stock in *Consular Relations between the United States and the Papal States: Instructions and Despatches* (Washington, D.C.: American Catholic Historical Association, 1945) and *United States Ministers to the Papal States: Instructions and Despatches, 1848–1868* (Washington, D.C.: Catholic University Press, 1933).

The best study of Pius IX's early life remains Alberto Serafini's *Pio Nono: Giovanni Maria Mastai Ferretti dalla giovinezza alla morte nei suoi scritti e discorsi editi e inediti* (Vatican City: Tipografia Poliglotta Vaticana, 1958). Serafini's work was finished by Giacomo Martina, who produced three additional volumes: *Pio IX (1846–1850); Pio IX (1851–1866)* and *Pio IX (1867–1878)* (Rome: Editrice Università Gregoriana, 1974, 1986, 1990), the most comprehensive studies of Pius IX's pontificate. In 1954 E.E.Y. Hales published *Pio Nono: A Study in European Politics and Religion in the Nineteenth Century* (New York: P.J. Kenedy and Sons, 1954), which utilized a wide variety of contemporary sources but not the Vatican Archives, which were then closed for the pontificate of Pius IX. Frank J. Coppa's *Pope Pius IX: Crusader in a Secular Age* (Boston: Twayne, 1979) had the advantage of access to the Vatican Archives and provides an account that focuses on the political events of the pontificate. The annotated bibliography in this last volume provides valuable information on Pius and his pontificate for English readers. Coppa has also written a study of Pius IX chief minister entitled *Cardinal Giacomo Antonelli and Papal Politics in European Affairs* (Albany: State University of New York Press, 1990) that provides information on the cardinal, the pope, and the pontificate.

The bibliography on Leo XIII is vast. Fundamental printed primary sources for this pontificate are the twenty-three volumes of *Leonis XIII, Pontificis Maximi acta* (Rome: Ex Typographia Vaticana, 1887–1905), *The Great Encyclical Letters of Pope Leo XIII*, edited by John J. Wynne (New York: Benziger Brothers, 1903), and the seven volumes of Leo XIII's writing, *Sanctissimi Domini Nostri Leonis Papae XIII allocutiones, epistolae, constitutiones* (Bruges and Lille: Desclée, 1887–1906). Eduardo Soderini provides a detailed study of this pope and his pontificate in his three-volume *Il pontificato di Leone XIII* (1932–33), the second volume of which has been translated into English as *Leo XIII, Italy, and France* (London: Burns, Oates & Washbourne, 1935). Briefer studies include William J. Kiefer, *Leo XIII: A Light from Heaven* (Milwaukee: Bruce Publishing, 1961); the older work by J. Bleecker Miller, *Leo XIII and Modern Civilization* (New York: Eskdale Press, 1897); and Edward T. Gargan, *Leo XIII and the Modern World* (New York: Sheed & Ward, 1961). Studies that are more focused include Thomas Joseph Shahan, *Leo XIII and the Hague Conference* (Washington, D.C.: New Century Press, 1902); Joseph Watzlawik, *Leo XIII and the New Scholasticism* (Cebu City, Philippines: University of San Carlos, 1966); and Lillian Parker Wallace, *Leo XIII and the Rise of Socialism* (Durham, N.C.: Duke University Press, 1966). On Leo's position toward the Anglican church and its orders, see Thomas Richey, *Leo XIII and Anglican Orders* (n.p., 1897), and, more recently, John Jay Hughes, *Absolutely Null and Utterly Void: The Papal Condemnation of Anglican Orders* (Washington, D.C: Corpus Books, 1896).

A number of significant primary sources, especially archival materials and collections related to the beatification and canonization of Pius X, have been printed and provide valuable material for understanding this pope and his pontificate. The archives of the Sacred Congregation of Rites in Rome contains *Romana beatificationis et canonizationis servi Dei Pii Papae X* (Rome: Typis Polyglottis Vaticanis, 1950) Vincent A. Yzermans has collected and edited the encyclicals and many of the other documents of Pius X in *All Things in Christ: Encyclicals and Selected Documents of Saint Pius X* (Westminster, Md.: Newman Press, 1954). Joseph B. Collins has collected, translated, and edited Pius X's catechetical documents in *Catechetical Documents of Pope Pius X* (Paterson, N.J.: Saint Anthony Guild Press, 1946). Volumes 6 to 14 of the *Acta Apostolicae Sedis* (1914–22) provide printed copies of the pertinent Vatican documents of the reign of Benedict XV. Among secondary sources, Robert Allthann's "Papal Mediation during the First World War," *Studies* (Ireland) 61, no. 243 (1972): 219–40, explores the role of Benedict in the peace negotiations between Germany and the Allies. This is also the focus of Konrad Repgen's chapter entitled "Foreign Policy of the Popes in the Epoch of the World Wars," in *The Church in the Modern Age*, edited by H. Jedin and others (New York: Crossroad, 1980), 35–95. Books that treat the subject of Benedict's role in World War I include Henry E.G. Rope, *Benedict XV, the Pope of Peace* (London: Catholic Book Club, 1940), in English, Giuseppe Rossini, *Benedetto XV, cattolici, e la Prima Guerra Mondiale* (Rome: Cinque Lune, 1963), in Italian, and Wolfgang Steglich, ed., *Der Friedensappell Papst Benedikt XV vom 1 August 1917 und die Mittelmächte* (Wiesbaden: Franz Steiner Verlag, 1970), in German. The comprehensive biography written by Walter H. Peters, *The Life of Benedict XV* (Milwaukee: Bruce Publishing, 1959) has long been the authoritative biography in English, utilizing the pertinent primary and secondary sources available. He did not have access to the Vatican Archives, as did John Pollard, who recently produced *The Unknown Pope: Benedict XV (1914–1922) and the Pursuit of Peace* (London: Chapman, 1999).

The early biographies of Pius XI cover only a part of his pontificate, including A. Novelli's *The Life of Pius XI*, trans. P.T. Lombardo (Yonkers, NY: Mt. Carmel Press, 1925) and those of Lord William Clonmore, *Pope Pius XI and World Peace* (London: Robert Hale, 1937) and of Philip Hughes, *Pope Pius the Eleventh* (New York: Sheed and Ward, 1937). More recently Marc Agostino has published a monograph *Le Pape Pie XI et l'opinion (1922–1939)* (Rome: École Française, 1991) that covers the entire pontificate and provides an assessment of the impact of his message in France and Italy. This pope's relations with the Fascist regime are explored in John F. Pollard's *The Vatican and Italian Fascism, 1929–32: A Study in Conflict* (Cambridge: Cambridge University Press, 1985) and Peter C. Kent's *The Pope and the Duce: The International Impact of the Lateran Agreements* (London: Macmillan, 1981). The concordats with Italy and Germany are explored in Frank J. Coppa, ed., *Controversial Concordats: The Vatican's Relations with Napoleon, Mussolini, and Hitler* (Washington, D.C.: Catholic University of America Press, 1999), while the lost encyclical *Humani generis unitas* is discussed in Georges Passelecq and Bernard Suchecky, *The Hidden Encyclical of Pius XI*, trans. Steven Rendall (New York: Harcourt Brace, 1997). Considerably more controversy surrounds his successor Pius XII, even after the publication of the 11 volumes of the *Actes et documents du Saint Siège relatifs à la seconde guerre mondiale* (Vatican City: Libreria Editrice Vaticana, 1965–81).

There are numerous works on the pontificates of John XXIII and Paul VI and the Second Vatican Council. These include the admirable biographies of Peter Hebblethwaite, *Pope John XXIII, Shepherd of the Modern World* (Garden City, N.Y.: Doubleday, 1985) and *Paul VI: The First Modern Pope* (New York: Paulist Press, 1993). The documents of Vatican II have been edited by Austin Flannery in *The Conciliar and Post Conciliar Documents* (Wilmington, Del.: Scholarly Resources, 1975). The five-volume *Discorsi, messagi, colloqui del Santo Padre Giovanni XXIII* (Vatican City: Typis Polyglottis Vaticanis, 1961–67) contains the official version of all the addresses of Pope John. Likewise, there have been innumerable biographies and publications of the works of John Paul II, including his *Crossing the Threshold of Hope* (New York: Knopf, 1994) and *The Encyclicals of John Paul II* (Huntington, Ind.: Our Sunday Visitor, 2001). Additional bibliographical references are appended to the end of each of the entries in this part under the heading "Selected Bibliography."

INDEX

Page numbers in **bold** indicate main entries.

Dopfher, Cardinal Julius, 526
Dosetti, Giuseppe, 524
Dreyfus affair, 469
Dumont, Jean, 395
Duns Scotus, 266
Durndus of Huesca, 128
Dyonisiana, 78

Eastern Christianity: in Alexandria, 3,
8–9, 44–46, 52, 56, 59, 76; in Constantinople, 8, 9, 35, 42, 44, 45, 55–
56, 57, 62, 76, 77, 91–92, 109; and
procession of Holy Spirit, 110, 142;
relations with papacy, 9, 34–35, 44–
45, 55–57, 59–60, 61, 62–63, 76–77,
81, 85, 90–92, 109, 110, 129, 142,
186, 187, 219, 222, 229, 232–33,
234, 240, 242, 246, 349, 458, 485–
86, 530–31
Eckhart, Meister, 197, 202
Ecumenism, 486, 506, 513, 515, 516–
17, 525, 526, 528, 530–31
Edict of Nantes, 395
Education, 466–67, 469, 493
Edward I, 164
Elagabalus, Marcus Antoninus, 27, 30
Eleutherius, 5
Elias of Cortona, 139
Elizabeth of Thuringia, 140
Elizabeth I, 336, 339, 352
England, 46–47, 48, 75–76, 78, 85,
222, 224, 284, 292, 330, 374; Tho-
mas Becket, 114, 117–18; Church
of, 525, 531; Edward I, 164; Eliza-
beth I, 336, 339, 352; Gunpowder
Plot, 367, 374–75, 379; Henry II,
116, 117–18; Henry III, 150, 160–
61; Henry VIII, 295, 299, 303;
James I, 352–53, 367, 374, 379;
John I, 123, 127, 130, 134; Mary I,
339; relations with France, 126, 164,
183, 210, 211, 214; relations with
Spain, 360; William the Conqueror,
81, 99, 100. *See also* Great Britain
Enlightenment, the, 329, 435, 436,
445
Enzio (son of Frederick II), 146–47
Ephesians, passages from, 77

Ephesus, councils of: Council of 431,
8, 46, 59; Council of 449 (Latro-
cinum/Robber Council), 9, 48, 56,
60
Epiphanius, 22
Epistle to the Corinthians (1 Clem-
ent), 18, 23–26
Erasmus, Desiderius, 193, 279, 293
Eskil of Lund, 114
Este, Alfonso d,' 284
Este, Borso d,' 256
Este, Cesare d,' 367
Este, Niccolò d,' 212
Estouteville, Cardinal William d,' 252
Estrées, François Annibal d,' 391
Ethelbert, 75
Ethiopia, 495, 501
Eucharist, the, 124, 142, 348, 528
Eugenius III, 83–84, 114, 116
Eugenius IV, 181, 185–87, **229–35**,
242, 245; charity of, 234; and conci-
liarism, 185–86, 225–26, 229, 230,
231–33, 234–35, 241, 250; and
Council of Basel, 225–26, 231–33,
234–35; and Council of Ferrara-
Florence, 222, 232–34, 240; curia
under, 234; nepotism of, 234
Eulalius, 41
European Economic Community, 506
Eusebius, 18, 22, 23, 25, 28, 53
Eutyches, 9, 56
Evolution, 478

Facundus of Hermiane, 62, 63
Faenza, 138
Fanfani, Amintore, 524
Farinacci, Roberto, 523
Farnese, Cardinal Alessandro, 308,
309, 312, 333, 340, 344, 353, 366
Farnese, Alessandro (duke of Parma
and Piacenza), 350–51
Farnese, Elisabeth, 419–20
Farnese, Giulia, 286
Farnese, Ottavio, 312
Farnese, Pier Luigi, 308–9
Fathers of the Church, 30, 84, 93, 94,
98, 188, 244, 349. *See also* Ambrose,
St.; Augustine of Hippo, St.; Basil,

INDEX

Serra, Daniel, 543

Servites, 347

Seven Years' War, 421

Sexuality, 30, 120; birth control, 442,
527–28, 529–30; homosexuality,
441, 503, 546

Sforza, Ascanio, 281

Sforza, Cardinal Guido Ascanio, 308

Sforza, Caterina, 269

Sforza, Francesco, 242, 256

Sforza, Ludovico, 280

Sforza, Muzio Attendolo, 222, 223,
225

Shepherd of Hermas, 22

Sicily, Kingdom of, 99, 116, 125, 126,
127, 134, 136, 145–46, 147, 148,
159, 160–61, 167, 198, 338; William
I, 114, 117

Siena, 136, 213, 250, 253, 257–58,
259, 269, 373

Sigebert of Gembloux, 117

Sigismund, 220, 225

Sigismund of Luxemburg, 231

Signorelli, Luca, 190, 273

Sigonio, Carlo, 348, 349

Sillon of Marc Sangnier, 478

Silverius, 60, 61

Simon d'Authie, 139

Simon de Monfort, 130

Simonetta, Cardinal Ludovico, 337,
344

Simon of Brie, Cardinal, 163

Simony, 81, 89, 91, 97, 99, 100, 118,
119, 191, 195, 221, 326, 337; definition, 79; and Innocent XII, 398–99;
and John XXII, 182; and Julius II,
282–83; and Leo X, 294, 295, 296;
and Pius II, 257; and Sixtus IV, 189,
268, 271

Siri, Cardinal Giuseppe, 527

Sirleto, Guglielmo, 348

Sistine Chapel, 190, 191, 194, 273,
285, 293, 304, 311

Sixtus III, 52

Sixtus IV, 181, 189–90, 191, 192, **265–
74**, 279, 280, 281; and Franciscans,
265, 266, 267, 358; and heresy, 272;
and indulgences, 271; and the Med-

ici, 269–70, 289; nepotism of, 268–
69, 271; Papal States under, 271;
and simony, 189, 268, 271; and Sistine Chapel, 190; as theologian, 266–
67; and Vatican Library/Archives,
190, 273

Sixtus V, 311, 341, 344, **357–62**, 365,
366, 373, 378, 390, 399; and Council of Trent, 360; curia under, 359;
and evangelization, 329–30; and
heresy, 328, 330; and modernization, 328–29; Papal States under,
326, 353, 358–60; as patron of the
arts, 325, 326; as reformer, 330, 359–
60; and Sixtine Vulgate, 327, 361,
369; treasure of, 359, 408, 423

Slavery, 257, 329, 341, 410

Slovakia, 503

Smedt, Émile-Joseph de, 514

Socialism, 439, 441, 453, 457, 468,
484–85, 494, 530. *See also* Communism

Society for the Propagation of the
Faith, 367, 485, 512

Society of Jesus. *See* Jesuits

Sodalitum Pianum, 478, 482

Soderini, Francesco, 300

Solimeno, Giuseppe, 401

Somaschi, 308, 368

Southern, R. W., 200

Soviet Union, 439, 440, 441, 500, 543;
Stalin, 434, 494, 501, 502, 503, 506.
See also Communism; Russia

Sozzini, Mariano, 250, 401

Spain, 55, 100, 111, 194, 200, 222,
283, 292, 301–2, 328, 339–40, 365,
366, 376, 384, 406, 409, 410, 438,
500, 506, 542–43; Charles I, 186,
193, 293, 300, 301, 302, 303, 310,
338; Charles II, 402; Charles III,
419–20; Civil War, 495, 501; and
Council of the Indies, 340; Ferdinand VI, 419; under Franco, 440,
507; Jesuits in, 419–20, 436, 450;
Philip II, 338, 344, 350, 352, 360,
368; relations with England, 360;
relations with Germany, 439, 468;
relations with Portugal, 417, 419;

ABOUT THE EDITORS AND CONTRIBUTORS

JAMES R. BANKER is professor of history at North Carolina State University in Raleigh, North Carolina. His important first book is entitled *Death in the Community: Memorialization and Confraternities in an Italian Commune in the Late Middle Ages*. Forthcoming is *The Culture of San Sepolcro during the Youth of Piero della Francesca*. He is the coeditor with Carol Lansing of the forthcoming volume *Florentine Essays: Selected Writings of Marvin Becker*.

JOSEPH A. BIESINGER, professor emeritus of history at Eastern Kentucky University, received his B.A. and M.A. from Loyola University in Chicago and his Ph.D. from Rutgers University. His areas of specialization include modern German history and the Holocaust, and he has published widely on these subjects. Among his most recent publications is a long article on "The Reich Concordat of 1933: The Church Struggle Against Nazi Germany," which appears in the volume *Controversial Concordats: The Vatican's Relations with Napoleon, Mussolini, and Hitler* (1999). He is currently working on a volume on modern Germany.

RICHARD J. BLACKWELL is partially retired from St. Louis University, where he has held the Danforth Chair in the Humanities. He has edited and translated many volumes of primary sources related to the history of science, including Giordano Bruno's *Essays on Magic* (1998). Among his books are *Galileo, Bellarmine, and the Bible* (1991) and *Science, Religion, and Authority: Lessons from the Galileo Affair* (1998).

UTA-RENATE BLUMENTHAL is ordinary professor of history at the Catholic University of America, where she directed the Program in Medieval and Byzantine Studies for many years. Her published monographs include *The Early Councils of Pope Paschal II, 1100–1110* (1978); *Der Investiturstreit* (1982); *The Inveiture Controversy: Church and Monarchy from the Ninth to the Twelfth Century* (1988) and *Gregor VII: Paspst zwischen Canossa und Kirchenreform* (2001). A selection of her numerous papers has been published under the title *Papal Reform and Canon Law in the 11th and 12th Centuries* (1998).

LORENZ BÖNINGER is an independent scholar based in Florence, Italy. He has produced numerous studies on late medieval and Renaissance topics. He has been a fellow at Villa I Tatti and is the editor of one of the forthcoming volumes of the *Medici Lettere*.

FRANCESCO C. CESAREO is professor of history and director of the Institute for Catholic Studies at John Carroll University. Among his recent publications are two books: *A Shepherd in Their Midst: The Episcopacy of Girolamo Seripando, 1554–1563* (1999) and *Humanism and Catholic Reform: The Life and Work of Gregorio Cortese, 1483–1548* (1990).

KATHLEEN M. COMERFORD is an assistant professor of history at Georgia Southern University. She is the author of several articles on the impact of the legislation of the Council of Trent, and of *Ordaining the Catholic Reformation: Priests and Seminary Pedagogy in Fiesole, 1575–1675* (2001).

FRANK J. COPPA is professor of history at St. John's University in New York, director of its Vatican Symposium, and director of the university's doctoral degree in modern world history. He received his B.A. from Brooklyn College and M.A. and Ph.D. from the Catholic University of America and is the author of a series of biographies, including *Pope Pius IX: Crusader in a Secular Age* (1979) and *Cardinal Giacomo Antonelli and Papal Politics in European Affairs* (1990). More recently he has published *The Modern Papacy since 1789* (1998) and served as editor-in-chief and contributor to *Encyclopedia of the Vatican and Papacy* (1999) and *Controversial Concordats: The Vatican's Relations with Napoleon, Mussolini, and Hitler* (1999). He is currently writing a volume on *The Papacy Confronts the Modern World*.

LAURA DE ANGELIS is ricercatore in the Dipartimento di Storia of the Università di Firenze. She has published studies on fourteenth and early fifteenth-century political history. Her articles appear in *Archivo Storico Italiano*, *Studi Storici*, and other important journals. She has a forthcoming book on the *Libri Fabarum*. She is editing one of the later volumes of the *Medici Lettere*, to be published by the Istituto Nazionale di Studi sul Rinascimento.

CHARLES F. DELZELL, professor emeritus at Vanderbilt University, received his Ph.D. from Stanford University. A specialist in Italian and papal history. His published volumes include *Mussolini's Enemies: The Italian Anti-Fascist Resistance* (1961), *Mediterranean Fascism, 1919–1945* (1970), and *The Papacy and Totalitarianism between the Two World Wars* (1973), among others. His article "Pius XII and the Outbreak of War," appear in *The Journal of Contemporary History* (October 1967).

BRENDAN DOOLEY is the chief of Research at the Medici Archive Project in Florence, Italy. He taught at several universities in the United States, including, most recently, at Harvard. Among his many publications are two recent books: *Morandi's Last Prophecy and the End of Renaissance Politics* and *The Social History of Skepticism: Experience and Doubt in Early Modern Culture* (1999).

ROY P. DOMENICO, an associate in the Columbia University Seminar on Modern Italy and Associate Professor of History at the University of Scranton, received his Ph.D. from Rutgers University. A historian of modern Italy, he has published *Italian Fascists on Trial, 1943–48* (1992), among other books. His article "America, the Holy See, and the War in Vietnam" appears in the volume *Papal Diplomacy in the Modern Age* (1994), edited by Peter Kent and John Pollard.

EDWARD D. ENGLISH is an independent scholar. He is working on a major study of the city of Siena. His books include *Enterprise and Liability in Sienese Banking, 1230–1350* (1988), and he has edited *Reading and Wisdom: The De Doctrina Christiana of Augustan in the Middle Ages* (1995). With Mark Meyerson, he edited *Christians, Muslims, and Jews in Medieval and Early Modern Spain* (1999).

The late **ROBERT B. ENO**, S.T.D. from the Institut Catholique in Paris was professor of church history at the Catholic University of America. His research focused on the fathers of the church in the Latin West, with a particular interest in social doctrine and the social structure of the church. He served for many years on the Lutheran–Roman Catholic Dialogue in the United States.

GERARD H. ETTLINGER was ordained a priest in the Society of Jesus in 1966. After completing a B.A. and M.A. at Fordham University, he earned a D.Phil. in the Theology Faculty of Oxford University, specializing in patristics and early church history. He was an assistant professor at the Pontifical Oriental Institute in Rome from 1972 to 1974 and associate professor and professor in the Theology Department at Fordham University from 1974 to 1989. Since 1989 he has been a professor in the Department of Theology and Religious Studies at St. John's University. His publications include a critical edition of the Greek text of two treatises by John Chrysostom, a critical edition of the Greek text of the *Eranistes* by Theodoret of Cyrus, and an anthology of readings, in English, from the church fathers on the theology of Christ. A translation of the *Eranistes* is scheduled for publication in 2003.

ROBERT C. FIGUEIRA is professor of history at London University. He pursued undergraduate studies at Wesleyan University under the tutelage of Robert L. Benson and graduate studies at Cornell University under Brian Tierney. His research focuses on medieval canon law and medieval papal legation. A recipient of grants from the German Academic Exchange Service, the Fulbright Commission, and the National Endowment for the Humanities, he currently serves as a board member of the South Carolina Humanities Council and advisory board member of the Stephan Kuttner Institute of Medieval Canon Law.

MARGERY A. GANZ is a professor and chair of the Department of History at Spelman College in Atlanta, Georgia. She has written on quattrocento Florentine political and social history. Her articles have appeared in *Rinascimento, Stanford Italian Review*, and *Renaissance Quarterly*. Her current project is entitled "Conspiracy as Civic Responsibility: The 1466 Plot to Oust the Medici."

KENNETH GOUWENS is associate professor of history at the University of Connecticut at Storrs. He is the author of *Remembering the Renaissance: Humanist Narratives of the Sack of Rome* (1998).

PATRICK GRANFIELD is professor of systematic theology and church history at the Catholic University of America in Washington, D.C. He is the author of numerous articles and books, including *The Papacy in Transition* (1980), *The Limits of the Papacy: Authority and Autonomy in the Church* (1987), *The Church and Communication* (1994), *The Theology of the Church: A Bibliography* (coauthor with Avery Dulles, 1999), and *The Gift of the Church* (2000), among others.

HANNS GROSS is professor emeritus of history at Loyola University, Chicago. His books include *Rome in The Age of Enlightenment: The Post-Tridentine Syndrome and the Ancien Regime* (1990), and *Empire and*

Sovereignty: A History of the Public Law Literature in the Holy Roman Empire, 1599–1804 (1979).

JOHN B. GUARINO, who received his M.A. from the University of Michigan, Ann Arbor, has recently retired from full-time teaching. Long interested in the eighteenth-century papacy in general and Benedict XIV in particular, he has presented papers on the subject before the New England Historical Association and the American Catholic Association. He is professor emeritus at Northern Essex County Community College in Haverhill, Massachusetts.

JACQUELINE A. GUTWIRTH is professor of history at Bronx Community College of the City University of New York. She is the editor of *Priorista (1407–1459) with 2 appendices (1282–1406) of Pagolo di Matteo Petriboni and Matteo di Borgo Rinaldi* (2001).

WILLIAM V. HUDON is professor and chairman in the Department of History at Bloomsburg University. He also serves as the executive director of Bloomsburg's Institute for Culture and Society. Among his recent publications is an article entitled "Religion and Society in Early Modern Italy: Old Questions, New Insights," *American Historical Review* 101 no. 3 (June 1996): 783–804, plus two earlier books: *Marcello Cervini and Ecclesiastical Government in Tridentine Italy* (192) and *Theatine Spirituality: Selected Writings* (1996).

RICHARD KAY has taught medieval history at the University of Kansas since 1967 and is now an emeritus professor. His recent publications include *Councils and Clerical Culture in the Medieval West* (1997), a translation of and commentary on Dante's *Monarchia* (1998) and *The Council of Bourges, 1225: A Documentary History* (2002), as well as articles in *Viator*, *Traditio*, and *Bibliothèque de l'École des chartes*.

JOSEPH F. KELLY is professor of church history at John Carroll University in Cleveland, Ohio. His area of expertise is the transition era from the church of the Roman Empire to the church of the early Middle Ages. His publications include seven books, fifty scholarly articles in European and American journals, and more than three hundred book reviews. He is past president of the North American Patristic Society and serves as book review editor of *Journal of Early Christian Studies*.

PETER C. KENT, professor of history at the University of New Brunswick, received his Ph.D. from the London School of Economics. He is an expert in papal relations with the broader world. His books include *The Pope and the Duce: The International Impact of the Lateran Agreements* (1999) and the work he has coedited on *Papal Diplomacy in the Modern Age* (1994). His articles on these and other subjects appear in a host of scholarly journals.

CAROL LANSING is professor of history at the University of California at Santa Barbara. Her books include *The Florentine Magnates: Lineage and Faction in a Medieval Commune, Power and Purity: Cathar Heresy in Medieval Italy*, and, *The Lament for the Dead*. With James R. Banker, she is the coeditor of the forthcoming volume *Florentine Essays: Selected Writings of Marvin Becker*.

ALISON WILLIAMS LEWIN is associate professor of history at St. Joseph's University in Philadelphia. Her book *Negotiating Survival: Florence and the Great Schism (1378–1417)* is forthcoming.

THOMAS F. MADDEN is associate professor and chair of the Department of History at St. Louis University. He is the author of *A Concise History of the Crusades* (1999), coauthor of *The Fourth Crusade: The Conquest of Constantinople* (1997), editor of *The Crusades: Essential Readings* (2001), and coeditor of *Medieval and Renaissance Venice* (1999). At present he is working on a general history of Venice in the Middle Ages.

FREDERICK J. McGINNESS is a lecturer at Smith College in Northampton, Massachusetts. He is the author of numerous articles and reviews in addition to a book, *Right Thinking and Sacred Oratory in Counter-Reformation Rome* (1995).

PHILIP A. McSHANE is an associate professor at St. Paul University in Ottawa. His dissertation for a D.S.R. at Strasbourg dealt with Pope Leo the Great. His major areas of interest are ecclesiology, missiology, historical theology, and patristics.

CAROL BRESNAHAN MENNING is professor of history at the University of Toledo. She has published numerous articles in scholarly journals, as well as a book entitled *Charity and State in Late Renaissance Italy: The Monte di Pietà of Florence* (1993).

NELSON H. MINNICH is professor of church history and chair of that department at the Catholic University of America. He received his B.A. and M.A. from Boston College, his S.T.B. from the Gregorian University, and his Ph.D. from Harvard University. A specialist in the Renaissance, Reformation, and Counter-Reformation, among other works he has published *The Catholic Reformation: Council, Churchmen, Controversies* (1993) and *The Fifth Lateran Council (1512–17): Studies on Its Memberships, Diplomacy,* *and Proposals for Reform* (1994) and has published a series of journal articles. He is associate editor of *Catholic Historical Review*.

EMILIANA P. NOETHER professor emerita of history at the University of Connecticut, received her B.A. from Hunter College of the City University at New York and her M.A. and Ph.D. from Columbia University. Her specializations include intellectual and religious history as well as modern Italian history. Among her books are *Seeds of Italian Nationalism* (1951) and, as coauthor, *Modern Italy: A Topical History since 1861* (1974). Her article on "Political Catholicism in France and Italy" appeared in *Yale Review* (Spring 1955).

GLENN W. OLSEN is a professor in the Department of History of the University of Utah, Salt Lake City. He has published widely on topics in ancient and medieval church intellectual, legal, and art history, as well as on modern subjects in theology, philosophy, history, and political thought. He is the author of the chapters on the church fathers and on the early Middle Ages in Glenn W. Olsen, ed., *Christian Marriage: A Historical Study* (2001).

SERGIO PAGANO is the prefect of the Vatican Archives. He is the editor of a large number of major primary sources on the history of the early modern papacy, including *I documenti del processo di Galileo Galilei* (1984). His most recent book is *Le ragioni temporali di un vescova: Maffeo Gambara vescovo di Tortona e il conflitto giurisdizionale con il senato di Milano, 1593–1596* (2000).

KENNETH PENNINGTON is Kelly-Quinn Professor of Ecclesiastical and Legal History in the School of Religious Studies and in the Columbus School of Law of the Catholic University of America. He is the author of *Pope and Bishops: The Papal Monarchy in the Twelfth and Thirteenth Centuries* (1984), *The Prince and the Law, 1200–1600: Sovereignty and Rights in the Western Legal Tradition* (1993), and *Popes, Canonists and Texts, 1150–1550* (1993).

CARLA PENUTI teaches at the University of Bologna in Italy. She is the coeditor, with Paolo Prodi and others, of two major collections of articles on the history of early modern Europe: *Introduzione allo studio della storia moderna* (1999) and *Disciplina dell'anima, disciplina del corpo, e disciplina della società tra medioevo ed età moderna* (1994).

JAMES M. POWELL, educated at Xavier University and Indiana University, where he received his Ph.D., is professor emeritus at Syracuse University and a corresponding fellow of the Royal Historical Society. He is author of *Anatomy of a Crusade, 1213–1221* (1986) and *Albertanus of Brescia: The Pursuit of Happiness in the Early Thirteenth Century* (1992). He edited *Innocent III: Vicar of Christ or Lord of the World?* (1994).

ALAN J. REINERMAN, professor of history at Boston College and secretary-treasurer of the Society for Italian Historical Studies, received his Ph.D. from Loyola University in Chicago. He is a specialist in papal and Austrian history. His published volumes include *Austria and the Papacy in the Age of Metternich* vol. 1, *Between Conflict and Cooperation, 1809–1830* (1979), vol. 2, *Revolution and Reaction, 1830–1838* (1989). His article "Metternich, Pope Gregory XVI, and Revolutionary Poland, 1831–1842" appeared in the October 2000 issue of *Catholic Historical Review*.

WILLIAM ROBERTS, who received his M.A. at Fordham and his Ph.D. from the City University of New York, is currently professor of history and director of the Public Administration Institute at Fairleigh Dickinson University and a member of the Advisory Board of the National Endowment for the Humanities. His books include *Prophet in Exile: Joseph Mazzini in England, 1837–1868* (1989) co-compiled with Frank Coppa, *Modern Italian History: An Annotated Bibliography* (1990), and as coauthor, *Sicily: An Informal History* (1992). His article "Napoleon, the Concordat of 1801, and Its Consequences" appears in *Controversial Concordats: The Vatican's Relations with Napoleon, Mussolini, and Hitler* (1999), and he is a major contributor to *Encyclopedia of the Vatican and Papacy* (1999).

JEAN-PIERRE RUIZ is associate professor and chairperson in the Department of Theology and Religious Studies at St. John's University in New York. He holds a doctorate from the Pontifical Gregorian University in Rome. His research interests in biblical studies include the Book of Ezekiel and the Apocalypse of John. He is past president of the Academy of Catholic Hispanic Theologians of the United States and president of the Mid-Atlantic Region Society of Biblical Literature. He serves as editor-in-chief of *Journal of Hispanic/Latino Theology* and is an associate editor of *Catholic Biblical Quarterly*.

MARGARET A. SCHATKIN is associate professor of theology at Boston College, where she has taught patrology since 1969. Trained at Fordham University and Princeton Theological Seminary, she specializes in the writings of St. John Chrysostom. Her books and articles have appeared in patristic series and journals, including Sources Chrétiennes, Fathers of the Church, and Christian History.

MICHAEL SLUSSER earned a D.Phil. at Oxford University and is professor of theology at Duquesne University, Pittsburgh, Pennsylvania. He is a specialist in the early development of the Christian church, its beliefs, and its life.

ROBERT SOMERVILLE, the Ada Byron Bampton Tremaine Professor of Religion and also a member of the Department of History at Columbia University, received his Ph.D. at Yale University. His primary research interests include the history of Christianity through the sixteenth-century Reformation, the medieval Latin church, the papacy in the High Middle Ages, and medieval Latin manuscripts. His publications include *Pope Alexander III and the Council of Tours (1163); Scotia Pontifica: Papal Letters to Scotland before the Pontificate of Innocent III; Pope Urban II, the Collectio Britannica, and the Council of Melfi (1089).*

CAROLE E. STRAW is a professor in the Department of History, Mount Holyoke College. A specialist on Gregory I, she is the author of *Gregory the Great: Perfection in Imperfection* (1988) and *Gregory the Great* (1996).

LOUIS J. SWIFT is professor emeritus of classics at the University of Kentucky, where he was also dean of undergraduate studies from 1990 to 1999. He received his Ph.D. from Johns Hopkins University and has written on the early Latin church fathers, particularly with reference to issues related to war and peace.

RICHARD J. WOLFF has authored numerous books and articles on Catholicism in the twentieth century. His books *Catholics, the State, and the European Radical Right, 1919–1945* (1987) and, as coauthor, *Dorothy Day: Le Mouvement Catholique Ouvrier aux Etats-Unis* (1994) focus on the relationship between Catholicism and contemporary political, social, and economic movements. In his *Between Pope and Duce: Catholic Students in Fascist Italy* (1990) and in his many articles on Giovanni Battista Montini, he discusses the development of the life and career of Pope Paul VI. He received his A.B. from Georgetown University (Phi Beta Kappa) and his Ph.D. from Columbia University.